The Girl In The Red Coat

The Girl In The
Red Coat

Roma Ligocka
With Iris von Finckenstein

Translated from the German by
Margot Bettauer Dembo

SCEPTRE

Copyright © 2000 by Roma Ligocka
English translation copyright © 2002 by
Margot Bettauer Dembo

First published in Great Britain in 2002 by
Hodder and Stoughton
A division of Hodder Headline

1 3 5 7 9 10 8 6 4 2

A CIP catalogue record for this title is available
from the British Library

ISBN 0 340 81906 5

Typeset in Sabon by Palimpsest Book Production Limited,
Polmont, Stirlingshire

Printed and bound in Great Britain by
Clays Ltd, St Ives plc

Hodder and Stoughton
A division of Hodder Headline
338 Euston Road
London NW1 3BH

For my son, Jakob

you were saved not in order to live
you have little time you must give testimony

Zbigniew Herbert: *Pan Cogito*
(translated by Jan and Bogdana Carpenter)

I

The Hotel Negresco in Nice on France's Côte d'Azur presides over the Promenade des Anglais like an enormous white ship. Its white awnings flutter slightly in the morning breeze. The sea is an almost supernatural blue.

Inside the hotel, pageboys in colourful uniforms with feathers in their hats dash across the red carpets. I walk through the enormous entrance lobby with its gleaming marble floor, past large flower vases from which billow red roses, and into the breakfast room.

The room is round, decorated entirely in tones of pink and brown; the effect is that of an antique Biedermeier carousel. White horses turn to the music of a barrel organ playing gentle waltzes. Countless little lightbulbs illuminate the scene. The paintings on the walls show pretty landscapes done in warm pastel tones. A life-sized doll in a quaint costume stands in the middle of the room; she has long, curly hair and her mouth is locked in a smile.

The windows are framed by heavy red-velvet curtains, the Venetian blinds lowered half-way. Sunbeams paint golden stripes on the floor and on the pink tablecloths. The waitresses all look like the big doll – they wear the same pink skirts that reveal the frills of their lacy knickers – only *their* smiles are real and a little tired. They bustle back and forth.

The room smells of chocolate and raspberries, of coffee and perfume.

I sit down at one of the tables.

The circular breakfast buffet in the centre of the room

looks like a work of art and immediately puts me into a euphoric mood. There are raspberries, strawberries, chunks of pineapple, red, yellow and green melon slices; pink-tinged ham artistically shaped into rosettes; salmon, sliced wafer thin and folded into stars; tiny halves of quail eggs topped with dots of caviar; jewel-like petits fours; mounds of gleaming raisin rolls; fresh orange juice flowing like a waterfall over a cliff of ice cubes; jams and preserves of many colours; honey and butter balls.

And that smell of raspberries and chocolate. I close my eyes. The sun's rays play on my eyelashes and scatter into golden dust.

I feel strangely carefree and happy in this place but I won't admit to this, for I am a superstitious old Jewish woman. I think of the beach and of the large green *chaise-longue* waiting for me there, of the cocktails the waiter will bring me while the sun warms my skin and I soak up and dissolve into the blue of the sky and the smell of the sea. For lunch I'll have a Salade Niçoise with a glass of Prosecco. And then there is that beautiful handbag I saw at Sonia Rykiel . . .

An elegant couple sits down at a table near mine, a little girl in tow. She stands staring at the life-size doll, then finally joins her parents. The mother has placed a huge goblet filled with strawberries before her. But the little girl doesn't eat. She merely puts her spoon into the glass, absently stirs the berries around, and gazes at the doll, which keeps smiling its wooden smile.

The little girl has dark curly hair and large black eyes ringed by dark shadows. She is perhaps five years old and looks very fragile. She pays no attention to me.

Suddenly I feel as though I am sitting across the table from myself in another life, another time. I look at the little girl I once was or might have been, and I know that she has everything I never had: a happy, safe childhood, a beautiful home and garden, strawberries, chocolate, toys, and parents who love her, parents who have enough money to pay for trips, piano lessons and birthday parties.

The life of the little girl passes before me like a Technicolor film of the life fate had cheated me of. I feel no envy – just the sharp pain of an old, unhealed wound. The little girl has the right to this splendid wholesome world. But I . . . I am an outsider only passing through. Does everyone see that I really don't belong here? I know that now they will see through my disguise, tear the clothes from my body, chase me out into the snow. Suddenly I feel cold and begin to tremble. I grip the soft cushions of my chair. The little lights on the carousel begin to flicker, the barrel-organ music grows louder, and faster, faster, round and round, pulling me down into the abyss of memory, back down into the dark hole. The ghetto.

It is always cold in the ghetto, ice cold, inside the house as well as out. Inside there's only the one kitchen stove for all of us and almost no coal. Outside, snow blankets the ground. There is no summer in the ghetto, no seasons at all, and no sunlight. Everything is dark and grey, always.

The ghetto has four large gates. We are not allowed to pass through these gates. It's absolutely forbidden. A tram runs on the main street, the number three. We are not allowed to get on to it. That's why it makes no stops here in the ghetto. It simply goes right on through. The people sitting in the tram stare at us through the steamed-up windows. A boy throws a few loaves of bread out of a tram window; they fall at our feet.

We stand on the street, freezing. Many, many people. There are people everywhere. Some have large dogs, and carry guns, and just watch. They shoot at who they want to, maybe at me too. We're the others. The Jews. We have to wait all the time.

The people with the guns have gold buttons and black shiny boots that crunch in the snow when they march by.

But mostly you can't hear that because they are constantly yelling and shouting. They yell, we obey. Anyone who doesn't obey is killed. I know that, even though I'm still very little. So little that I reach only up to the knees of the men in the shiny boots. When one of them comes near me, and I hear the black boots crunching and see the dog with the sharp teeth panting right next to my head, I feel even smaller than usual. That's when I try to make myself invisible. Sometimes it actually works, and I dissolve in the icy wind and the yelling, and my grandmother's cold, thin hand. She holds me tight, but I'm not there any more.

Grandmother is always there. When the waiting is over she takes me back into the kitchen, then takes off my red coat. It's a beautiful coat made of soft red wool, and it has a hood. She sewed it for me herself. With her thin cold hands Grandmother warms my feet; I can't feel them any more. She sets me on top of the table while she stirs a pot on the stove. Then she comes back with a bowl of steaming porridge that has little lumps swimming in it. She tries to feed me, but I turn my head away. The porridge is disgusting, the lumps, revolting. I don't want to eat it. I feel sick. The other people scold me. The hot kitchen is full of noisy strangers with sweaty, smelly bodies. One of the men grabs the bowl from Grandmother's hand and swallows the gruel in one gulp. My grandmother doesn't say anything. She sits down at her sewing machine again and clatters away. I'm glad the man ate the disgusting stuff. Lucky for me there's nothing left now.

At some point my mother comes home. It's already dark outside. I'm lying in my little crib but can't sleep because people are everywhere, making all kinds of sounds. They snuffle, groan, grumble and curse. They slurp and smack their lips, and some of them cry. My mother embraces me wearily. Her soft brown hair no longer smells of flowers the way it used to. It smells funny and sharp. 'You smell funny,' I say.

My mother smiles. I can tell she is sad. She is always sad. 'That's just the disinfectant,' she says.

'What's that?' I ask.

She doesn't answer. Instead she pulls her suitcase out from under the bed, takes out a small bottle, and opens it carefully. She lets a drop fall on her wrist and rubs it in. Then she closes the bottle, hides it again in the suitcase, and lifts me out of my bed. 'Better?' she asks. Now she smells like flowers again.

'Hello, Tosia, I'm back.' It's my father. He comes into the room, lifts me up, gives me a kiss. My father has a deep voice and his eyes are black, like mine. He embraces my mother. 'You smell good,' he says. 'I brought some potatoes.'

They go into the kitchen. That's where the other people are. I hear their voices, but I can only understand fragments of words because there is so much noise. I have the feeling that they are talking about me. 'Those eyes!' says my mother. 'If only she had blue eyes, like Irene!'

'And her hair is so dark,' says another woman, whose voice I don't recognize. 'That's not good for getting by. But maybe we could do something about that.'

'Poison?' my mother asks. She sounds horrified.

'No way!' my father cries out, and there's a dull thud, which makes me flinch. He probably hit the table with his fist. He does that sometimes when he's very angry. He's probably angry with me because I'm not the way I ought to be. I'm wrong.

Shots ring out in the street, a scream pierces the night. The conversation in the kitchen stops. After a while they begin to talk again, and finally I fall asleep.

Suitcases, handbags, bundles, an overturned baby carriage are strewn all over the street. Why doesn't anybody pick them up? Grandmother pulls me away. It's still snowing. We stand in the street and wait. We stand here every day. Every day is the same. Every night is the same. There's no sleeping in the ghetto. There's no dusk and no dawn, only boots coming up the stairs, dogs that bark, men who yell. Doors that are ripped open, people who scream, beg, implore, moan, grumble and curse. The light never really goes out, it is never quiet.

And every day, every night, strangers arrive, more and more of them. They talk, jostle and push, and they touch me. There are always a lot of people around me: outside in the narrow streets and inside in the small, dirty kitchen where the women cook and fight for a spot at the stove, and in the big, dark room that we share with the strangers and where Grandmother sits calmly at her sewing machine and sews. My little bed stands there too. A different family lives in each corner of the room. There is no bathroom; the toilet in the hall is used by everyone and is constantly clogged. The stink is horrible. It makes me sick every time I go in there. Still, I never let Grandmother go by herself. Otherwise she might not come back.

I am always cold, always sick and feverish, but still I have to wait outside in the cold with the others. They wrap a cloth soaked in a bad-smelling liquid around my neck; it's called methyl alcohol. They put me on my bed, undress me, hold little round glasses over a candle till they're hot and stick them on my naked back. Grandmother tries to soothe me. 'It's called cupping,' she whispers in my ear. 'It will make you well again.' But I don't believe her. I panic every time, struggle, whimper. The little glass cups make a disgusting, smacking sound when they're taken off at last. I'm afraid of them and I'm even more afraid of the strange people who touch me all over with their cold, damp hands. What's more, the glass cups don't make my cough better.

'She's so weak,' my mother says.

When Father comes home, he proudly takes a small bottle out of his coat and presses it into my mother's hand. 'Cod-liver oil,' he says, 'so that my little girl can get well.' Mother throws her arms around his neck, the strangers nod in approval. I warily watch my mother as she pulls the cork out of the bottle, gets a spoon and pours some yellow, oily slime into it. She tries to put it into my mouth, but I'm quicker than she is. I escape and hide behind my grandmother. My mother says, 'Roma.' Rarely does her voice sound that stern. The other people also urge me to take it. 'You must swallow it!' they say. 'You have to do what your mother tells you.'

I hide my head in my grandmother's skirts. Here they can't find me and force me to swallow that yellow slime.

'Come here, Roma,' my mother calls. 'Please, child . . .' In spite of her soft tone I can hear the annoyance in her voice. It's better for me to stay where I am.

'Come here immediately and swallow it,' my mother yells. 'It's liquid gold!'

She tries to grab me. For the first time in my life I'm afraid of her. But not of my grandmother: she doesn't budge. Her back is a dark, safe mountain. She doesn't say a word.

My mother manages to get hold of my hand, tries to drag me out from behind Grandmother's skirts. I struggle with all my might, whimpering, fighting.

'I won't swallow that gold! I don't want to, no!' I wail. But my mother's hand is like iron. It grips mine. And suddenly I hear a funny cracking sound and feel something like an electric shock in my wrist. I start to cry.

My mother pulls me towards her, I no longer struggle, my hand hurts too much. It hangs there, all crooked. My mother drops the spoon and the liquid gold splatters on the floor; it smells of fish.

My mother puts her hands up to her face in horror. 'What's wrong with your hand?' she stammers. 'My baby! Roma, I'm so sorry.'

She tries to hold up my hand but it droops again. It hurts. The people in the room are talking in loud voices, all at the same time. They stand in a circle around me. Each of them wants to look at my hand, take hold of my arm and paw me.

Then my father rescues me. He lifts me up without saying a word and carries me through the dark, smelly hall out to the street. I lean my head against his shoulder. I'm exhausted and my hand hurts so much.

The old doctor puts a hard white bandage around my broken hand. Now it doesn't hurt as much. I'm proud of my bandage.

On the way home I see some of the men in the shiny black boots cutting off an old man's beard. They yell and shout and laugh while they're doing it. 'Don't look at that,' my father whispers, and holds me tight. He walks a little faster. But I can't help turning round. The old man is crawling on the ground and they keep kicking him with their black boots till he's not moving any more.

Grandmother has told me that my parents sold a gold ring to buy the cod-liver oil and that they only want the best for me. That doesn't make sense. I'm not angry with my mother any more. I proudly tell everybody that she broke my hand, and then I show them the bandage.

My mother doesn't like that. Is she still angry with me?

She no longer forces me to swallow the yellow slime. But she does force me to eat other things. She says, 'You have to eat to live,' and doesn't understand that I can't do it. She continually tries to feed me, always stuffing food into my mouth, and I regularly spit it out again. My gagging and my nausea drive her up the wall. When I'm freezing – and I'm always freezing – she wants me to eat. It's a constant battle. 'See, you're cold because you're so thin and you don't eat enough. Come on, eat something, then you'll feel warm.' But that's not true. I'm cold whether I eat or not.

My mother has to leave the house while it is still dark

outside, and when she comes home late in the evening she is tired and pale. Once I asked Grandmother what my mother does all day long. 'Sweep the streets and clean toilets,' was her brief answer. My mother is often so exhausted she can scarcely get up in the morning. And she's cold, like me. Even though *she* eats.

My father, too, is never home. Grandmother says he works on a construction gang. Then she is silent and doesn't answer any more of my questions. She simply keeps on sewing. The clatter of the sewing machine always reassures me.

One day a man brings my mother home in the middle of the day. She collapsed at work, he says. And when the doctor comes he says she has a high fever. I show him how well my hand has healed, but he's in a hurry. 'Don't you have any medicine for her?' Grandmother calls after him.

'No, there's nothing left,' he says, and his voice sounds bitter. 'Keep her warm, and give her plenty to drink.'

I'm glad that my mother has a fever and has to be kept warm because I can lie down next to her in the bed and warm myself on her hot body. I feel good in the glow of her fever: it is as hot as the fire in the stove, and I have it all to myself.

There comes a day, a special day, that's different from all the others. It's my birthday. Now I am three years old, and my other grandparents and Irene come to visit me. I don't know these grandparents. I have seen this grandfather about whom my mother talks sometimes only once before; he is her father. I was still very little then. It was in his bakery. They put me into a breadbasket, and I saw his large red face with a white twirled moustache hovering above me. He was laughing and smelt of fresh bread, and he was holding a gold chain with a ticking watch that he dangled in front of my nose. It's my earliest memory.

Now here he is again, here in the ghetto. He is different

In the ghetto: grandmother Anna (left), Uncle Szymon with his wife (third and fourth from left), mother Teofila (fifth from left). Roma's family are hiding the armbands they wear with the Jewish star on them for this photograph (about 1941).

from the other people – a distinguished man. I can tell immediately because he pays no attention to all the people around us. They are like thin air as far as he's concerned. He is wearing a dark coat with a fur collar, a stiff hat, and in his waistcoat pocket there's the gold watch. He sits down on my parents' bed in our corner of the room and looks at me for a long time. Then he sighs.

I'm sure he saw that I have dark eyes like my father. Not like Irene who is just coming into the room. How beautiful she is! Her blue eyes sparkle and her blonde hair makes me think of sunbeams. She is wearing a blue hat.

Grandmother Anna looks severe and serious. She is wearing a high-necked dress and a white blouse; under her chin is a golden brooch with a face on it. Shiny little spheres dangle from her ears. Her grey hair is pinned up in a knot; her hands are folded. She smiles at me, but I back away. I want to go to my real grandmother who, I see with relief, is just then entering the room, accompanied by my parents.

Now everybody is here. They lift me up and pass me around. Grandfather still smells of bread and tobacco. Irene takes me in her arms, and I touch her golden hair. Grandmother Anna pulls a package out of her handbag. I'm allowed to unwrap it by myself. It's a wonderful white knitted dress with a round collar and little blue embroidered flowers. Mother puts it on me. I'm proud and feel very beautiful in my new dress.

They all love me very much, I think. Or do they? They look at me with such sadness, wrinkle their foreheads and whisper among themselves. So softly that I can only understand bits and pieces.

'We have to . . . tomorrow morning at six . . .'

'Resettlement . . .'

'. . . only two suitcases . . . Resettlement . . . warm clothes . . .'

'Dress warmly,' my mother says. She embraces Irene. 'Please don't go, Irene,' she begs, 'you mustn't go! You look so good, so Aryan.'

'No,' Irene says. Her face is set. 'I have to go with Mama and Papa.'

'Oh, let her stay here. She's only sixteen years old! She's blonde. She's got to stay here!' my mother implores Grandmother Anna. Suddenly there are tears in her eyes. She grabs Irene's arm. Is she going to break her hand?

Grandmother Anna looks away and gets up. 'We have to go,' she says stiffly. 'We'll let you know as soon as we arrive. In the country.'

Grandfather puts on his stiff hat. He coughs. His eyes twinkle. He winks at me.

Grandmother Anna, Grandfather and Irene stay only a little while longer. Not long enough for us to get to know one another. They're already standing at the door. I can still see Grandmother Anna's earrings sparkle, and Irene's blue hat.

'But she's only sixteen!' my mother calls after them.
Then they go out into the darkness. Out of my life.
I never see them again.

'I want to be blonde too, like Irene,' I tell my mother. She
nods. Again she has tears in her eyes. Better if I don't say
any more. It's evening, and they all stand around the kitchen
table, singing. This is called 'Kaddish'; it is a prayer for the
dead in a foreign language I don't understand, but I feel their
deep sadness, see their glassy, unmoving eyes. The sadness
and the pain in the song almost overwhelm me.

At some point I am tired and fall asleep.

Suddenly someone wakes me. I'm lifted up and carried into
the kitchen. I can tell they're planning to do something to
me, I look round for my grandmother. But she isn't there.

There's a bowl on the table. They pour a bad-smelling
liquid from a green bottle into it. Now they take hold of me.
I'm supposed to dip my head into the bowl. I struggle, cry
and kick. But resistance is futile. There are many strange
hands, hands forcing me to do things I don't want to do. I'm
told to close my eyes tight, hold a towel in front of me, and
dip my head into the disgusting liquid. My eyes are burning.
Then they pour warm water over my hair, dry it off. My eyes
and my skin still burn.

I wonder whether I should cry, but by now it's probably
too late. And anyhow I'm not supposed to cry: there's always
too much noise in this overcrowded apartment.

Later my mother puts a mirror into my hand. 'Look how
beautiful you are,' she says. 'Now you look like Irene.' And
then she cries again.

I look in the mirror. My hair is blonde.

But my eyes are still not blue.

The loudspeaker booms: Jews must hand in their fur coats. We
are in a long line of people, on the street, waiting. Grandmother

holds me by the hand. The men in boots stand guard.

Grandmother is carrying my mother's fur coat under her arm, the big brown soft one that's so warm and cuddly. I hope I'll be allowed to keep my beautiful red coat. Even if it isn't as warm as Mama's fur coat.

It's ice-cold and snowing. I'm freezing. There's a pile of fur coats lying in the street, the snowflakes fall on them, first dancing in the air then covering the coats in a thin white layer.

I'm allowed to keep my coat.

It's almost dark by the time we get home, and I'm trembling. 'She has a fever again,' my grandmother murmurs. My mother lifts me up. Her eyes are all red.

We need new identity cards; ours are no longer valid.

'It's impossible,' my father whispers. 'An Aryan identity card is more expensive than gold.'

Always the same words, KENNKARTE, ARISCH. That's German for 'identity card' and 'Aryan,' my mother tells me. She doesn't explain the meaning of the words, but I know you need both those things to stay alive. And we don't have them. My mother understands German. I hate German. You have to shout when you speak it, and there are only a few words:

HALT! – STOP!
LOS! – GET GOING!
SCHNELL! – HURRY UP!
VORWARTS! – FORWARD!
KOMMALHER! – COMEOVERHERE!
AUFSTEHN! – GET UP!
AUFMACHEN! – OPEN UP!

All of them mean the same thing: fear.

I look out of the window. There are pieces of furniture standing in the street. They are shiny because they're wet. It's been raining for days. Grandmother says it's spring.

*   *   *

Still more people are now living in our house. Four instead of three people per window, my father said to my mother. Why did he say that? Anyway, nobody looks out of the window. Even I don't any more. Because it is forbidden now; the punishment is death. My mother warned me that anyone who opens a window or looks outside is going to be shot by the Germans. That's because our house borders on the Aryan residential district.

There are two windows in the dark room where we sleep. My crib is gone, I now share a bed with my parents. It's warmer there, even though I often feel that I can't get any air, that I'm suffocating. The room has a sweetish smell. The air is stale and heavy.

The sewing machine isn't here any more either. The new people now sleep in the spot where it used to stand beneath the window. I miss the reassuring clatter of the sewing machine. Grandmother sews by hand now. Her knobbly fingers are quick and skilful. She sews dresses for people and mends their things. For that we get a little bread or tea or a handful of flour.

We sit in the dark kitchen and wait. Like rabbits in a burrow. My grandmother once told me about rabbits. They're small, soft animals with long ears and they can run very fast when they're being chased. They get chased most of the time. Then they quickly run into their underground holes and they're safe there.

I'd like to see a rabbit some day.

I keep hearing a new German word, 'AUSSIEDLUNG.' It means 'resettlement', but I don't know what that means, and Grandmother doesn't want to explain it to me. Everybody is constantly talking about it. I sense how afraid people are when they talk about it; it must be something terrible, this word.

I see my father only rarely now, and my mother's face looks grey. When she's home she stuffs food into my mouth.

There's no time for anything else. Luckily I have my grand-mother.

It is night and they're coming to get us.

At least, that's what I think whenever I hear their boots on the stairs, their shouting, and the harsh barking of the dogs. Then I quickly make myself invisible. Will they find me? My heart is pounding in the darkness. The pounding is much too loud. They're going to hear it.

But they don't find me, not this time. They bang on the door; the dogs are panting. 'KENNKARTEN!' they yell. They take the fat man with the beard who always snores so loudly at night and also the woman who dipped my head into the bowl. And the twins from upstairs; I sometimes saw them on the staircase. Even though I hold my breath and hide under the blanket like a rabbit, I can hear every-thing. The sobbing and pleading of the woman. And the wailing protest of the fat man, the rapid shuffling of his feet while he hurriedly packs his suitcase. The twins cry softly.

Then they are gone. It's over, and I'm relieved they didn't find me. I want to snuggle up to my mother, but she is stiff with fear. Is she dead? I tug her sleeve. 'Go to sleep now, Roma,' she whispers. The sound is as hollow as if it came out of a tunnel or a deep well. I don't dare say anything, don't dare to move, to breathe. I have to go to sleep. But then I hear them again. It isn't over yet. They are continuing their search in the next house, and in the one after that, and the one after that. People scream, dogs bark, men shout. It goes on like that all through the night.

In the early dawn, still half asleep, I hear the tramping of feet in the street, mixed with the shouts of the Germans.

LOS, LOS! RAUS, RAUS! WEITER! SCHNELL, SCHNELL!

Where are they all going? There are so many feet, big ones and small ones.

Slowly the sound of the tramping feet recedes; the barking of the dogs and the yelling fades, seems far away now. Maybe they'll come back to get me. It isn't over.

It's only the beginning.

Like the others, I'm standing in the big square, waiting.

I don't know whether it's hot or cold. There's no difference any more. I'm wearing my red coat and carrying my little suitcase. The beautiful knitted dress I got for my birthday is in the suitcase. It's already much too small for me. There are also two pairs of stockings in the suitcase. I forgot to take the rest of my things. We had no time to pack.

People are all carrying heavy suitcases and bundles, and all are wearing coats and hats. It looks as if we're going away on a trip. But where are we going?

Nobody dares to ask the men in the boots. They are inspecting our papers; they are sorting the people. None of us knows what we're waiting for and what will happen to us. It could take a second or hours to find out. It feels like an eternity.

Sometimes someone tries to run away. Anybody who tries to run away is immediately shot. They pull groups of women and children out of the crowd. My aunt Dziunia is among them. Suddenly she runs across the square, tries to escape. Shots whistle through the air, she falls down. Right next to me. She has lost one of her shoes. A couple of people drag her to the side of the road; there they add her to the other dead bodies.

My grandmother and I clutch each other's hands tightly. That's the only thing I can still feel. We are very quiet, we don't move. If someone shouts, cries, or makes any sort of sound, he is shot.

I don't want to be shot.

Now some trucks drive into the square. Alarm spreads through the crowd like a sudden blast of wind. Many people leave the group and run towards the trucks, others are driven there by the men with sticks.

My grandmother holds on to me tightly.

The people are loaded into huge trucks. The men in boots drive them with blows, the dogs snap at their heels. A few of those already up in the trucks defend their spots with their elbows and fists. They kick at those who want to climb up. Some don't make it and fall back down; many simply drop everything; others are buried under their heavy baggage; these are shot immediately. Dead people lie next to me on the ground, and I see blood flowing out of their bodies, discolouring the white snow. Is it snow at all, or dust?

Snow or dust, there's no difference any more. Blood streams over the cobblestones. Everywhere, scattered baggage, suit-cases, handbags, velvet-bound books. The screams and the yelling combine to make one continuous bellow. I stare into the eyes of the dead people lying next to me. They look as if they were made of glass – wide open, extinguished.

And yet they look at me imploringly.

I close my eyes so that I don't have to see the eyes of the dead. I try again to make myself invisible and it works.

Now I am far, far away, and nothing can touch me.

The people in the apartment are shouting to each other, 'We're supposed to leave the house and go out on the street!' They grab anything in sight, run down the stairs.

I want to run after them, but Grandmother stays where she is. She sits on her chair, sewing. I hear boots in the hall, the dogs barking; they're coming upstairs, into our apart-ment. I'm numb with fear. Grandmother gets up, takes hold of me and pushes me under the table. Then she stands in front of it, to protect me.

It all happens very quickly. The door is ripped open. I see the black shiny boots. I see my grandmother's legs and small feet in grey slippers that dig themselves into the floor and are swept off as though they were two dry little branches in a storm. I hear Grandmother struggling and screaming desperately for help. I have never heard her scream before. Her screams are the worst thing I have ever heard. They break my heart into pieces.

I want to get out from under the table and hold on to her – but there is this black, snarling dog directly in front of me, blocking the way to my grandmother. Threads of spittle drip from the dog's jaws on to the dirty floor. And so I stay under the table, sitting there like a rabbit and putting my hands over my ears so that I don't have to hear her screams as the men in the shiny boots drag her off and push her down the stairs.

Many hours later I'm still sitting there when my father comes home. Next to me is the empty chair with the brightly coloured pillow on which Grandmother always sat. My father looks for me, spots me under the table, sees the empty chair. I know that he knows everything. He sits down on the floor next to me, holds his head in both hands, and worldlessly sways back and forth.

I want to tell him everything that happened, but I can't speak. I have lost my voice. I don't ever want to leave my hiding place under the table. I will stay there for ever.

Later my father sits down on the edge of the bed, still swaying silently back and forth. He looks like the children I've seen who were also rocking themselves like that at the side of the road. My mother comes home, drops her handbag when she sees him, sits down next to him. They embrace in silence.

I would like to join them, have them put their arms around me, but I can't leave my hiding place.

Behind me, where the sewing machine used to be, someone is sobbing.

I spend the whole night under the table. I close my eyes, but my ears hear everything.

The men in the black boots are on the move, picking up more people.

At dawn heavy cars drive through the streets.

Sabine, my mother's younger sister, comes to see us. 'Rominka,' she says to me, 'Rominka, what a pretty girl you've turned into!' I think Sabine is a pretty girl. She has such a nice laugh and looks jolly, not sad like my mother. She has a colourful kerchief tied over her dark hair.

'How do you always manage to look so good?' my mother says in admiration.

Sabine earns money. She sells things.

'Do you have a real shop?' I ask.

She laughs and taps the small plaid suitcase she carries with her. 'This is my shop.'

I would love to know what's in the suitcase, but she doesn't open it.

'Please be careful,' my mother warns. She sounds worried. But Sabine doesn't worry about herself. She is worried about her husband, Krautwirth. He is an engineer, one of the first to go into the camp; that was months ago already.

'What's going to happen to Krautwirth?' She always calls him only by his last name. 'I can't live without Krautwirth,' she whispers, and leans her head on Mama's shoulder.

But a moment later she's smiling again; she embraces me, holds me tight, kisses me, picks me up and swings me through the air. 'Rominka!' she says. 'My sweet little Rominka! Just wait. If you continue to look as good as this you'll have all the men at your feet.'

While I wonder what Sabine means by this and whether she's talking about the dead people who were lying at my feet in the snow, my mother says softly and sadly, 'She looks just like you.' Then she walks Sabine to the door.

'Be careful!' my mother says, and kisses her goodbye.

Day by day the fear gets worse. And the shouting. Nobody

Teofila (left) and her sister Sabine (about 1933).

speaks in a normal voice any more. Either they're shouting or they're crying or they're whispering. When we have to go out on the street, we always scurry. Like thin, grey animals. We sit in our hiding place and watch what they're doing with the other animals. They're constantly picking up people and killing them. Everybody whispers: 'Who will be next to go?' Any of us could be next.

They all scurry and whisper. There are only brief news reports, rumours, pieces of paper pressed into one's hand. Mother no longer goes to work; she hides at home and takes care of me.

One day Sabine's plaid suitcase is lying in the street, open and empty. And then somebody comes and hands my father a golden ring. It isn't unusual for somebody to come into the kitchen with a bag of potatoes or one or two cabbages, and my father gives him a ring for it. But this time it's my father who is given the ring, and he doesn't give the man anything in return. He hugs the man, and they sit down on the bed together. I come out from under the table. My father's face is chalk-white and he looks like an old man. The ring is on the table. It has a red stone into which are scratched two intertwined symbols. I want to put it on my father's finger and he lets me. Wearily he looks at the ring on his finger. 'It's beautiful,' I say.

'It is Bernhard's ring,' my father says. His voice sounds as if it were far away. 'It is my brother's signet ring.'

'They're picking up the children. They won't let us take them along,' my father whispers. 'We have to get Roma out somehow. Quickly, before it's too late.' As usual I'm sitting under the table, wishing once again that I had no ears. No matter what I hear, it makes me afraid. That's how it must be for the rabbits with their long ears. They hear everything.

The grown-ups talk all the time. Their conversations are about documents, identity cards, identification papers, emigration, deportation, hiding places. Who goes, you first, I first. Or do we want to die together?

I quietly repeat this sentence, over and over again. We want to die together. To die, die, die . . . They wonder what they ought to do with the children. Can one even keep them?

'Whole families are killing themselves, they want to die together,' my mother says. 'There's practically no poison to be had. You can scarcely get any cyanide.'

Cyanide, I say to myself, a nice word.

'Roman got out,' my father says quietly. 'There's the hole

in the wall. And after all, now that she's blonde . . . It ought to work with a sleeping pill.'

Run away! cries a voice inside me. They're planning to do something with you again. Save yourself! Hide! Quick! But where should I go? I'm already sitting in my hiding place. The only hiding place I know. I'm not safe here. But I have no choice. There is no such thing as safety.

Then they explain things to me. 'Somebody will take you out of the ghetto,' they say. 'You'll be with good people and you'll survive.' Then they give me something to drink and try to shove me into a suitcase. I panic. I fight for my life, I scratch, kick, bite. The only thing I can't do is yell. My mouth is dry, as if it were glued shut, and my eyelids are as heavy as lead. I know I'm going to suffocate in the suitcase. I haven't been able to breathe for a long time anyway; fear is choking me.

'She's going to suffocate,' my mother screams. I can hear her muffled voice through the thick suitcase cover. All around me it's pitch black, cramped. I can't move. I can't breathe. I'm trapped, and I'm going to suffocate.

Time stands still. My heart stands still.

Then the suitcase is ripped open. Light floods over me, I have to blink, take a deep breath. Where am I? Am I dead already?

My mother pulls me to her and holds me tight, covering my face with kisses; hers is all wet with tears. 'I can't do it,' she says again and again. 'David, I simply can't do it.'

My father sighs, deeply, heavily. He puts his head in his hands and says nothing. He is thinking.

We are standing in a long line of people. We wait, my mother and I. It is very, very hot; the sun beats down on my red coat. My legs are so tired I can scarcely stand. And I am terribly thirsty. But I know I have to stand there. The men in boots have their guns trained on us and they're watching us. One of them is smoking a cigarette. He is as tall as a tree, and under his hat you can just see where his hair begins. It is shiny blond, his eyes as blue as the sky. He does not smile. Why should he? Because an ugly little girl with black eyes stands in front of him? A Jewish child? I would like to keep looking at him, but I'm afraid to look into his face. That's forbidden.

'WEITER! LOS!' I'm being pushed forward by the crowd behind me, and now I can't see the man in the boots any more.

'KENNKARTE!' They are checking documents. Right in front of us a young woman with a baby in her arms is dragged out of line by two men in boots. She cries and screams, but that just makes it worse. The blond man grabs the child away from her and throws it on the ground. Its head hits the cobble-stones with a dull thud.

My mother holds my hand a little tighter. 'Don't look!' she whispers. 'Don't be afraid . . .' She says that whenever she's afraid.

We have been given a piece of blue paper, and for a moment my mother is truly happy. In the evening she shows it to my father. 'We have a Blue Paper, we're fit for work,' she keeps repeating, 'Maybe everything will still turn out all right.'

Then she stuffs some food into my mouth.

My father is silent. He is thinking.

In the big square there are many, many people again standing next to or sitting on their baggage. The trucks are here again. And the men in boots with their big cars. They bellow commands. They're herding the old and the sick people together. Many can't walk properly. I see an old man on crutches fall down in the crush. They beat him on the head with their gun butts and throw him aside like a bag of rubbish.

It is still unbearably hot. My throat burns like fire. My

mother has the blue piece of paper in her pocket. She is trembling.

We sit down on our suitcases. We wait.

Cries, shots, blows. Yelling. I would like to put my hands over my ears, but that is forbidden.

We wait. Hours pass.

Suddenly, a boy is standing next to me, my height, maybe a bit taller. He is wearing a coat that's much too big for him and a cap that keeps slipping over his eyes.

He smiles at me.

Terrified, I hold my breath. Smiling is forbidden!

I smile back briefly.

Have I seen this boy before? He looks familiar.

Oh, yes. I've known him a long time. All my life. He is my friend. I think his name is Stefuś.

We have to keep very quiet.

He is holding a small pebble in his hand. We aren't allowed to move. But we play a game, a kind of ball game. He slides the pebble into my hand, I slide it back into his. Back and forth. Again and again. The pebble becomes damp and warm. It is nice, smooth, and it belongs to us.

I have a friend.

Then suddenly Stefuś is gone. He has seen his mother being pushed on to a truck by one of the uniformed men. He runs towards her. Something clatters at our feet. Stefuś falls down.

Did he trip?

Why doesn't he get up?

I see his feet, his much-too-large shoes. The shoelaces are untied. That must be what made him trip.

The little pebble rolls out of his open hand, rolls across the cobblestones, lies there, still.

As still as Stefuś. Why doesn't he get up?

I get the answer in the little red rivulet that seeps out from under his coat.

They drag him away.

'Mama . . .'

'Don't look, child,' she whispers, 'don't look.'

'I have the identity cards,' my father whispers proudly. 'They are stolen, genuine. Aryan identity cards. Your name, darling, is now Ligocka. And I also have a hiding place for us. It's a good one.'

They are sitting at the table again, talking. Very quietly, secretively. The others aren't supposed to hear. And I sit in my hiding place under the table and listen. 'Ligocka . . .' my mother murmurs. 'I wonder if the child can remember that? L-I-G-O-C-K-A. We're going to have to drill it into her. Our lives could depend on it.'

But my name is Liebling; I don't want this new name; my name is Liebling.

'Ligocka,' my mother says again. She sighs and blows her nose.

'How much did you have to pay?' she whispers. I peep out from under the table. My mother looks around her. But the other people aren't paying any attention to her. They have enough problems of their own. In the corner a woman is washing her hair. Two others are arguing. A thin, bearded man sits on a chair staring straight ahead.

My father shrugs. 'Almost everything we had,' he says, and there is bitterness in his voice. He strokes my mother's hair. She leans against his shoulder and closes her eyes.

'I don't want my name to be Ligocka!' I say, in a loud voice. 'My name is Liebling, like yours.'

They pull me out of my hiding place and try to persuade me. They practise the new name with me until I am tired. I crawl back under the table.

They go on talking for a long time, but I don't hear them any more.

I sit under the table and think of Stefuś.

We are always waiting, waiting for nothing. We wait day and night. Nobody knows what will happen tomorrow. We are sorted out, like merchandise, we're constantly being sorted out, encircled, street by street, house by house. Some old people are now also colouring their hair. They do it to look younger so they won't be deported. So that they will be put to work. But youth is no guarantee either. There is no guarantee for anything. We have no rights. Our papers are examined, the choice is made, randomly, in accordance with a scheme known only to them. Sometimes it's the women's turn, another time the men's, sometimes the younger people, another time the older ones. Fear paralyses us, because any move you make, any word you speak could be the wrong one. Everything is forbidden. Yet we never know whether we aren't doing something that's even more forbidden. Or from which direction the bullet will come. We try to look like the rocks, like the walls, try not to exist. And never to let go of the hand we are holding. If you let go of it, it might be gone in an instant. People leave and simply don't come back. You just get used to a face, and it's gone.

My father isn't here any more. Where is he? 'Płaszów,' my mother says. She is standing at the stove, looking for an onion she had put in her apron pocket. I saw the thin woman take it, but I don't say anything. I'm glad because now that she doesn't have the onion I won't have to eat anything. Płaszów . . . I know that name. It's the name of a camp. They load people into trucks and drive them to the camp. That's what people say. I heard them say it.

My mother is grumbling to herself. 'Those gangsters,' she mutters, 'filching my little bit of food. Stealing the clothes off my body.'

Ever since Grandmother went and is not sewing any more we scarcely have anything to wear. My clothes are worn out and too small. My mother's beautiful dresses have almost all been stolen.

'Is Papa coming back?' I know I shouldn't ask, but I have to know.

My mother doesn't answer.

She dresses me in my red coat, kneels before me and buttons it carefully. Her hands are trembling. 'Come,' she says, 'take your suitcase. We're leaving.'

The voice in my head warns me, but I don't dare ask what my mother plans to do. She, too, is carrying a suitcase as well as a big bundle under her arm.

'Quickly,' she says, as we go down the dark flight of stairs, past the stinking toilet. I hold my nose, I hurry, trip. My mother clasps my wrist, pulls me along.

On the street the men in boots are walking back and forth. They are talking to each other, laughing. I stop.

'Hurry!'

Past the men in boots. They are absorbed in conversation, don't notice us. I feel the iron grip on my wrist loosen a little.

We turn into a narrow alley, then into a rear courtyard. On one of the balconies laundry is flapping on a clothes-line. Cooing pigeons sit on the wet pavement.

'Here we are.'

She pulls me into a doorway.

We are standing in a small shop. Other people are here too. They have suitcases and bags. As always. Nothing new.

But the shop is new to me. I've never seen a shop like this before. I look up. On the shelves and on a table in the middle there are brushes, paintbrushes, bottles, pails. And paint, paint everywhere. Everything is colourful. There are big crates with coloured powder, colourful snow. Dark red, gold-green, sky blue . . .

I dip my finger into some bright yellow powder, smear it on my face. My mother pulls my hand away.

'No!' I shriek.

She draws me close to her, holds me tight. I feel her whole body trembling.

A short, fat man stands behind the counter. He pulls open a drawer out of the wall. The walls of the shop are made up of many drawers. He pulls out a big lower drawer; he looks funny as he bends under its weight. In the place where the drawer was there is now a black hole. 'This way, get down, hurry up!' the man says. It is both a shout and a whisper.

The people jump into the black hole with their bags and their suitcases.

Now I'm supposed to jump too. I don't want to. I back off, terrified. I cling to my mother, holding on tight. I don't want to go down there.

'You go first!' the man yells at my mother. 'Hurry, hurry up.'

I don't want to let go of her, but a hand grabs me, another covers my mouth.

My mother disappears into the black hole. I struggle with all my might, kick, fight, flail my arms in despair. I can't breathe any more. The cooing of the pigeons, so loud . . .

Then they let go of me; someone gives me a hefty push. I fall.

I fall down into the black hole.

It is pitch dark all around me. Black as night. I lie on damp, rotten straw. It sticks to my hands, my face. It smells bad. The other people are here too, the ones who were in the shop. Strangers I don't know.

My mother is here. Takes me in her arms. She stuffs a piece of zwieback in my mouth. It is damp and sticky. I spit it out, begin to wail.

'Keep quiet,' someone hisses angrily. My mother puts her hand over my mouth.

Gradually my eyes get used to the darkness and I can make out the shadowy contours of the other people hiding here.

All the way up on the wall there's a tiny barred window.

Through the dirty glass you can occasionally make out the shape of running feet. I hear their clatter and the cooing of the pigeons. Coo, coo, coo . . .

It is cold. I am freezing. I wish I were back under the kitchen table. After a while I decide to explore, to see where we are. Once off my mother's lap, I crawl around on the damp floor.

I discover something in a corner of the room. It is cold and stiff. I feel the thing with my hands. It has a belly, a throat . . . it's like a rigid human body, like a corpse! And worms are crawling out of its belly! I am horrified, gripped by sheer panic, I scream.

For the first time in my life I scream, as shrilly and as loud as I can. It is also the last time I ever scream. They pounce on me like an octopus with a thousand arms, grab my arms and legs, hold on to me. They press their hands over my mouth. Try to choke me. I can't breathe; I begin to lose consciousness and can no longer fight against all those hands. I get weaker and weaker.

As if through a fog I hear my mother's imploring voice in a shouting kind of whisper, 'Let her go, please let her go! She'll never scream again, I swear she'll never scream again. Never! Please let her go!'

My mother tugs at the hands that are holding my mouth closed. The hands loosen, finally let go. I struggle for air, gasp, spit, breathe. I am alive.

Outside, deathly silence. Only the cooing of the pigeons.

Later my mother takes me over to the corpse. 'It's only an old dressmaker's dummy. Don't be afraid.'

That's what she always says when she's afraid.

Hours pass, days, weeks. Maybe months. Time stands still when you live in the dark. I don't know how long we stayed huddled in that black hole, and I never will know. My mother wants to make me drink a sweet milky tea. It's called *Bawarka*. I spit it out. It tastes disgusting.

A man hands my mother a bottle. Before I can put up a fight they pour the liquid into my mouth. It's warm and burns my tongue. 'There's vodka in the tea,' the man whispers. The vodka tastes horrible, but it feels good. Warmth spreads through me. Everything including my fear becomes dim. For a while I relax.

Again and again we hear shouting above us in the street, shots, dogs barking – the raids. People pound on the hatch in the floor above. We recognize the voices of those pounding and begging. 'We know you're there,' they call. 'Let us in, let us in. Save us!'

We remain silent and don't move. We can't let them in. They wail, they beg. They cry. All around me there's weeping. They howl like dogs.

'Have pity! Sarah, let us in! It's me, your sister. Rachel, it's me, Joseph! Your Joseph! Open up! Save us! It's me, Rosa!'

I put my hands over my ears.

Then, it is quiet again. Only the pigeons, cooing.

I hear the stranger next to me sobbing softly. 'My sister, my little sister,' a woman's voice wails. 'Oh, Rosa, Rosa . . .'

They all whisper feverishly in a jumble of voices. That was my mother, they sob, my brother, my friend. Now they'll have to die.

Why didn't we let the other people in?

'There is no room for everybody down here,' my mother whispers. 'We would suffocate. They would find us. If one of us had let them in, the others down here would have pounced on him.'

In the grey dawn, holding my mother's hand and almost blind from the darkness, I leave the hiding place in the cellar. I am four years old.

It's an ice-cold, ice-grey day. The streets are empty; the houses too. The dead are silent.

30

Many suitcases and bundles lie scattered on the pavement, a hat, handbags. Traces of blood stain the grey, trampled snow.

A work gang is tidying up, throwing the suitcases on to a hand-cart, sweeping the bloody snow into a heap.

I no longer know where I am. Who I am.

'Your name is now Roma Ligocka,' my mother whispers into my ear. 'Don't forget that, don't ever forget that, no matter what happens!'

The men in the work gang surround us. It's all done inconspicuously. They quickly lift me up on to the cart, put me down among the suitcases, and throw a blanket over me. Their cleaning pails clatter. The wheels of the cart bounce on the cobblestones. I hear the regular swish-swish of the brooms sweeping away the bloody snow.

We are rolling through the big gate into the other, the Aryan world.

Behind us is the almost totally deserted ghetto.

It seems to me that I am no longer a child.

The day my mother and I left the ghetto was 14 March 1943. Years later – and years before I saw or even heard of *Schindler's List* – I understood the significance of the date.

In 1939 3.3 million Jews were living in Poland, more than in any other European country, and most of them in the cities. Jews constituted 14 per cent of the population of Poland. King Kasimir the Great of Poland had brought them to his country in the fourteenth century to promote its economic and cultural development. In contrast to what happened in other European countries, only a small number of the Polish Jews became assimilated.

Immediately after the Germans occupied Poland in 1939, they began to issue a growing flood of regulations regarding the Jews. They were registered, given special identification cards, and forced to wear the Star of David. Their bank accounts were blocked, their property confiscated, and they could no longer be gainfully employed. They were forbidden to travel or to drive cars. Pets were prohibited; certain streets, shops and restaurants were off limits.

The compulsory resettlements began. The Jews were forced into ghettos located in the shabbiest parts of town. They were allowed to leave these 'residential districts' only to do forced labour. Isolated from the rest of the population, they had to work for starvation wages, or even for no wages at all, in factories that produced goods essential to the German war effort, or at other menial jobs. Overcrowding, hunger, disease, epidemics and death were daily facts of life in the Jewish ghettos.

At the start of the war about 60,000 Jews lived in the city of Kraków. An estimated 225,000 Jews lived in Kraków Province, the Vaivodship of Kraków. Only 15,000 survived the war, many because of help from Polish citizens.

In March 1941 the Jews of Kraków were crammed into some 320 decaying and dilapidated little houses in what had been a working-class district on the right bank of the Vistula river. At first the ghetto comprised about 17,000 inhabitants. Then, in May 1941, Jews from the environs of Kraków were resettled there as well. The number of people 'per window' rose from three to four. Sanitary conditions were indescribable.

The tightly guarded ghetto was first encircled by a wall; later barbed wire was added. It was forbidden to leave without permission on penalty of death. Increasingly harsh coercive measures, deliberate cruelty and brutal round-ups took Jewish lives, day in and day out. In the autumn of 1941 alone, some 2000 people were either deported or murdered on the spot, especially those without documents or job. The majority of these were orthodox Jews.

In January 1942 the Wannsee Conference decided on the 'final solution of the Jewish problem'. Deportations had already begun, but until then there had been no concerted efforts to exterminate the Jews.

In June 1942, countless people were shot in the Kraków ghetto. Then, in two large-scale 'actions', the Germans began to carry out the 'final solution' with deportations. Thousands were assembled and shipped direct to the extermination camp Bełżec, where they were murdered. This was still being done with diesel exhaust fumes.

Another 6000 Jews were deported from the ghetto on 28 October, 1942. The Germans took between 12,000 and 15,000 people directly to the extermination camps. Those who remained were deported to the Płaszów concentration camp, which had recently been erected on the site of two destroyed Jewish cemeteries at the edge of the city.

That same month, the Jewish resistance group ŻOB planted bombs in the Café Cyganeria, the Esplanada, and the Skala cinema, all located in the centre of the city.

The brutal SS Untersturmbannführer Amon Göth took over command of Płaszów in February 1943. The number of camp inmates grew rapidly, from 2000 to 25,000. Many wasted away as a result of starvation, heavy physical labour, disease and beatings. Many were killed by Göth himself.

The now-reduced Kraków ghetto was divided into 'Zone A' and 'Zone B' – A, for 'those able to work', and B, for 'those unable to work'.

To save ammunition, the children still left in the ghetto were ordered to line up, and then were shot with only one bullet each. The men of the security force, armed with axes and iron rods, flushed out any Jews still hiding in the ghetto. Those found were either shot or sent to Płaszów.

At 11 a.m. on 13 March, 1943, on the orders of SS Obergruppenführer Scherner, the Jewish Council announced that the ghetto was to be evacuated by 3 p.m. The Jews still left in Zone A were taken to Płaszów. Those in Zone B were loaded onto a train that took them directly to their deaths in the East. Amon Göth, carrying a weapon and followed by his dogs and his men, raced through the almost empty ghetto streets. It is said that within a few hours on 13 and 14 March some thousand people were shot on the spot.

The ghetto was declared 'Judenrein', that is, 'cleansed of Jews'. It was thoroughly cleaned up in December 1943. The remains of the wall were taken down and the quarter was reopened to Poles who wanted to live there.

Until late 1944, transports of men, women and children from Płaszów were taken directly to the death chambers of Auschwitz, Mauthausen, and Gross-Rosen. The last transport from Kraków reached Auschwitz one day before the Red Army arrived.

Today somewhere around a hundred Jews are registered as residents of Kraków.

2

Kraków is enormous, strange and eerie. Sleet falls without let-up. I have never seen so many houses, so many horse-drawn cabs and trams. In spite of them the city seems depressed, almost silent. There are few people on the streets and they are all in a hurry. We are freezing, my mother and I, and we walk quickly. We're carrying our suitcases. Our Aryan identity cards with the strange name 'Ligocka' are in our pockets. Our hearts are pounding.

My mother is walking very fast, too fast for me. I stumble along behind her. Nobody pays attention to us. Nothing extraordinary about a tall blonde woman and a little blonde girl in a red coat, carrying suitcases. There is a war, and many people are on the move.

My mother says nothing. I sense how tense she is, how confused she is by the daylight and the many streets and alleys. But she knows the way. We avoid the major streets.

She's determined, keeps going. Her steps are getting quicker and quicker. She is afraid. I know she is looking for a particular house. A place where we will be safe. Our new hiding place.

Now she has stopped and is looking around, breathing heavily. I clasp her hand tightly, feeling her fear growing. She has lost her way.

A man unlocking his shop on the other side of the street casts a suspicious glance at us.

Keep going.

She hurries ahead, pulls me along behind her. I am tired, exhausted, still I don't dare complain.

Again she stops, looks about her nervously. No one is following us, no one is chasing us.

Or is that . . . ?

Suddenly she flinches. Footsteps behind us on the pavement. Coming closer.

But it's only an old woman dragging a bag of coal. Her head is lowered; she shuffles past us without looking up.

Again, my mother stops, to think. Or is she too exhausted to go on?

'This way,' she says; her voice is firm. I can feel her relief. Apparently she now knows where we are. We are walking down a long street at the end of which is a large stone gateway. Behind that, a courtyard with tall old houses.

'There it is,' my mother whispers. 'Just a little further.'

The street seems endless to me. But we have no choice, we have to keep going.

It takes for ever, but we make it. Finally we're there.

Suddenly a man steps out of the shadows of the arched gateway. The gold buttons on his uniform glitter. His black boots gleam. He has a black moustache and small, piercing eyes. 'Halt! Police!' he yells at my mother in Polish. 'Show me your identity card.'

I feel the shiver that runs through my mother's body like sharp pinpricks. She lets go of my hand, puts down her suitcase, gasps for breath, searches through her pockets.

'Here,' she stammers, and hands him our new identification documents.

He takes them and leafs through them, looks at the photo, then at my mother, then down at me, back again at the photo.

'Ligocka,' he says, drawing the name out and chewing on one end of his moustache. 'Are you Aryan, Mrs Ligocka?'

My mother nods, lowers her head.

A grin spreads across the man's face. His moustache twitches.

'You're lying!' he barks. 'You're Jews! I know you. I know

all about those things. You're not the first Jews I've caught here. You're coming along to Montelupich with me.'

I don't know what Montelupich is, but from the look on my mother's face it means death for us. We have walked into a trap.

She's trembling all over, searches through her pockets again.

'Please,' she begs, and presses something golden into his hand, 'please let us go . . . the child and me . . .'

He takes the jewellery, examines it, bites down on it with big, yellow teeth. Then he slips it into his pocket.

'All right,' he mutters. But then the moustache twitches again. He grins. 'Ha, you think you can bribe me, you dirty piece of Jewish rubbish? I'm going to take you where you belong. To Montelupich.'

'Wait, please . . .' My mother's face is white as snow. She again rummages through her pockets, presses something else into his hand. 'Here, take this . . . it's all I have . . . let us go, I beg you . . .'

He pockets the jewellery, looks at her, enjoying her fear. Waits.

'You're lying,' he growls. 'You have more. Hand it over, or . . .'

It goes on like that. My mother trembles, cries, pulls jewellery out of her pockets. He takes it, puts it away, and asks for more, ever more. His face is red and he is sweating.

I am tired, terribly tired. I kneel down on the cold ground, next to my mother. Nothing matters any more. I want to sleep, to dissolve . . .

The golden rings slip out of my mother's hands. They glitter on the wet cobblestones, diamonds sparkle in the gutter.

I see the sparkle, the boots, the sleet that falls on everything, quietly, steadily, endlessly.

A voice in my head shakes me awake. Suddenly I clearly sense that my mother cannot continue like this. Her strength is all gone. She has given up.

I have to save her. I have to save us.

I put my arms around the boots of the policeman.

'Please take the jewellery,' I beg him, 'and let us go. Please, what good is it to you if you hand us over? They're going to kill us. Let us go, please.'

Tears run down my cheeks. He looks at me. Looks into my black eyes. Then he gestures wearily with his hand. 'Oh, all right, go on. But make it quick. Before I change my mind.'

We run. Behind us the policeman bends down and picks up the jewellery out of the gutter.

We are still running. It's a race against time. Curfew is approaching; by dusk everyone has to be off the streets; otherwise you can be shot, even if you're not a Jew.

The clocks on the church towers strike. Another fifteen minutes have passed, a half-hour, an hour. The trumpet sounds from atop the Church of Our Lady, marking each hour. My mother flinches every time.

We run and run. We climb up flights of stairs and down again. We knock on doors and ring doorbells. We beg and ask if we can stay.

'Only for one night . . .'

'I'm a distant cousin of yours from the country . . .'

'We know each other from school. I'm a close friend . . .'

'Our parents were friends. My daughter and I are just passing through . . .'

My mother keeps thinking up different stories, tries desperately to remember addresses from earlier times. Tries to think of people who are not Jewish who could help. Of friends from school, former housemaids . . .

Everywhere doors are slammed in our face.

We keep going, and going.

Along streets and alleys. Across squares and through back courtyards. Up and down endless stairs.

My legs feel like lead. I am exhausted and have to force

myself to take the next step. Only fear keeps us going.

Soon it will be curfew time.

Again the metallic sound of the trumpet.

We keep going but our steps are slowing. We have no strength left.

A brief rest stop on a park bench. My mother pulls a stale piece of zwieback out of her pocket. It smells of the cellar hole. I shake my head.

'Where can we possibly go now?' she whispers.

Just then she sees a basement window in the house across the way. It is slightly ajar.

'Come on!'

My mother looks around; the street is empty. She pulls me over to the little window. I'm supposed to climb through it. I resist, whine. My mother sighs.

'Then I'll go first.' She bends down, opens the window, puts one leg through, suddenly suppresses a cry of pain. She carefully pulls her leg back out. She has cut herself on an iron hook and is bleeding.

She ties a white handkerchief around her leg. It slowly turns red. I'm sure the cut hurts; walking is hard for her; she limps.

Meanwhile it is gradually getting darker. She stops, looks at one of the many church tower clocks.

'Only one hour left.'

She moans.

'We need a doctor,' she whispers, 'I can't go on with this leg.'

My mother reads the name on the brass plaque, 'Dr Groschen' – 'Dr Penny.' What a jolly name.

The doctor himself opens the door. He sees the bloody handkerchief wrapped around my mother's leg. 'Come in.'

He leads us into his consulting room. In the next room a canary is chirping. There's a clock on the wall. My mother keeps looking at it nervously while the doctor examines her leg.

'How did this happen?' He looks at my mother through gold-rimmed glasses.

She doesn't reply.

He bandages the leg and washes his hands. 'It looks worse than it is, Teofila. Soon it will stop bleeding.'

My mother, who was slumped in a chair, sits up in surprise.

The doctor looks into her eyes. 'Your name is Teofila, isn't it? Teofila Abrahamer? I operated on your brother Jakob a few years ago. Gallstones. Remember? You often came to the clinic to see him.'

He dries his hands, carefully hangs up the towel, and sits down.

My mother, who had turned pale, blushes. She speaks hurriedly, insistently. 'Please help us . . . please hide us, only for one night . . . it's almost curfew time.'

For a moment the doctor says nothing, looks at her. Is thinking it over. 'Wait,' he says, 'wait . . .'

His glance moves from my mother to the wall clock, then rests on me.

He stands up abruptly.

'I have a wife and children, understand? Do you understand? Please leave.'

Again we're on the pavement. My mother seems dazed.

The church tower clock strikes many times, and the sky is already dark grey.

'Only half an hour left . . . but Johanna must live somewhere around here. She used to work for my parents, in the kitchen . . .'

We run into a dark entry hall; the heavy wooden door shuts behind us with a loud bang. It's so dark we have to turn on the light in the stairwell. Looking out of the lobby window I can see the gas lamps being lit on the street.

My heart is thumping like mad.

Slowly we climb up the wooden steps. They creak and groan. First floor, second floor.

We stop in front of a door with a brass nameplate.

'Kiernik? . . . I wonder if this is it,' my mother says.

I press the golden bell button.

We hear footsteps. The door opens.

An angel stands before us. A blonde angel.

She is wearing a polka-dotted dress and radiates warmth, light and friendliness. The angel is beautiful, bright like the sun, golden blonde, even more beautiful than Irene.

Temporarily safe: Roma in the arms of Manuela Kiernik (about 1943).

'Manuela!' a harsh voice calls from inside the apartment. 'Close the door immediately. Don't let anyone in.'

But the angel doesn't reply. Her friendly blue eyes look at me. 'Well, come on in. Come in, you sweet little strawberry,' she says.

We don't have to be asked twice.

Quickly the angel shuts the door behind us.

Are we safe here?

'Just temporarily,' the angel says. 'Just for tonight, Mother. Please. Look at the little strawberry. The little *Poziomka* . . . She's so tired, cold and hungry.'

The other woman gives me an angry look. She has a hooked nose, wrinkles on her forehead and a stern face. Her dark hair is tied in a knot at the back of her neck.

My mother politely calls her *Pani* Kiernikowa, Mrs Kiernik.

'Out of the question,' she says, and presses her thin lips

together. 'As though we didn't have enough trouble already.'

I don't like Mrs Kiernikowa. She scares me. Hard to believe that she should be the mother of the blonde angel.

'Helene!' a thin but powerful and commanding voice calls, from somewhere at the back of the apartment.

We are standing in the entry hall. I can't see the person the voice belongs to. It comes from a room at the end of the corridor, the door to which is slightly ajar. The voice sounds as though the person would not put up with any answering back.

The Kiernikowa woman obeys the voice. She turns around and with quick, firm steps she walks into the room at the end of the corridor.

I hear an undecipherable murmuring. My mother puts her arms around my shoulders. She is afraid. The blonde angel smiles at me.

Mrs Kiernikowa comes back. Her face looks even more sullen than before, as though she has suffered a defeat.

'All right,' she says, without looking at us, 'but only for one night. Take them down to the cellar, Manuela.'

The cellar, like the black hole we were living in before, is dark and damp. There's a pile of coal in one corner, a bedframe leaning against the wall. Manuela drags out an old mattress and hands us a blanket. As she leaves she puts something crumbly into my hand. A piece of cake. 'I'll be back tomorrow morning,' she whispers to me. Then she goes quickly, leaving us alone.

My mother heaves a deep sigh, puts me down on the mattress, covers me. Wearily she curls up next to me. '*Mazel tov, mazel tov,*' she mumbles, half asleep. She is so exhausted that she immediately falls into a deep sleep.

I, on the other hand, am so excited, I can't get to sleep. I lie there in the dark, holding the sticky, damp cake crumbs in my fist, and I think of Manuela.

*   *   *

We are awakened by a loud creaking. Scared to death, we jump up from the mattress. They've found us!

But it's only the cellar door, only Manuela who has come to get us. 'Quick,' she whispers, 'it's already light outside. Come upstairs with me. It wouldn't be good if the neighbours discovered you here.' We take our suitcases and, still rubbing our eyes, we stumble along behind her, up the stairs to the third floor, to the Kierniks' apartment. Manuela locks the door behind us and takes a deep breath. No one has seen us.

'First of all, come to the kitchen with me. You need something warm to drink,' she says, and takes my hand. 'Well, *Poziomka*, were you able to sleep down there?' I nod. I still can't believe that all this is real and not a dream. My blonde angel really does exist. And she's calling me *Poziomka*, 'little strawberry', just like yesterday!

The kitchen is big and bright, not at all like the kitchen in the ghetto. Shiny pots and pans hang on the wall. The big round wooden table is clean and there are coloured cushions on the white chairs. A fire crackles in the big tile stove. It is warm and comfortable here. I especially like the floor. It's black and white.

Manuela asks us to sit down and brings us hot tea, bread and jam. My mother gives me a brief, stern glance. It means, 'Eat!' Obediently I take a bite of the bread. But I eat it only because *she* gave it to me; I even drink a little tea.

Manuela speaks very seriously with my mother. To my relief it seems that Mrs Kiernikowa isn't here. Maybe she doesn't even live here and maybe we can stay for a while. How I would like that? Swinging my legs back and forth, I gaze at Manuela's golden hair, which gleams in the lamplight. Just then, the door opens.

A small figure with long white hair stands in the doorway. She is wearing a white nightgown and would have looked like a ghost if she hadn't reminded me so much of my grandmother. The same determination in her eyes. The same friendliness in her face. Only not as thin and small and stooped.

And her voice is completely different. Clear and commanding. It's the same voice we heard coming out of the room down the hall last night. 'Manuela,' she says.

Manuela who is sitting with her back to the door, turns around. 'Yes, *Babcia?*' *Babcia* means grandmother. So it's Manuela's grandmother who is standing there. Memories of my own grandmother come flooding over me. I can't eat any more and put the bread back on the plate.

'Eat!' says my mother's look. She is sitting silently next to Manuela, stirs her tea, doesn't dare speak.

'This is your cousin from Rzeszów, Manuela,' the grandmother says, in that peremptory voice that doesn't allow any answering back, 'and this one' – she looks directly into my black eyes – 'is her little daughter. They are visiting us. For an indefinite period of time. Your cousin's husband was killed in the war – think up a story. You can do it better than anyone else. In any case, they can stay. Is my tea ready yet?'

Having said that, she sweeps majestically out of the kitchen. We stare after her, open-mouthed.

Manuela pours tea out of a kettle into a cup and puts it on a tray. 'Once Grandmother has spoken, the case is closed,' she says, smiling. 'Nobody in this apartment would dare contradict her. Certainly not my mother.' She winks at me and carries the tray to her grandmother.

Mrs Kiernikowa completely disagrees with the grandmother's decision. She comes home late from work and doesn't say a word when she sees us sitting in the kitchen. She takes some vegetables wrapped in newspaper out of her large bag and starts to clean them. My mother jumps up to help her. Wordlessly Mrs Kiernikowa hands her a knife.

I look at Manuela. She smiles. 'If you like you can look at my album,' she says. I beam.

I have never seen anything more beautiful than Manuela's album. In it there are shiny papers in the most glorious colours, even silver and gold. 'Those are sweet and chocolate wrappers,' she explains, 'I collect them. Smell!' She holds the album up to my nose, and it smells marvellous and sweet, of things with wonderful names I've never heard of before. 'Chocolate' – it sounds foreign and mysterious and brings on a strange longing.

Manuela shows me the whole apartment. It is gigantic, has a gleaming wood parquet floor and smells of floor wax. Manuela herself smells like violets.

The nicest room is the parlour. It has a carpet that looks like a flowery meadow. A massive, dark sideboard, in which there are coloured glasses and plates of fine genuine porcelain, stands against the wall. I must not touch anything, says Manuela. There is a vase that is almost as tall as I am, and a blue velvet sofa with many embroidered cushions on it.

Some pretty little stuffed figures sit on the sofa. Two of them have long hair and wear elegant lace dresses. They have blue glass eyes and long eyelashes. The third has short, brown hair and wears a shirt and green trousers. It's a boy.

I stare at them. 'What's that?' I ask Manuela.

She laughs. 'Haven't you ever seen a doll before, *Poziomka?*' She takes the stuffed figures, and one by one she puts them into my arms. 'This one is Eva, this is Violetta, and this one here is Jacek. Do you like them?'

Trembling with excitement, I gulp, can't speak because I'm overwhelmed. Manuela sees the expression on my face, laughs again, and takes back the dolls. 'Maybe you'll be allowed to play with them if you're very good,' she says, and replaces Eva, Violetta and Jacek neatly among the pillows. I nod. My heart is close to bursting with longing for the dolls, but I know that they don't belong to me and that I must not touch them.

There's also the room that belongs to Manuela's brother,

Dudek. Manuela shows it to me only briefly. Hanging over the bed is a beautiful big rug with flowers. The next room is the grandmother's room. 'She stays in bed all the time,' Manuela tells me. 'She might be asleep just now, and we don't want to disturb her.' But the door is slightly ajar, and as we pass I catch a glimpse of the grandmother; her head is nestled against several pillows, she's wearing glasses, and she's playing cards.

'You can sleep on the couch in Grandmother's room,' Manuela says. I am glad because I was almost sure we'd have to spend the night in the cellar again.

And then she shows me an elegant bathroom with shiny tiles and something that she calls a 'bathtub'. 'You fill it with warm water and then you sit down in it,' she explains. The thought makes me shudder.

Finally there is Manuela's room, which she shares with her mother. The room smells of violets. Pink curtains hang at the tall windows and a pink coverlet is spread over the wide double bed. There's a low table with a pink pleated skirt and a big round mirror on the wall above it. Bottles and little flasks and jars stand on the table.

From now on pink will be my favourite colour.

Manuela takes my hand and leads me back into the kitchen.

Days and weeks pass, and we are still at the Kierniks'. To be allowed to be near Manuela is happiness. Whenever she is with me, I feel the touch of another world, a glittering, magical world I have never known, but for which I yearn and under whose spell I have fallen.

It is Manuela's world and mine – not my mother's. Grief and worry, death and horror don't belong here. And neither does fear. But I, with my dark eyes and my bleached-blonde hair, really have no right to be a part of this world either. It's tempting to feel safe here in this big, bright apartment, and I shouldn't give in to temptation.

There is no safety.

I often look out of the window at the street, for hours at a time. Out there children are playing. How I yearn to be allowed to play with them.

But that's forbidden. I hear the trucks drive by and the rasping voices coming out of their loudspeakers: IT IS FORBIDDEN . . .

Manuela tells us they are pulling people off the tram and taking them away as hostages, *Zakładnicy*. Or simply shooting them. Many people are shot right there on the street, she says, horror in her voice. Just today, she says, they again shot several people because they found leaflets on them. I don't know what leaflets are, but I am not surprised at Manuela's news. People getting shot is just part of our everyday lives. Why is she so upset?

I also know that the men in boots search houses at night to catch people who are hiding, people like us. I know that nobody is supposed to see me or hear me, that I must not attract attention, and that under no circumstances must I leave the apartment. The neighbours have been saying things like, 'Oh, your cousin seems to be staying with you for quite a long time, isn't she? The little one has such dark eyes. But you . . .'

Not for a moment do I forget that our new world is only on loan to us. We are being hidden, but we could be discovered and shot at any time. And Manuela, the grandmother, Mrs Kiernikowa, and her son, Dudek, are all risking their lives for us. I know all that from Mrs Kiernikowa, who never tires of repeating it.

My mother and Mrs Kiernikowa are in the kitchen for hours, baking. The cakes are then sold. This way we have a little more money to live on.

Since dawn today they've been making rose-petal marmalade. You stir fresh rose petals with sugar till it turns into a pink mush. Your fingers get blisters from all that stir-ring. After that the rose-petal marmalade is spooned into little golden-yellow doughnuts. The mountains of doughnuts look lovely and smell wonderful, but I don't feel like eating any.

'Would you like to try one?' Mrs Kiernikowa asks, and I can tell that she is forcing herself to be friendly.

'No, thank you,' I say. I am sitting on a chair looking through a big book with unusual pictures.

Mrs Kiernikowa gives me an indignant look because I've turned down her offer. Then she turns to my mother, who is standing at the stove using a ladle to dip the doughnuts into a big pot full of hot fat.

'The child is too thin, she eats hardly anything,' she says, in a voice full of reproach. 'And so pale, probably anaemic. You really have to put your foot down, otherwise she'll become ill. And you know what trouble that's going to cause us. We can't possibly have a doctor come to the house because then they'll find out. I'll buy something at the market for the little one today – but it's going to be expensive.'

My mother caves in after this scolding. She looks through her pockets and presses a narrow gold band into Mrs Kiernikowa's hand.

'Here, take this. Perhaps you can get some liver some-where, or spinach . . .'

Mrs Kiernikowa nods. Later, after she has packed up the doughnuts and left the house, my mother lets her anger out on me. 'See, Roma? Haven't I been telling you all along? "Anaemic," she said! You need iron, vitamins. You have to eat, do you hear me? We ought to be grateful that we have anything to eat at all! You're going to be the death of us with your stubbornness.'

She puts a plate of boiled red beetroot in front of me. 'Eat that,' she orders, her hands on her hips. 'You may not get up from the table till the plate is empty!'

That evening I'm still sitting in front of the full plate when Manuela finally comes home and rescues me.

The following day I am ill, running a high fever.

'You see?' Mrs Kiernikowa snorts. 'I told you so. Now the child is ill because she hasn't eaten anything. Under these circumstances you cannot stay here. Please leave, right now.'

Manuela isn't here, and the grandmother is asleep. Without saying a word my mother packs our suitcases. She is crying. Then she helps me put on my red coat and we leave.

Down the stairs, out into the street. The front door closes behind us with a dull thud.

I feel terribly cold, even though it's warm and bright. The sun is shining and there are little green leaves on the trees. In spite of being cold, I feel a surge of life. It's because of the fresh air, the sunshine on my skin. It's spring. A wonderful feeling.

But at the same time I know, as always, that our lives are in danger.

My mother takes my hand and we walk rapidly down the street as if we have a definite goal.

'Where are we going?' I ask.

'Be quiet,' she says. 'Don't be afraid.'

No one stops us, and we soon arrive at the outskirts of the city. Behind a tall wooden fence there are many little gardens and tiny wooden houses. Bright flowers bloom in the beds. I am delighted at the sight, and for a brief time I forget my fever and the danger.

'Look, Mama, look at the beautiful flowers!'

But she pays no attention to me. She pulls me over to where a few boards are missing in the fence. We crawl through, walk over to one of the little houses, try the door.

It is locked.

We try the next little house and the one after that.

In the market square in Kraków (from left): Roma's parents David and Teofila; next to them Teofila's sister Irene and her brother Jakob (about 1936).

Finally we're in luck; one of the doors isn't locked, and we slip inside.

Sunlight falls through cracks in the walls of our hiding place on to dust-covered garden tools hanging on the wall, spider webs spun between flower-pots, old sacks, and bales of straw in the corner. My mother puts down her suitcase, forms the straw bales into a bed, and covers me with the sacks. I feel very hot. There are eerie, rustling sounds, and I'm scared. 'Mama,' I whisper.

She puts her cool hand reassuringly on my forehead. 'Those are just mice, darling. Don't be afraid.'

Mice? I don't know what that is. In any case, my mother is afraid of them. Are they dangerous?

'What do they look like?' I ask.

'Like rats,' she explains with a shudder, 'only a little bit smaller.'

I know what rats are. I think of our stay in the dark hole, of the black shadows scurrying across the floor, of the sound of many tiny feet, of the screams of the people outside . . . I don't want to think of that.

'Mama,' I beg her, 'please tell me a story.'

The Café Maurizio on the Kraków market square served the best *cassata*, the best ice-cream in the city. They also had chocolates decorated with nuts and marzipan, jars filled with bright-coloured sweets, and cakes and pastries in all shapes and colours. You sat at small round tables in softly upholstered armchairs and talked in low voices while quick, polite waiters in long starched aprons served you. Cocoa came in cups made of thick brown chocolate. After you spooned up the mountain of snowy whipped cream and sipped the creamy cocoa, you could bite into the cup and eat it. Then you had this great feeling in your tummy – soft, full, warm, wonderful. Happy.

On Sundays when they went to the Café Maurizio with their mother, Tosia – that was Teofila's nickname – and her little sister Sabine used to wear white dresses and huge white bows in their hair. They also wore white dresses and bows in their hair when they were taken to school in the mornings in a horse-drawn cab. They went to a Catholic convent school, not a Jewish school. Their parents thought culture and education were very important, and the convent school – run by nuns in snow-white, pleated coifs – was considered stricter and better. They were taught European literature, art and music, and they learned etiquette and languages. Tosia also took German.

At home in the Abrahamers' big *Jugendstil* villa on the outskirts of the city, the bookshelves held the works of German writers like Goethe and Schiller. The family spoke Polish and sometimes German, but only rarely Yiddish. Tosia's father, Jacob Abrahamer, had built the house. He was wealthy, had a moustache, and was a good businessman. In addition to a big bakery, which made the best wholewheat rolls in Kraków, he owned sprawling estates and the mills from which came the flour for his rolls. His passion was raising horses, which he kept in barns at the far end of the huge garden. Some of them were so handsome that well-known artists used them as models.

Jewish holidays were celebrated in the large drawing room with its carved dark furniture, grand piano, and thick soft carpets. There Tosia and Sabine, their little brother Jakob, and later also Irene, would join their parents and their many relatives around a huge dinner table covered with the red gold-embroidered velvet tablecloth. They would eat roast turkey with round dumplings called *Kluski*. The turkeys had been fattened by the farm girls, or sometimes even by the mistress herself, so that their meat would be more tender; or there might be crispy roast goose, or ducks stuffed with apples. There would also be carp with raisins and almonds, chopped goose liver with onions and eggs on white bread, jellied chicken with egg, and sweet-and-sour borscht made with cherries and beetroot. Dessert consisted of cold sweet plum soup and mountains of cakes. Anna Abrahamer could bake marvellous cakes: apple strudel, cherry cake, nut torte, and raisin cake made with yeast dough. The grown-ups drank raisin wine, walnut schnapps, raspberry liqueur and plum brandy. Father made these himself from fruit that grew in the garden . . .

My mother sighs. Her voice had become quite wistful as she recounted all the good things they used to eat back then and because the memory was so beautiful. I like it when she tells me about those days, even though I don't know what roast goose is or how chocolate tastes. My mother's stories are fairy-tales about another world that has nothing to do with my life. It's as though she had lived on an island that has sunk beneath the sea, as though Noah's flood had come between us and that life. I never thought that I, too, could ever have had a right to it.

'Mama, what does chocolate taste like?' I am getting sleepy. The fever and looking for a place to hide have made me tired.

'Oh,' she says, and there is a strange gleam in her greenish brown eyes, 'the taste of chocolate is so wonderful, it's impossible to describe. Sweet and sticky, like milk and honey, like jam and cake, but much better.'

The sun is setting, and the birds are twittering. I think of the flowers in the garden and of Manuela who smells of violets. My mother pushes a piece of bread into my mouth and lies down next to me. We sleep.

My fever is gone. It's pouring with rain and we're once again standing in front of Manuela's apartment with our suitcases. Mrs Kiernikowa opens the door. She sizes us up with a gloomy look. Nobody says anything.

Then we hear footsteps down in the lobby. Someone is coming up the stairs. The steps creak.

Mrs Kiernikowa grabs my arm, pulls us into the apartment, quickly closes the door behind us.

'Well, go on, take your shoes off. The floor is going to get all wet and dirty,' she grumbles, and disappears into the kitchen.

My mother squeezes my hand hard. We pick up our suitcases and tiptoe down the hall to the grandmother's room. She hugs us without saying a word, is happy that we're back. She smells of old tea and valerian. The covers on the quilts we used before haven't been changed.

Manuela is glad we're back too. She is sitting in her room in front of the mirror that hangs above the table with the pink skirt, patting her face with a big powder puff. Her long blonde hair is pinned up and decorated with little black bows. She looks in the mirror and sees me standing behind her. Thin, small, serious and dark-eyed.

'Do you want some too, *Poziomka?*' She laughs and flicks the soft puff over my nose. It tickles and makes dust. I laugh awkwardly. 'Don't always look so sad,' Manuela says gravely, and frowns. Then she takes a little red stick and paints her mouth with it. Suddenly she looks quite different.

'Manuela!' a peremptory voice says. The grandmother is standing in the doorway, as always wearing a long white nightgown. 'Don't put on so much makeup, child. You look like a paintbox.'

Arifche Wohnung

MIESZKANIE CHRZEŚCIJAŃSKIE

Nazwisko

A sign like this gave a household some protection from raids.
[German on sign reads 'Aryan Household']

Manuela sighs. Then she gets up, takes my hand and pulls me into the parlour. 'Come, I'll show you something.'

I'm terribly excited. Manuela opens the sideboard. In it is a black box containing a loudspeaker like those I've seen on the trucks, only much smaller.

'This is a record player,' Manuela explains solemnly. 'And now watch . . .'

She takes a black disc out of its cover. On the cover is a picture of a beautiful blonde woman.

'Marika Rökk,' Manuela says over her shoulder. She places the disc on the black box and sets a long, silver, metallic thing on it. Then she pushes a button. The black disc begins to turn and I hear a lovely female voice singing a song:

> *Ich möchte so gerne*
> *Ich weiss nur nicht, was*
> *Mein Herz möchte dies*
> *Mein Verstand möchte das . . .*

I so much would like
I just don't know what.
My heart would like this
But my head would like that . . .

I am dumbfounded. Over and over again I look at the photograph on the cover, stare at the turning black disc, shape the words with my lips, 'I so much would like . . .'

Manuela laughs. The song is finished. She puts the black disc back into its cover, pushes the button on the box and closes the sideboard.

'Do you know her? Marika Rökk?' I ask Manuela.

She shakes her blonde curls. 'Oh, no, *Poziomka*,' she laughs, 'Marika Rökk is very famous. She lives far away from here. She's German.'

I can't believe that Marika Rökk is German.

I don't see Manuela's brother Dudek very often. He is completely different from Manuela – big, strong and silent – but he, too, is blonde. Mostly he comes home only in time for curfew or not at all. Sometimes he brings a few men along; they sit in the kitchen and talk for hours. I think they have a secret, but I realize that I'm not allowed to know what it is. So I don't say anything, slip away into a corner with a book. Once Dudek pats me on the head as he passes by, and I'm surprised and pleased that he even noticed me.

I spend the days sitting at the window or in the kitchen, or in a corner with a book. Mrs Kiernikowa and my mother bake cakes and talk. They talk about men.

'Men are scoundrels. All of them,' Mrs Kiernikowa says, and her thin lips become even thinner. I wonder what a 'scoundrel' is. In any case, nothing good. Mrs Kiernikowa talks herself into a tizzy. 'He had one affair after another, all with young, pretty things. And then he went off to Warsaw and made it big in politics, left me here with two little children.

I often didn't know how I was supposed to cope all by myself
– work, raise the children, pay for the food . . .'

My mother sympathizes, but lets Mrs Kiernikowa do the
talking. She is a good listener.

'But now I'm glad he's gone. I wouldn't take him back,
not even if you paid me. And if he were standing at the front
door right now, I'd slam it shut in his face!'

My mother is searching for something comforting to say.
'But your children, you can really be proud of them,' she
says.

Mrs Kiernikowa heaves a deep sigh. 'If only you knew,'
she murmurs, 'if you only knew . . . Manuela's head is full
of fancy ideas. And Dudek . . .'

She suddenly breaks off in mid-sentence. 'And you, Teofila?
Is your husband a scoundrel?'

My mother smiles. 'Oh, no,' she says, in a soft voice.
'Certainly not. He waited seven years until my parents finally
gave us permission to marry.' Her eyes are shiny with unshed
tears. 'If only I knew whether he's still alive . . .'

That evening, after we're in bed, I ask my mother about
my father and what that business with the seven years was
all about. She holds me close in the dark and tells the story.

It happened on a beautiful hot summer day. Tosia was fifteen
years old, sitting in the gazebo in her parents' garden, reading.
It was her favourite spot. The garden with its flowers, fruit
trees and berry bushes was so large that no one in the house
could see her here, and even if they called her she wouldn't
hear them. Whenever her parents gave a party – and they
did frequently – a band in the gazebo would play romantic
popular songs and ladies and gentlemen in fine clothes would
dance under colourful Chinese lanterns. Tosia and her sister
would hide behind the bushes and watch the dancers, hoping
to see one of the couples sharing a secret kiss. Sooner or later
one of the servants would appear, grab the two protesting

girls by their collars and haul them back to bed. But Tosia couldn't sleep and would lie awake in the dark, breathing in the perfume of the evening primroses that drifted in through the open window and surrendering to the music that was filled with such strange longing it sent her into a turmoil she had never felt before.

On that particular summer day she was listening to the humming of the bees, and relaxing in the warm sun. Eventually she put down her book, closed her eyes and dozed until she forgot the world around her.

Suddenly she felt someone's lips on hers. Startled out of her half-sleep, she was not sure whether she had been dreaming or whether it really happened, this gentle sensation of someone's lips on hers, arousing both shock and tenderness in her.

It was real. A young man with tousled hair and black eyes stood before her. He was wearing a threadbare jacket and a shirt open at the neck – a *preposterous* way to dress. He looked irresistible.

David Liebling excused himself, blushing bright red. He was shocked by his daring. How could he have taken the liberty of kissing this girl? A poor Jewish boy barely eighteen years old . . . He had climbed over the wall of these rich people's garden to fill his pockets with fruit to take home to his mother and three brothers. What had got into him? Certainly he was known all over town as a daredevil. His mother had always had trouble with him and his brothers from the time they were quite little. The neighbours were used to seeing Maria Liebling dragging her boys home by the seat of their pants, scolding them because they had been up to another of their pranks or had stolen something. 'That poor woman,' they would say, shaking their heads, 'she really doesn't have an easy time of it with that pack of rascals and her husband dead. Four boys! It's a miracle she manages at all.'

Actually it wasn't a miracle. It was Maria Liebling's iron will and hard work that did it. She took in sewing to feed her family, working day and night. She hardly slept. She did the cooking and cleaning early in the morning while the children were still asleep. Then after school she would lock her sons in their room so that they would do their homework, only to discover that they had climbed out of the window, leaving behind a note saying, 'Mama thinks we're studying, but we're not studying.' Still, she was proud of her sons, even though not a day passed when she didn't have to read them the Riot Act.

David stared at Tosia, and Tosia stared at David. For a brief moment the buzzing of the bees and the twittering of the birds in the garden stopped. Then David turned round, jumped over the wall with one leap and was gone.

Teofila felt hot and dizzy. She took her book and went back into the cool house, flopped down on her bed and buried her face in the pillows. Something new had entered her life, and she didn't know what to make of it. She couldn't tell her mother about what happened, her mother who was always busy managing the household. And certainly she couldn't talk about it with her father. He had just come back on the train from a business trip to Vienna and was now relaxing with a cigar and a glass of liqueur in the semi-darkness of the drawing room. Sabine, who was only thirteen, was too young. And the servant girls who took care of the children could not be entrusted with such a secret. So Tosia kept it all to herself, and it was quite some time before she realized why she no longer had any appetite and couldn't sleep at night. It wasn't until David had climbed over the wall a few more times and his kisses could no longer be considered a coincidence, not even with the best of intentions, that she had to admit to herself that she was head over heels in love.

*　　*　　*

'What does that mean, Mama, "in love"?' I ask. It is the first time I've heard those words. My mother hesitates. She clears her throat, but her voice is still husky, 'Being in love is like . . . like . . . like chocolate.'

'And the seven years of waiting?' I ask, not at all satisfied with her answer.

'I'll tell you about that another time, darling. It's time to go to sleep now.'

When her voice has taken on that certain tone, it's useless to ask more questions. It means she doesn't want to tell me any more stories, and I can no longer get through to her. She hides like a snail in its shell. Disappointed, I say good night and roll over on my side.

'. . . the smell of the blood still: all the perfumes of Arabia will not sweeten this little hand . . .'

Somebody shouts, 'Kill them! Kill them all!'

I'm hiding behind the high-backed blue sofa in the parlour. The piece of bread I was supposed to eat but can't is squashed in my hand. That's why I slipped away and came here and, besides, I love to look secretly at the dolls.

But then these people suddenly came into the room and I had to hide quickly. They didn't see me and started to argue and shout and yell. Manuela is with them.

'Kill them! Kill them all!' a man's voice shouts. I peep out carefully from behind the sofa. The man is lying on the floor, on the flowered carpet. He presses his hand over his heart, then his head rolls to the side.

Suddenly he grins and gets up again. I sigh with relief.

There are other men in the room and a woman, too. I know them. They sometimes come to visit Manuela. I remember their names: Adam, Halina, Jerzy, Tadeusz.

'These are my friends,' Manuela says, whenever they come, and then she closes the door to the parlour. All you can hear is a strange jumble of voices.

'Die!' Adam yells. 'They must die . . .'

I flinch, make myself as small as I can. Are they talking about us? I hear them laugh. Now they're talking quite normally to each other and they're laughing.

But then again. 'Children! My children! They are all dead!' Halina cries out and bursts into tears.

Why are they saying these things? There aren't any Germans here. Who would kill them?

I come out from behind the sofa, run over to Manuela, grab her hand and hold it tight. Manuela knows immediately what's wrong. She kneels down and looks into my eyes.

'It's just pretend,' she says. 'You don't have to be afraid. We're rehearsing for a play.'

A play? Is killing a play?

Later she explains, 'This is an acting school. My friends and I want to become actors. We perform stories that are in the thick books you sometimes look at. Books by Mickiewicz, Shakespeare . . . But you must never, never tell anybody. Otherwise we'll all be put in jail, because it's forbidden.'

That doesn't surprise me at all, I know what FORBIDDEN means. Everything we do is forbidden, is dangerous. Always.

'May I pretend too?'

She doesn't answer. Instead she goes to her room and brings back a fat album that I haven't seen before. There are many photos in it, of beautiful blonde women in fine dresses, and elegant men. They all have a soft, dreamy look in their eyes.

'Greta Garbo,' Manuela says, 'Marlene Dietrich, Clark Gable – they're famous actors.' Her voice is full of admiration. I see a woman lifting her skirt up high; she has long legs. Slowly I read, 'Il-se Wer-ner.' And, then, a little girl no bigger than me. How pretty she is! With curly blonde hair in a ruffled dress. Who is that?

Her name is Shirley Temple. It's as if a spell has been cast on me. I can't get my fill of looking at this little girl. Shirley Temple, I keep repeating, Shirley Temple. I stare at the photo until I know every button on her dress, every bow on her shoes.

'I'd like to be an actress too,' I say to Manuela. My mouth is dry; my heart is pounding – with excitement now instead of the usual fear.

She nods absent-mindedly. 'Maybe. When you're grown-up,' she says. Why is she saying that? She doesn't seem to know that I will never grow up, that one day they'll come to get us, that children are shot. I will not grow up. Don't want to grow up.

Manuela closes the album. I would love to look at it again, but she doesn't have any more time for me. To distract me she gives me a present. 'Here,' she says, and presses a photo into my hand, 'Marika Rökk, you like her a lot, don't you? I have copies of her picture.'

Breathless with joy I hold the photo close to my chest.

The actors are all tall men with shining eyes and loud laughs, and they all like me. 'Our little friend,' they call me, and that makes me proud. One of them, Tadeusz, a thin, lanky man sometimes puts me on his shoulders and carries me around the room. That is marvellous because things look completely different from up there and I feel as though I could fly. I can also see that Tadeusz has a little bald spot on his head and that there's dust on the crystal chandelier.

'And now a wood comes towards Dunsinane . . .' Halina groans, and points at the stove in the corner. I see the forest as though it were really here. I see the invisible people with whom the actors are talking. I love pretending.

Manuela and the actors read to each other from fat books, they roll their eyes, prance through the room, and shout at one another. I try to copy them. 'Fetch me the handkerchief, Desdemona.' I squeak. They all laugh and applaud. They say I have talent. That makes me feel ever so proud.

Pretending has a lot to do with 'love', a word that's like

'chocolate'. Being in love. I ask Manuela if she's in love. She laughs and her cheeks turn pink. 'The questions you keep asking me, *Poziomka!*'

I'm sitting at the kitchen table in front of a full plate. There's a thick slice of brown liver on it. It's good for the blood, they say. I hate liver. I hate blood.

My mother and Mrs Kiernikowa are talking. I sneak away. There's nobody in Dudek's room. I tiptoe in, intending to crawl under the bed. But there's not enough room for me. Something hard and metallic lies under the bed: guns. I know what they are; the men in boots always carry them. And there are also small, round, shiny things; I don't know what they are. They roll around easily . . .

I hear someone cry out and I recoil. Mrs Kiernikowa is standing in the doorway. I've never seen her look like that, pale and furious.

The grown-ups say what I did was very, very bad. Even Manuela is angry with me. Because now I know too much. You have to leave early tomorrow morning, Mrs Kiernikowa says angrily. And again my mother's lips are white and thin. We have to leave. But it never comes to that.

Because that night the men in the shiny boots and the gold buttons come again.

AUFMACHEN!
KONTROLLE!
KENNKARTEN!
LOS!
SCHNELL!
AUFSTEHEN!

I can hear the shouting from far away, and I crawl under my blanket. I know all this, it's very familiar: the hard sound of boots on the stairs, the slamming of doors, fists pounding, the eager sniffing of the dogs, the hoarse voices of the men giving orders.

Now they're in the hall. They search through everything, the kitchen, the living room, Manuela's room, Dudek's room. They approach the grandmother's room, our bed. Mrs Kiernikowa has told us to pretend to be asleep whenever there's an inspection. I don't make a move under my quilt. I can feel the pounding of my mother's heart, just as in the ghetto, her fear, her rigid body. I hear the grandmother pretending to snore softly.

They rip open the door and turn on the light. I blink sleepily. But all the time I'm wide awake.

'This is my sick mother. And this is Teofila Ligocka, my cousin from Rzeszów and her daughter,' Mrs Kiernikowa explains, in a strained voice.

'Identity cards!' one of the two men in boots barks.

My mother sits up, rubs her eyes, pretends she has been fast asleep. I can tell immediately she's not a very good actress. Making a lot of fuss she gets our papers out of the suitcase under the couch and hands them to the men in uniform. Do they notice that my mother's hand is trembling? Maybe they're accustomed to that. But maybe it annoys them. They look at us suspiciously.

I jump out of bed, kneel down and begin to pray. My mother taught me to do that so they won't suspect we are Jews: 'Our Father, who art in heaven . . . Mary, Mother of God, have mercy upon our . . .'

I reel off the words, get confused and start again from the beginning: 'Our Father . . .'

The men in boots hesitate. They stop at the open door and stare at me. One of the soldiers sees the photo of Maria Rökk on my night-table. He picks it up with two fingers, looks at it for a long time, smiles. Then he says something to the other man and they leave.

'*Poziomka* played her part well!' Manuela says, and gives

me a kiss. 'Very well done. What a fabulous actress!'

We're all squatting around *Babcia*'s bed, still trembling with fear. The grown-ups confer in whispers. I sit on Manuela's lap.

We're allowed to stay, even to sleep in Dudek's room. In the wide bed under which lie the guns. Dudek has to sleep on the couch in his grandmother's room.

I feel proud. 'We have much more space here,' I say to my mother, who doesn't seem at all happy as we stand in Dudek's beautiful big room with our suitcases. 'It's because I played my part so well.'

I touch the flowers in the carpet hanging on the wall above Dudek's bed, trace the curved lines with my finger. I sleep much better in the new bed. The blue lilies have a calming effect; it's as though they are singing me to sleep.

My mother buttons her coat.

We are by ourselves in the apartment except for the grandmother. She is still asleep.

I run to get my coat, quickly throw Maria Rökk's photo into my suitcase.

'No,' my mother says. Her voice shakes a little.

I look at her, surprised.

'You stay here,' she explains. 'with *Babcia* Isdebska. I have to do something. I'll be back soon.'

I panic. I cling to her legs.

'I'm coming too,' I sob. 'I want to die with you!'

My mother tries to free her legs from my arms. 'You can't come,' she says. 'It's too dangerous.'

'Please, Mama,' I implore, clinging to her like a burr. If she goes off by herself, I'll never see her again.

'All right,' she says, and sighs when she sees she can't get rid of me. 'But only this once, do you hear me? And you mustn't say a word, is that clear? Leave your suitcase here.'

She wipes my nose, and I cover her face with kisses. I know she's actually glad I'm going with her.

The bell above the door clatters.

We step into a hairdresser's shop.

I've never seen anything like it. The room is full of mirrors and smells of flowers. Snippets of hair are scattered on the floor. A man with foam on his face is sitting on a high chair. He has a big napkin tied around his neck, and his head is tilted back. A thin man with yellowish skin scrapes the foam off with a long silver knife.

A blonde woman sits on another chair reading a magazine. She has lots of golden curls and a red mouth like Manuela after she's used the colour stick. A bright circle of hair, looking like a radiant sun, lies at her feet on the floor.

The yellowish man turns to my mother. 'Yes, what is it?'

'I'd like to pay the bill for the permanent wave,' my mother says.

The man gives an imperceptible start. 'Please excuse me for a second,' he says to the man in the chair, and puts the silver knife into a pot. Then he and my mother go through a curtain into the back room.

Enthralled by all the interesting things, I just stand there as though rooted to the spot. There are little coloured bottles and combs in all sizes, a strangely shaped sink, mysterious pots and little containers on the shelves, and near one wall, a big machine that looks like a silver hat . . .

Just then the blonde woman looks up from her magazine and sees my reflection in the mirror. She smiles at me with her red lips.

I smile back. The woman is blonde and beautiful; she looks very nice. Something draws me to her. The feeling is so strong that I forget everything else. I run over to her and climb up in her lap.

She's a little surprised by this. 'Oops,' she says kindly, 'who is this sitting in my lap? What's your name, little one?'

I'm just about to answer her when I remember that I'm not allowed to talk to anyone. I close my mouth and say nothing.

'Did you forget your name?' the woman asks, and laughs.

Just then my mother comes out from behind the curtain, followed by the yellowish man. Both stare at me in the mirror. I recognize the horror in my mother's eyes and know immediately that I have done something wrong.

'What's your little girl's name?' the blonde woman asks my mother.

My mother is groping for words. 'Eh . . . Roma . . .' she says. 'Roma, please come here, we have to leave now.'

It's impossible to miss the threatening note in her voice. I quickly climb down from the blonde woman's lap and run over to my mother. She grips my hand.

'Well, then, till next time,' my mother says to the yellowish man, who is again scraping at the other man's face with the knife. He nods.

'Goodbye, Roma,' the blonde woman calls after me. I don't dare to turn round. The bell above the door clatters as we leave the hairdresser's shop.

'The woman was German,' my mother says to Manuela. 'I'm sure she was German.'

My mother is still angry with me. Now she and the Kierniks are again talking about what the child knows and what she doesn't know, what she'll say if someone asks her.

I'm a problem for everyone. A danger to all.

I feel guilty and stare at the newspaper lying on the kitchen table. It was wrapped around the vegetables my mother is washing in the sink. I already know a few letters of the alphabet. Manuela taught them to me. I make believe I'm reading the newspaper so that I don't have to hear their conversation.

Manuela notices the grim expression on my face.

Trying to cheer me up, she asks, 'What are you reading there, *Poziomka*? The classifieds in the *Kraków Messenger*? No respectable Pole would read that rag. It's put out by the Germans. Do *you* think it's interesting?'

I nod, my eyes glued to the newspaper. Manuela sits down next to me, puts her arm around my shoulders, 'Shall I read to you?' she asks. Again I nod. The main thing is to get them to stop talking about me.

'"Miscellaneous",' Manuela begins. She reads beautifully. Everything takes on a life of its own. Even the most boring things sound like a story when Manuela reads them. That's because she's an actress.

Little Girl's coat (for 5-year-old), black dress for slender woman, selling cheap. Karmelicka 54

'That's almost too small for you, isn't it, *Poziomka*?' Manuela asks. She reads on.

Identity card No. 3792 made out to Helena Marek. Stolen 10/11/43.
Wedding rings, earrings, sofa, child's crib for sale. Rajska 4.
Beautiful Christmas presents: used watches, jewellery, silverware, for sale at lowest prices. Szewska, 7/1

My mother sighs.

Singer sewing machine for sale, in good condition. Adolf Hitler Platz 38.

My grandmother . . .

Diamonds. Sell or buy. Reasonable prices. Kraków, Dietla Street 15.
Christian second hand store, buy, sell. Record players, furs, carpets, shoes, quilts. We pay highest prices. Lobzowska Street 103.

Identity card stolen, issued at the Kraków Registry Office, made out to A. Konieczna.

'Were our identity cards stolen too?' I ask. Manuela quickly reads on.

Old pictures, paintings, buy and sell. Free appraisals. Art gallery. Kraków. Łobzowska Street 59.
Furs, fox collars, coats – will take on commission. Stradom 6.
Singer sewing machine, good condition, covered drive belts, lady's fur coat, small size, Smoleńsk 39.
Down quilts in good condition, we buy, Hauptstrasse 10.
Excellent psychologist, fortune teller and handwriting expert can look into the future and the **fate of missing persons.** Include exact date of birth and 20 Złoty in letter. Address all mail in care of editorial offices.

Manuela clears her throat before she continues.

Hair colouring, waving, expert service. Sława Company, Kraków.
Better class young woman, clean, must know how to cook, with excellent knowledge of German, wanted for refined household. Kraków, Aussenring 12/6.
Holes in clothing invisibly mended. Workshop. Kraków, Starowiślna 43.
Certificate of Aryan ancestry scientifically researched by accredited genealogical researcher (world-wide document retrieval). Kraków, Retoryka Street 174/Vienna, Türken Street 1.
Overnight accommodations, clean, discreet. Jana 30/4.
For sale, cheap: Used clothing, bed sheets, carpets and other nice things. Kraków, Karmelicka 80 (store).

'I can well imagine where they got those things,' my mother says. She dries her hands and sits down with us.

Overnight accommodation for discerning individuals.
Kraków, Radziwiłowska 14/2.
Overnight accommodation for travellers. Sebastiana 34/4.
Bargains: used household linens, men's trousers, suit, fur
coat, men's travel shaving kit, patent leather shoes. Dietla
19.
Christian second-hand store is urgently seeking: Italian
candlesticks, silver trays, best quality bed linens, table
linens, down comforters. Lobzowska 103.
Two-week-old infant – female, available. Please contact
'No. 6248'.

Manuela takes a deep breath, reads on.

Bedbugs and other vermin exterminated, disinfected.
AZOT. Kraków, Krakowska 27.
Restaurant 'Alt Krakau' seeking German-speaking staff.
Records, German music, light classical and classical, for
sale every day. Marka 81.
As Christmas presents we recommend: silver cigarette cases,
sugar servers, spoons, crystal goblets, and other gifts.
Kraków, Sławkowska 26.
Learn German in 3 months. Kraków, Długa 30/1.
Fur coat for little girl, with hood, in good condition, a
bargain. Sienna 1.
Young boy missing. Left his home 17 September. He is 12
years old, blond, blue eyes. Send information to editorial
offices.
German Army looking for volunteers for temporary service.
Report at: Böcklin Str. 19.
Singer sewing machine . . .

'*Et cetera, et cetera.*' Manuela's voice sounds angry. She
crumples the newspaper and throws it into the stove. It's the
first time I have seen Manuela lose her temper, and I am
quite shocked. I'm sure it's my fault.

Roma Ligocka

My mother gets up and goes back to cleaning vegetables.

A few days later when Mrs Kiernikowa puts us out again I realize what a good thing it was that Manuela read the classified ads to us. 'They've been increasing the number of inspections recently,' Mrs Kiernikowa had said, 'and, as you know, Gestapo headquarters is just round the corner. You've got to leave.'

We took our suitcases and left. One last look at the beautiful flowered carpet hanging above Dudek's bed. How nice it would be if we lived here. But by then we're already standing on the street.

Where to? My mother feverishly considers the various possibilities. There's an icy wind blowing; it's winter again. The puddles between the cobblestones are frozen. It's too cold to go back to the garden house.

But then she remembers the classifieds: 'Overnight accommodation for discerning individuals . . . Radziwiłowska 14/2,' my mother mutters and grabs my hand.

The street is in a dirty, run-down neighbourhood in the Kraków suburbs; the house at number fourteen looks anything but inviting. Grey stucco crumbles from the low façade, the windows are opaque with dirt. An emaciated cat sits by the front door and stares at us with hostility. We ring the bell.

Slow, shuffling footsteps approach. A fat woman opens the door. Her face is red and puffy, her hair stringy. She is wearing a dirty striped bathrobe.

'We're not buying anything.' Her voice is brusque and unpleasant.

My mother says something about a classified advertisement, overnight accommodation and discerning individuals.

'Come in.'

We're in a dark narrow hall stuffed with armoires and chests. It smells of cabbage and cat faeces.

'This way.' The woman shuffles along in front of us, stops at a door.

'First you pay,' she says to my mother, and looks at us with the same hostility as her cat.

My mother rummages through her pockets, pulls out a couple of banknotes. The woman grabs them like a fat frog snapping up a fly. She opens the door.

It's almost dark in the room; the curtains are drawn. A massive, carved double bed takes up nearly all of one wall, dirty quilts are piled on it; a sofa is pushed up against the other wall. At least four armoires fill up the spaces between them.

'You can use the double bed,' the woman says to my mother, sounding almost resentful. She slams the door as she leaves.

'Quiet!' says a voice in the semi-darkness. It comes from the direction of the sofa. Only now do I see that we're not alone in the room. A shapeless form lies on the sofa, sleeping – or at least trying to sleep. We step closer and put our suitcases down. My mother offers polite apologies for the disturbance. The figure's fat behind is turned towards us, but she sits up now in order to look at us. I am amazed. The woman has two colours of hair, dark and light, the hair is parted in the middle. I've never seen anything like it. I want to ask her why it's like that, but she looks at me so angrily from under her thick black eyebrows that the words stick in my throat.

'A child,' she sighs, 'that's all I needed.'

My mother makes a startled sound. 'Professor,' she says, 'what are you doing here?'

The two women seem to know each other and begin to chat quietly, excluding me completely. I sit down on the edge of the bed and undress. I'm terribly tired.

'You can go to sleep, Roma,' my mother says, over her shoulder. 'I'll join you in a minute.'

I crawl under the dirty covers. The quilts are repulsive; they smell like the air in the hallway. The room, the professor, the apartment disgust me.

Roma Ligocka

I think of Marika Rökk:

I so much would like . . .
I just I don't know what . . .

Moments later I'm asleep.

I am awakened by loud banging on the front door.
The Germans!
But it can't be the Germans. The man outside isn't shouting: he's begging, pleading.
'Please, let me come back in, Sophie, my jewel. Please. I'm your husband. You can't possibly hold that little bit of vodka against me . . . Come on, open the door, my dove. It's curfew time . . .'
But apparently Sophie wouldn't think of letting him in. I hear them bickering.
'Don't behave so hysterically, sweetheart,' the man's voice sobs. 'You're too hysterical, you really are.' The banging lets up a little and finally it stops. It is quiet again.
'Go back to sleep,' my mother whispers in the darkness. She is lying next to me under the heavy, bad-smelling coverlet. Maybe the bed belongs to the man the fat woman didn't let in. I shudder at the thought. But my eyelids are heavy, and I fall asleep again.
Not for long, though. Suddenly I feel a funny tickling on my body, a prickling and crawling, all over. I throw back the quilt and look for the light switch.
'Mama!'
'What's the matter now?' the professor grunts. My mother finds the switch, turns on the lamp next to the bed. I pull up my undershirt to see what's itching me.
'*Gewalt geshriben!*' my mother cries out in horror, and covers her face with her hands. That's Yiddish, and it means something really terrible. I look at myself. A black stripe

72

stretches across my body. I don't understand, look more closely. Now I see that the black stripe is moving. It consists of many single black dots, little living things crawling and creeping across my skin. I try to wipe them off, but they cling to me.

'Mama!'

'It's all right, child. Ssh. I'll pull them off. They've attached themselves to your skin . . . don't be afraid . . .' My mother bends over me; I can tell she's disgusted. She picks the bedbugs off my body with her fingertips, quickly and purposefully, like a pigeon picking up breadcrumbs. Then she squashes them on the floor with her shoe. It's a silent, gruesome battle, interrupted only by gruff sounds coming from the professor, who is complaining about my yowling and the night-table lamp being on.

By early morning my mother is finished. My entire body is red and swollen. We don't dare turn off the light, because the bedbugs would come back in the dark. The professor has gone back to sleep. We lie silently next to each other, my mother and I. A thin stripe of grey morning light touches our exhausted faces. No use trying to sleep now.

'Tell me more about love,' I whisper.

My mother sighs.

'It was so long ago . . .'

It wasn't long before Tosia's mother realized that her daughter had a secret. She would often walk in the garden by herself, and at dinner she didn't even touch her favourite dessert, apple strudel with raisins. But her mother thought it better not to say anything, just to wait and see. After all, that's what her own mother had done years before when she introduced her sixteen-year-old daughter Anna to Jakob Abrahamer, the young man the family had carefully chosen for her. Anna was sixteen years old then, and from that time on she was convinced that love was a rather practical matter.

Like the plum trees in the garden, love developed and grew with time, required a little nurturing now and then, and produced fruit now and then, but there was no reason to waste a lot of words on it.

The riddle of Tosia's secret was solved sooner than expected. She had tired of playing hide-and-seek, and boldly decided one day to invite her beloved to her house. 'Oh, by the way, I'm going to ask David Liebling to the Sunday tea dance,' she said over her shoulder after supper, running hastily upstairs to her room to avoid seeing her parents' reaction. Jakob Abrahamer took the cigar out of his mouth and looked questioningly at his wife.

Anna nodded. 'It certainly looks like it.' She sighed. 'But I have no idea where she found this David Liebling. I can only hope that he comes from a good family. Oh, well, we'll see.'

On Sunday, punctually at five, David appeared for the tea dance. He had brought a bunch of flowers for Anna Abrahamer and wore a starched white shirt and a brand-new straw hat. He was polite and charming and kissed Mrs Abrahamer's hand. But it was all in vain.

'He comes from an *unacceptable* family,' Anna explained to her daughter, after the last guests had left. 'There can be no question of your marrying him, Teofila.'

Tosia burst into tears. Not that David had even asked her to marry him; what disappointed her was her parents' re-action. They had called her Teofila, like the nuns at school – as though she were a stranger. They had no inkling of their daughter's emotions, and they had no idea what love was. They were narrow-minded and heartless. Well, Tosia would show them.

From that day on she refused to eat. She sat at the table silently and didn't touch her food. She lost weight and became thinner and thinner. The circles under her eyes deepened, but her eyes burned with defiance.

'Oh, please eat something,'
Anna urged her eldest daughter.
'You have to eat to stay alive.'
But Tosia wouldn't hear of it.
If she couldn't have David, she
didn't want to live.

In spite of his family background, David now came to
visit every Sunday. His manners
were flawless, his shirts always
freshly ironed. He was continuing his education at night
school, had started a construction company, and one day he
came to ask Jakob Abrahamer
for Tosia's hand.

Teofila at twenty (1931).

Jakob Abrahamer poured David a glass of plum brandy,
offered him a cigar, and closed the french windows to the
drawing room. Even Sabine, who was experienced in such
things, couldn't find out anything of importance by looking
through the keyhole. All she could catch were a few scraps
of conversation.

'They're talking about you,' she said to Tosia, who had
already guessed as much and was now bent over her books
at the desk in her room, pale and tense.

After at least an hour, the french windows opened again.
Jakob Abrahamer and David Liebling had come to an agreement. As used to be the custom in Jewish families in the old
days, David would have to wait seven years for his Tosia and
would use that time to build a solid financial foundation for
his future family. The two men shook hands.

After David put on his hat and left, Tosia crept down to
the kitchen and ate a huge piece of apple strudel.

'And you really waited seven years?' I ask, deeply impressed, even though I can't really imagine such a span of time. In any case, it seems like a long time.

'Yes,' my mother says, and a smile flits across her face. 'I was twenty-three years old when we finally got married. By that time I had already left school and gone on to college.'

'College?' I had no idea that my mother had a profession.

'Actually I wanted to be a doctor,' she says, a little sadly, 'but your father did not want me to work. We wanted to have a lot of children, you know. At least five . . . and so I went to a secretarial school instead. That's where you learn to write letters on a typewriter.'

Writing letters sounds pretty boring. Being an actress is a much more exciting profession. But the thing about children, that makes me think. I would have liked to have sisters and brothers. I am always so alone.

'I'd like very much to have a little sister!' I blurt out.

My mother pats me on the head and quietly gets out of bed. 'I said the same thing to my mother when I was little.' She sighs. 'I'll tell you what happened another time. Now we ought to leave this place and get something to eat.'

We tiptoe out of the dark room. The professor's rhythmic snoring never stops. And then we're back on the street.

Snow has fallen overnight. A white world, glittering and untouched, stretches before us. The contrast between the purity of the snow and the horrible ordeal of the previous night almost hurts. I close my eyes, take a deep breath. Cool, fresh air fills my lungs – it feels good.

We go to a bakery and buy two pieces of cake, then to a little park where my mother wipes the snow off a bench. We put down our suitcases and sit down to eat breakfast. All around us everything is beautiful and peaceful. I watch some children on their way to school, throwing snowballs at one another and laughing. They're wearing bright-coloured hats and carrying schoolbags on their backs. They are only a little older than me. How I'd like to be one of them, running around in the snow, and screaming whenever a snowball hits me in the head.

My mother interrupts my daydreaming. 'Eat,' she says sternly. She is thinking about where we should go next. I can almost always read her mind.

'Back to Manuela,' I say, without hesitation. My mother nods. What choice do we have? We have no home, only a hiding place where our presence is a constant danger to the lives of the people who hide us. But in spite of that maybe they'll take us back. At least we have to try.

We're lucky. They take us in again. In the kitchen my mother tells Manuela about our night with the bedbugs. I stand at the window in the parlour watching the dancing snowflakes. I think of Maria Rökk, who so much would like and doesn't know what.

But suddenly I know what *I* would like. I would like to make snowballs! Quietly I open the window. Thick white snow lies on the windowsill like the sugar my mother sifts over the doughnuts. I put my hand in it. It is soft and cold and melts under my warm fingers. I lick them. Actually I hoped the snow would taste like sugar, but it has no taste. I begin to form little snowballs, tiny white spheres, one, two, a whole lot. I'm so busy, I don't notice that Mrs Kiernikowa has come into the room.

'You bad girl! Look what a mess you've made on the parquet floor. Everything is wet and full of snow. And it's freezing in here. You're going to catch a cold at the open window. Then you'll be ill again.'

Her words rain down on me like hailstones. I try to make myself invisible, but it doesn't work. Maybe I've forgotten how. While I wonder whether I ought to hide behind the sofa, the grandmother comes into the room. As always she's wearing her nightgown, has thrown a crocheted shawl over her shoulders. She looks very angry. Oddly enough, she isn't angry with me but with Mrs Kiernikowa.

'Close the window, and don't make such a fuss, Helene!' she snaps at her daughter, and I have the feeling that Mrs Kiernikowa would also like to make herself invisible or hide behind the sofa.

The grandmother continues her scolding. 'The poor child is scared to death of you! How can you get so upset about a little bit of water? Roma is going to wipe up the floor and that will be that. It would be better if you spared your nerves, Helene. There are really worse things nowadays than a puddle of water.'

With that she rustles off, her head held high. Mrs Kiernikowa closes the window, mumbles something unfriendly and leaves. I get a pail and a rag from the kitchen and wipe up the water, making believe I'm Cinderella and Mrs Kiernikowa is the cruel stepmother. That gives me a wonderful feeling of superiority.

And, besides, I finally have learned how to make snowballs.

Mrs Kiernikowa, my mother and Manuela have been baking for days, and the apartment smells of cinnamon and cloves. The actors have brought little packages for Manuela, and Tadeusz even had a big one for me. But I'm not allowed to open it, not yet. I'm also not allowed to go into the parlour because that's where the tree is. A real tree! I saw Dudek dragging it in. But nobody will tell me what this is all about. Not even the grandmother. 'It's Christmas,' she says, with a mysterious smile that makes many creases form around her eyes. I like the way she looks.

Everybody is excited and busy, except for me. I have no idea what Christmas is. I sit in the kitchen reading the newspaper. By now I can read pretty well. After all, I'm already five years old.

The old world order has come to an end following the violent struggle we have witnessed among the nations. A new Europe is emerging. Naturally, such a rebirth is connected with tremendous changes that require not only great effort but also great sacrifice . . . Sometimes we think the world turns around us, but this is not the case . . .

I don't understand any of this, and it's boring. I turn the page. 'Christmas in Kraków,' it says.

Our city with its many churches has always been the religious capital of Poland where all holidays have been celebrated festively, especially Christmas. The traditional Christmas Eve dinner begins with three kinds of soup (fish soup, almond soup with raisins, and borscht with mushroom-filled pierogi). Then comes herring. After that, three kinds of fish: carp in grey sauce, pike in saffron sauce, perch with mayonnaise, and finally, biscuits with poppy seeds and honey . . .

The table is set with a snow-white cloth and under the tablecloth there's traditionally a bundle of hay. In affluent homes Christmas Eve dinner consists of twelve courses . . .

'What are we having for dinner this evening?' I ask Manuela. She looks at me in surprise. '*You* want to know what we're having to eat, *Poziomka?*' she asks me, 'That's a change!' Then she looks at the newspaper I've been reading and takes it away from me. 'Didn't I tell you that no decent, self-respecting Pole would read this German propaganda?' She skims the article. 'Twelve courses . . .' she says, with bitterness, 'as if people had anything to eat during this war . . .' She crumples up the newspaper and throws it into the stove. 'We're having something very, very good tonight,' she says solemnly. 'We've actually been able to get a real carp. I'm sure you'll like it.'

I sigh. Whenever they say something like that I'm pretty sure I won't like it.

*   *   *

I have to wait in the kitchen until I almost can't stand the suspense any longer. At last Manuela takes my hand and leads me into the parlour. And there is the shining tree! It reaches almost all the way up to the ceiling, and fastened to its branches are lighted candles. The entire room is full of a golden light. We all stand there, enchanted, and sing beautiful songs about the little Jesus who had no shirt and had to sleep in a stable and whose mother didn't know where she could go.

Of course we are all dressed in our best. Even the grandmother got out of bed for the occasion and is wearing a dark dress; I hardly recognize her. Manuela has lovely bows in her hair; my mother is wearing her flowered blouse, and somehow even Mrs Kiernikowa looks nicer wearing a lace collar and golden brooch. I have a large white bow in my hair and am wearing a dress that is a little too short on me. I'm growing fast.

The Christmas tree is the most beautiful thing I've ever seen. It sparkles all over and is decorated with toys made of wood, glass, and porcelain: little coloured angels, stars, birds of paradise, horses, and little sledges. Among them hang brightly wrapped sweets and tiny red apples. I'm allowed to touch these precious, glittering things; it's as if we're in a fairy-tale.

Then we eat dinner in the parlour, and there really is a white tablecloth with hay under it. I don't remember how the fish tasted, but at Christmas everything tastes good. Because it is so elegant and festive.

First I unpack the big package from Tadeusz; it was lying among the other packages under the Christmas tree. Inside is a fat book called *The Secret Garden*. Manuela promises to read to me every day. She gives me a little velvet-covered book. When I leaf through it I'm disappointed to see that all the pages are blank. But Manuela explains to me that it is a diary. I can write whatever I want in it, and I can also let other people write in it, their thoughts, a poem, or just their names. I immediately paste Marika Rökk's photograph into it.

My mother has made me a dark-blue pleated skirt in which I look grown-up enough to be going to school. I also get a present from the grandmother: a lovely little bag that she crocheted herself, the kind that grown-up women use.

I think I have never been as happy as I am on this Christmas Eve. It's almost as if I had a family and a real home. I am allowed to stay up as long as I want, and nobody comes and pounds on the door.

Later Mrs Kiernikowa and my mother wash the dishes. The grandmother and I stand at the open window and listen to the stillness of Christmas night. First we hear the nostalgic melody sounded by the St Mary's Church trumpet. And then the bells of Kraków begin to ring, many dark and bright bells, sad and joyful bells, big bells and little bells.

Once we're in bed, I ask my mother whether in the old days she celebrated Christmas the same way. 'No,' she says. 'Jews don't celebrate Christmas. We have different holidays.'

Too bad. 'Did you at least get presents?' I ask her.

She laughs a little in the dark. 'Of course,' she says, 'we had marvellous presents when I was a child. For every birthday there was something golden, a ring, a necklace, a little pin, and whenever my father came back from one of his trips to Vienna, he brought us presents. Once he gave me a glass paperweight. When you shook it, tiny snowflakes fell gently on a small village with a church. And once he gave me a musical box. That was my favourite.'

'What's a musical box?' I ask.

'Mine was a box made of gleaming mahogany. Little porcelain dolls turned on its lid while lovely waltz music played,' she says dreamily. 'The dolls were dressed elegantly, the ballerinas wore little tulle skirts, the male dancers dark dress

81

suits. You could wind up the musical box again and again, and the music would play and the figures would turn . . . But now you really have to go to sleep, Roma.'

She covers me with the quilt and gives me a kiss. Christmas has made me tired and before long I am asleep.

I think I dreamt about the musical box all night, but also about the Christmas tree. And the song about the little Jesus who didn't have a shirt or a home. Whatever happened to him and his mother?

3

I'm standing in the Kierniks' living room behind the white
lace window curtains, watching life out there, a life I'm not
allowed to take part in. By now I know each crack in the
wall across the way, each skylight and each cobblestone. I
counted all the church towers long ago. Pigeons flutter up
and settle on the roof of the house across the street. I hate
pigeons. Their cooing makes me sick.

Dark scraps of cloud drift across the grey sky; gradually
dusk descends over the city's roofs and spires. People scurry
into their houses like rats; then the street is empty. It is shortly
before six o'clock and curfew starts at six.

Everyone knows you get shot if you're still on the street
after six. And if people can't manage to get home in time,
they spend the night with friends, or knock on some stranger's
door. Once Tadeusz and the actors slept on the living-room
floor here when their rehearsing went on too long. That was
very nice. Tadeusz told me fairy-tales till late into the night.

After curfew a ghostly stillness sets in. I can make out the
shadows of two uniformed men on the corner.

Just as I'm about to turn away from the window to go to
the kitchen, I see two big boys running across the street. One
disappears into the doorway of a house. The other keeps
running. One of the uniformed men looks at his wristwatch
and draws his pistol. The church clock strikes. The shot and
the stroke of the clock are as one. The boy falls to the ground.
The two uniformed men continue talking to each other as
though nothing has happened.

My mother has come up behind me. 'Those gangsters,' she

says. Then she covers the window with black paper, as the regulations require.

In the evening Manuela reads to me from the new book Tadeusz gave me for Christmas. *The Secret Garden.* It's a wonderful book. On the jacket there's a picture of a little blonde girl in a beautiful garden. That's me. The flowers are in bloom and a robin sits on the little girl's shoulder.

We've already read two chapters, and it's terribly suspenseful and sad. The little girl is all alone and has no one to play with. Whenever I hear the children shouting and yelling in the back courtyard I think of the little girl. True, our courtyard is no garden, but there is a beautiful tree growing there. In the last few days it has put out many fat buds. Now I sometimes hide on the kitchen balcony and watch the children. They can't see me up here.

But unfortunately my mother does see me. She grabs me by the collar and drags me back into the kitchen, closes the door to the balcony and locks it. 'Roma,' she says half reproachfully, half gently, 'you know that no one, absolutely no one, must find out you're here.'

I have to promise to behave from now on.

Today we found out that my father is still alive. A young blonde woman named Ella came to see us. She is Maria's sister, and Maria is the wife of Uncle Szymon, Papa's brother. Ella is hiding in the house of her friend, a Polish engineer. She has Polish identification papers, and because she looks good and not at all Jewish – blonde-dyed hair and light brown eyes – she can go anywhere without arousing suspicion.

We don't know how she got our address. My mother almost fainted when Ella suddenly turned up here. She brought us a small package; in it was Father's ring. It's now lying on the kitchen table, just as it did when we were still in the ghetto. The red stone has two entwined symbols etched into it. Now that I can read I know that they are two letters of the alphabet: B and L.

I remember my father saying, 'It's Bernhard's ring.' I remember how his voice sounded – heavy and faraway, as though coming out of a deep well. But I can't picture his face any more. I only know that he had dark eyes, like me.

Ella stays only a short while. She says my father gave her the ring while he was still with the Płaszów construction gang. But she doesn't know where he is now.

After Ella has left, Mrs Kiernikowa asks, 'How could she have known that you're

Small pleasures: Roma on the Kierniks' balcony (about 1943).

staying with us?' She doesn't seem glad that my father is still alive.

But my mother is so happy she doesn't even notice Mrs Kiernikowa's frown. Her eyes have a moist gleam, and she makes believe that she's terribly busy putting the pots back into the cupboard. While my mother is running back and forth in the kitchen making loud noises with the dishes, Manuela says pensively, 'I wonder whether he's still in Płaszów. I heard they're breaking up the camp.'

My mother doesn't answer. She makes an extra loud clatter with the pot lids. 'I have no idea. But he's alive!' she says finally. 'The ring is a sign of life!'

I remember that Bernhard was dead when the ring was brought to my father. But I don't say anything.

It's wonderful to see my mother happy for once.

Later when she has time to sit down next to me, I ask her, 'Tell me more about you and Papa.' She slides a little closer, and while she speaks she turns the ring with her fingers.

'As you know, your father had three brothers,' she begins. 'This ring belonged to Bernhard, the second youngest. The oldest brother is Moshe. He is Roman's father – do you still remember your cousin Roman? He gave you your bottle when you were about six months old. They smuggled him out of the ghetto through a hole in the wall after Aunt Dziunia, his mother, was . . . I wonder whether he's still alive.' She sighs.

I try to remember him, but I can't. Still, I've heard the name Roman often; after all, it's almost the same as mine.

'Anyway, next came your father, David, then Bernhard, then Szymon. I don't know very much about the origins of the Liebling family. But I do know they were always very poor. Your great-grandfather had seven daughters. Every time another girl was born, he had a fit, cursing, banging doors and getting drunk. Finally he was blessed with a son who turned out to be a good-for-nothing. He was known all over town as a skirt-chaser. He played cards, and later became an army officer. They say he once created a scandal by galloping diagonally across the Kraków market square on his chestnut horse. His father and sisters idolized him. He was killed in the last war. This son had one daughter after another. His daughters were all very good and courageous Jewish women. Your grandmother Maria was one of them.' My mother pauses briefly and pours herself a cup of tea.

I use this time to think things through. It is all very confusing. Why did Great-grandfather have a fit every time a girl was born? And what was that about the skirt-chaser who was known all over town and who also had one daughter after the other? I'm about to ask my mother but she goes on with the story.

'Maria got married very early to a young man named Samuel Liebling. He constantly changed jobs and was never successful at any of them. He tried being a commercial representative, unsuccessfully; then he ran a restaurant. There is a story that goes back to that time. One evening, when your grandfather came home from the restaurant, he put a bag filled with the day's receipts on the table and went to bed. Your father and his older brother took everything out of the money-bag and folded the pretty coloured notes into little boats. After a while they got into a fight and tore up each other's boats. When they realized what they'd done, they flushed all the scraps down the drain, and so once again Grandfather had no money.'

'Were they punished?' I ask, thinking what a dreadful prank that was.

My mother smiles. 'You know your grandmother! No Jewish mother would ever allow her children to be beaten. But I'm sure she gave them a good scolding.'

'And Grandfather?' In a way I feel sorry for him because he never had any money and always had such bad luck.

'Well, unfortunately he died rather young; he was only thirty-five. And when he died, your grandmother Maria was pregnant with their fourth child. She kept jumping off the top of the armoire, trying to lose it. But nothing worked.'

Another of those puzzling sentences. But now my mother doesn't look as though she wants to go on telling stories. Suddenly she looks very sad again. Thinking of my grandmother makes me sad too. I often think of her. Still, one of these days I'll have to ask my mother why one would jump off an armoire when one wants to lose a child.

They've thrown us out again. Although I'm not sure why, I believe it has something to do with the ring. 'Too dangerous,' Mrs Kiernikowa kept saying, shaking her head. 'Someone could have been watching her. I don't want to see her here ever again.' She meant Ella. They were talking quite loudly, Mrs Kiernikowa and my mother. And it sounded very reproachful. My mother pleaded with her to let us stay, but this time not even the grandmother was able to stop her putting us out on the street. They had put us out so often, I don't even remember each time. Still, every time it happened it was awful.

Who could help us now? My mother is thinking. Again she runs down the short list of people she knows from before. There's a classmate from the convent school, and the Polish maids . . .

Yes, that might be a good idea. One of the maids had especially liked my mother because my mother always gave her her cast-off clothes. Didn't she live somewhere in this neighbourhood?

We start off, walking fast, up one street and down another, searching for the correct address. But we can't find it.

Around lunchtime we go into a little bakery to buy something to eat. No one is there except us. My mother sees fresh raisin rolls on a shelf behind the counter. She puts down her suitcase and rings the bell.

The assistant, a gaunt, older woman with short curls and a crooked mouth, comes out from behind a curtain. Her eyes shining, my mother asks for two raisin rolls, even though she knows I don't like raisin rolls. The woman takes two and puts them into a paper bag. Then she pushes the bag across the countertop, all the time staring at my mother. Suddenly she cries out, 'But you're old Abrahamer's daughter! Teofila, right?'

My mother is petrified. For a few seconds no one says anything. Then my mother grabs my hand and her suitcase and dashes out of the shop – without the rolls. We walk rapidly down the street, around the corner, look back. No one has followed us. We take a deep breath. '*Mazel tov, mazel tov*,' my mother whispers, almost inaudibly. She sighs with relief and wipes her brow.

But now we don't have anything to eat, and after this experience my mother is so afraid of being recognized she doesn't dare enter another shop. In Kraków everyone knows everyone else, of course.

We keep searching. Finally my mother thinks she's found the right street, the right house. 'Here it is,' she says, but doesn't sound at all sure. 'On the fourth floor.'

We climb the stairs. Second floor, third floor . . . As we reach the fourth floor, my mother realizes she has made a mistake. All the names on the nameplates are unfamiliar.

Just as we're about to leave again we hear shouting downstairs.

AUFMACHEN!

The Germans! They're pounding on doors, coming up the stairs. Where can we flee?

As far away as possible from them. We race up more stairs. All the way to the top where there's a heavy iron door that leads to the attic. My mother pushes down on the door handle. We're in luck – the door isn't locked. Quickly we slip through while the tramping on the stairs draws nearer and nearer. We close the door behind us.

But now we're in a trap. No sound can reach us through the iron door. It is quiet and dusty up here, only a little light comes through the small slanted skylight. Wet underwear is hanging on a long washing-line.

My mother is looking for a place to hide. There is none. The room is empty. Except . . . there's a wooden tub standing in a corner.

We crouch down behind the tub. It is much too small to offer us real protection. My mother is panicky. She fiddles with her coat, her blouse, pulls out a small pouch I've often seen before. Whenever I ask her what is in it, she won't tell me.

'Here,' she whispers, and hands me a capsule from the pouch. 'Here, take it. Hold on to it and swallow it when I tell you to.'

I stare at the capsule. It isn't a piece of bread and it isn't something horrible to eat. It is something deadly serious. 'What is it?'

'Cyanide,' she whispers. 'Do as I say.'

I take the capsule and hold it in my damp little fist. It burns like fire.

My mother is holding her capsule too. She stares wide-eyed into the half-dark attic. Listening, listening. But we don't hear anything, don't know if the door will be ripped open any minute by the Germans.

I suddenly realize that I don't know how I'm supposed to swallow the capsule without water. 'But I don't have any water,' I whisper.

My mother whips around. 'It'll work without water too,' she hisses. 'You can simply bite on it.'

'But I need water,' I wail.

'Keep quiet! There's no water here. Just do as I tell you!'

I know I can't swallow the capsule without water. Can't bite down on it either. Can't do what I'm told, can't die . . . In despair I begin to cry. The tears run down my cheeks.

My mother is almost beside herself with fear. She holds me close, tries to choke off my sobs inside her coat, pats my head, tries to calm me, to console me, all the time listening for sounds outside the door.

'Sssh . . . be still . . .'

But the beating of her heart under her coat is so loud and so rapid that I can't calm down. I cry, softly, till I have no more tears. I hold on to the cyanide capsule until the attic gets dark and there is silence. The underpants on the washing-line look like ghostly shadows, not moving.

We pass the night behind the tub, covering ourselves with our coats.

When it gets light outside, my mother wipes my nose and puts the capsules back in the pouch.

'It's over,' she says wearily. 'Let's go.'

We have no choice but to return to the Kierniks, my mother

says, since we couldn't find the former maid.

We climb the stairs to the Kierniks' apartment. Their creaking is familiar by now. I think of Manuela and the grandmother, and I'm afraid they'll send us away again.

When we reach the third floor and I'm just about to put my finger on the gold button of the doorbell, the door to the neighbour's apartment opens. Startled, we turn round. My finger drops from the doorbell. A nice-looking man is standing in the doorway. He has silvery hair, neatly parted, and a friendly smile. He's wearing shiny black boots and a uniform with gold buttons. A German, I know it immediately. A nice German? He smiles at me; I've never seen this sort of thing before.

Now he even squats down and stretches his arms out towards me. 'Little lady,' he calls, beaming. And some other words besides. I don't understand what he's saying, but I like him, run towards him. He catches me and lifts me up.

At that moment the door of the Kierniks' apartment opens and Mrs Kiernikowa peers out. When she sees me in the arms of the nice German, she freezes. Horrorstruck she looks at my mother, who looks equally appalled. No one speaks. The nice German senses that something isn't quite right and stops smiling.

Suddenly Manuela's curly blonde head appears behind Mrs Kiernikowa. Her blue eyes grow larger as she realizes what's going on, but only briefly. Manuela is a good actress.

'Teofila!' she cries, and embraces my mother. 'How nice that you're finally here. Come on in!'

She pushes my mother and Mrs Kiernikowa inside. Then she turns to the German officer. 'My cousin,' she explains, with a radiant smile. They say a few words to each other that I don't understand, but I sense no danger. Then the German takes me into his apartment and closes the door. We sit down together in a rocking chair in the living room. I think it's nice to sit on his lap. He smells good, like a man who has just shaved. A nice man. I'm not at all afraid, even though I know he's a German. He won't hurt me. He likes me, strokes my hair, smiles, talks to me. But I don't understand what he's saying.

A woman enters the room. He says something to her; I hear the word '*Enkelin*'. I like the sound of it; maybe it's a name?

The woman asks me in Polish what my name is. I automatically give my little speech: 'My name is Roma Ligocka and I come from Rzeszów and my mother is a milliner and I don't know where my father is.' I speak very eagerly and in my excitement I almost splutter because this is the first time I've had the chance to recite the story that my mother made me practise so often I can practically say it in my sleep. They both laugh, and again he says, '*Enkelin, Enkelin,*' and he gives me a biscuit with something brown on top, something sweet. Then they send me home.

I ring the bell at the Kierniks, thrilled and proud that I was given a biscuit and that I did so well. My mother quickly takes my arm and pulls me into the kitchen. Manuela and Mrs Kiernikowa are already there, waiting. And now all three pounce on me.

'What did you say? What did you tell the man?' They stand around me like big, dangerous birds, stretching their necks and flapping wickedly.

'What did you say?'

They frighten me. Hesitantly I repeat my speech: 'My name is Roma Ligocka and I come from Rzeszów and my mother is a milliner and I don't know where my father is.'

'Tell the truth!' Mrs Kiernikowa says, in a shrill voice. 'Otherwise you'll have to stand in the corner all day long.' I back away from her.

My mother squats down and puts her arm around me. 'Roma,' she pleads, 'Roma, please, you know we could all be killed. Did you really not say anything?'

'No!' I whisper. 'I mean, yes! I said my name is Liebling, no, I mean Ligocka and I come from Rzeszów . . .' Now I'm totally confused; I start to cry and get the hiccups.

Manuela takes me in her lap. 'Come now,' she wheedles, 'come now. *Poziomka*, tell me the truth. I'll give you a lovely picture of some actors for your album. But you have to tell the truth. What did you really tell the man?'

'My name is Roma Li-Li—' I sob. Suddenly I don't know what I said any more. I'm afraid they're going to punish me, do something to me. Maybe they'll just make me stand in the corner, but maybe we'll all have to die now.

They all keep on at me, so that I no longer know what my real name is and what I really said and what I didn't say and who I am. The more they bombard me with questions the less I know, and finally I can't say anything at all.

'Bring her here!' I suddenly hear the grandmother's voice coming from the hall; for them it's an order, but for me it's deliverance. They let me go and I sit down on her bed. 'Close the door!' the grandmother says, and Mrs Kiernikowa closes the door, but not without first throwing me another worried look.

I'm trembling, and my hands are very cold. 'Don't be afraid,' the grandmother says. 'Just let the hens go on cackling.'

I don't quite know what she means by that, but gradually I calm down. It always feels good to be with the grandmother. She shows me how to play cards, and I tell her that the man gave me a biscuit.

After a while she calls my mother in. 'Everything's all right,' she tells her quietly. '*Poziomka* is a clever girl. She would never say the wrong thing!'

I nod eagerly. No, I would never do that.

Ella told my mother that father's youngest brother, Szymon, is hiding nearby. This gets my mother terribly excited.

'We have to go to see him,' she says. 'Maybe he knows something about your father.'

And so we take the risk and go to see him.

But Uncle Szymon knows nothing about my father. For two years he has been hiding in a niche behind an armoire and hasn't seen anyone. He's very thin and pale. That's because he never gets any fresh air, my mother says.

A nice woman has hidden him in her apartment. She is Polish and her husband is German. During the day, while the husband is at work, Uncle Szymon is allowed to walk around in the apartment and stretch his legs. In the evening before the husband comes home, he has to go back into his hiding place. It's pretty cramped in there. It would be just right for me, but my uncle can only stand up or squat.

'How do you sleep?' I ask.

'Standing up,' he says, and smiles at me, 'It works all right.'

'And how do you go to the toilet?' I ask.

Uncle Szymon's pale face turns red. 'Don't ask,' he mutters. 'I go when he's gone.'

The nice woman's husband is a German officer. When my mother hears that, she practically has a heart-attack. '*Gewalt geschrieben*! What if he finds you, Szymon?'

But she already knows the answer. We all know the answer. No one speaks.

'But what about his wife? And the child?' My mother is horrified, and I think I know why. Having a child around is dangerous. Children can blurt out everything.

The woman, you see, has a son. He's about as old as I am, has smooth, short, blond hair that's parted on one side, and his name is Dieter.

Szymon doesn't answer. The woman says her husband often brings other officers home in the evening. They sing German songs. They also talk about the Jews they have killed, the way they'd talk about animals they shot. And Szymon, hiding behind the armoire, has to listen.

'But so far everything has worked out all right,' the woman says. 'Maybe he's safer with us than somewhere else – as long as the boy doesn't say anything to his father . . .'

She looks at Dieter a little anxiously, but he shakes his head and smooths his hair. 'You can depend on me, Mama,' he says, in a deep voice. I can tell right away that what he says is true. We can rely on him.

Dieter is really very nice. For the first time in my life I'm allowed to play with another child. Except that time with Stefuś, but that was a long time ago. Dieter shows me the apartment. He always wears short *Lederhosen* and white knee socks. His thighs and knees are pink and naked. 'German children are hardened to cold,' my mother says. 'They don't catch colds easily!' And she gives me a meaningful look.

Dieter has a collection of wooden ships of all sizes, and we're allowed to float them in the sink. We play hide-and-seek while the grown-ups talk in the living room, and sometimes we play ball. It's just wonderful.

'I love you,' Dieter says one day, while we're playing hide-and-seek and I have just discovered him hiding under his parents' bed. 'And when I grow up, I'm going to marry you.'

I agree, and we secretly kiss in the broom cupboard.

Unfortunately nothing ever comes of our wedding plans because I'm allowed to see Dieter only one other time. And it's entirely my fault.

I stole something.

We were playing nicely. Dieter had gone off to hide, and I was looking for him in the bedroom. His mother had one of those dressing-tables with a little skirt, like Manuela's, only this one was light blue. Anyway, there was a dish full of golden rings. I picked one up, and it sparkled and glittered beautifully. Suddenly I remembered that my mother's birthday was coming up soon. I was sure she'd be very pleased to have such a ring. Once she told me Jewish people always give each other something made of gold for their birthdays. So I put the ring into my panties, and then after a while I found Dieter who was hiding behind the woodpile in the kitchen and I forgot about the whole thing.

But that evening, at the Kierniks', I remembered the ring. I got out the lovely silvery foil paper Manuela had given me, one of my few prized possessions. The word 'Chocolate' was printed on it. I used to smell it and think that I could catch a fleeting aroma of the mysterious chocolate. Now I sniff it one last time, wrap the ring for my mother in it, and hide the precious little package behind the guns under the bed.

On the morning of my mother's birthday, I wake up early because for the first time in my life I have a present for someone. My excitement grows by the minute, but my mother doesn't want to wake up. Finally I can't stand it any more. 'Mama, Mama, Mama!' I whisper. 'Happy birthday, Mama. Look, I have a present for you.'

My mother smiles. She sits on the edge of the bed, takes the silvery package and unwraps it. The ring rolls on to the floor, stops in front of her feet. She turns into a stone statue. Her face is white marble and she is very, very angry.

'Where did you get this?' she asks, her voice ice-cold as she picks up the ring.

'It's a surprise,' I say, realizing immediately that I must have made a terrible mistake. 'It's a birthday present. For you . . .'

The statue emits a strange sound, a mixture of moaning and suppressed weeping. 'Roma,' she says, 'where did you steal it from?'

Steal? I just picked it up. After all she . . . the woman had so many rings. 'I only wanted to . . .' I stutter, my face flushed.

Bit by bit my mother gets me to tell her that the ring was on the dressing-table in the bedroom of Dieter's parents.

Horrified she puts her hand to her lips.

'No! This ring belongs to Dieter's mother. Do you have any idea what that could mean for your uncle, for us all? Now she'll throw him out of the house and then he's as good as dead.'

Though I know very well that each and every step we take could mean death for us, I hadn't thought of that when I hid the ring in my panties. Now I realize everything I do can have dreadful consequences, that anything I do, every word I say, may lead to death, that actually everything is punishable by death. That I make myself guilty by even the smallest offence and that I have always been to blame for everything. I am bad, bad, through and through.

It would be better for everyone if I were no longer around.

As soon as she can my mother drags me back to Dieter's apartment, and I have to beg the nice woman's pardon and give the ring back to her. I am terribly embarrassed and wish the earth would swallow me, but she just laughs and pats me on the cheek.

'It's all right,' she says. 'Children are like that. Go and play with Dieter.'

But today it's no fun being with Dieter. We argue because he no longer wants to marry me. 'I'm not going to marry a thief,' he says, and I start to cry. Somehow everything is over between us. Uncle Szymon, too, is very reserved today; he's probably angry with me. We say goodbye to each other, and he crawls back into his cave behind the armoire.

The nice lady washes the tea-cups so that her husband won't see them when he comes home.

'No harm done,' she says, as my mother is putting on her coat.

'Thank you for everything,' my mother says sadly.

Dieter shakes my hand. He doesn't look at me, stares at his feet instead. 'Goodbye,' he mumbles.

We never see each other again. We don't go to visit Uncle

Szymon any more. When everything was over, he left his hiding place behind the armoire. And shortly before the end of the war, Dieter and his parents went back to Germany.

I often think of Dieter. Whatever happened to him?

It's hard to be alone all the time. Spring has arrived, but the last snow still lies on the ground. It's dirty. The warm sun is making it melt, and there are many puddles in the street, big ones and little ones. I stand at the window and watch the children in the street jump into the puddles; they're laughing and playing hide-and-seek. I want to play with them so much that it makes my arms and legs itch with longing.

I just *have* to be with those children.

My mother, Mrs Kiernikova and Manuela are in the kitchen. I tiptoe down the hall to the front door of the apartment. Turn the big, golden doorknob. Slip into the stairwell.

It is quiet, empty and cold there. I'm scared. I know I shouldn't be doing this. But then I hear the children laughing outside on the street.

I *have* to!

With clenched teeth I go down the stairs. My hand slides along the polished banister.

One flight and then another . . . and now I'm already on the ground floor.

Suddenly I hear footsteps behind me. Someone grabs me by the collar, drags me back up the stairs and into the apartment.

'Roma!' my mother gasps. She had run very fast to catch up with me. And she is furious. 'How can you do this? You're putting our lives in danger!'

I hang my head. 'I know, but I wanted so very much to play outside.'

They've put their heads together to confer. Probably about how I can be kept in the house. But then I hear Manuela talking about a garden. Does she mean the garden in the book we're reading? The girl in the book has discovered a secret garden. It's hidden behind a high, thick wall. But she found the key to the little gate in the wall. Now she goes to play in the garden all the time, plants flowers and tides the flower-beds. Spring has come and everything is beginning to bloom . . .

'Roma.' My mother is gently shaking me. Are the Germans here again? But I don't hear anything. It's absolutely still and quite dark outside. I'd like to go back to sleep, so I turn over and pull the covers over my head. 'Come, Roma,' my mother whispers and pulls the covers off. 'I have a surprise for you!'

A surprise? Now, I'm wide awake and quickly slip on my clothes.

'Dress warmly,' my mother urges. She's already wearing her hat and coat, ready to go out. What is she planning to do? Have the Kierniks evicted us again?

She puts a finger to her lips, 'Sssh.' I nod obediently. Everybody is still asleep, the grandmother, Manuela, Dudek, and Mrs Kiernikowa. Only Mother and I are awake. We sneak down the stairs. It's so exciting. What kind of surprise can this be?

A carriage is standing at the front door. Just like a fairy-tale. We get in quickly so that no one will see us. Where are we going?

I've never ridden in a carriage before. Of course I've often seen them; in Kraków there are many horse-drawn cabs. People take them when they're in a hurry. Are we in a hurry? The carriage rattles and shakes as it rolls over the cobble-stones; I cling to the leather upholstery, peer out of a crack in the dark canopy, listen to the clattering hoofs of the horse – almost bursting with suspense. My mother doesn't say a word, just smiles mysteriously.

And then we've arrived. We climb out of the cab and I'm

allowed to pet the soft nose of the handsome brown horse. He smells good, and his breath is warm and alive in the cold morning air. But there's no time to dawdle because a man is already waiting for us. He's wearing a sort of uniform but it's completely different from what the Germans wear. A big bunch of keys dangles from his belt.

He waves to us, indicating we're to follow him. The pebbles of the path crunch under our feet. The man unlocks an iron gate; we go through it.

And suddenly we're standing in the middle of the Secret Garden.

I'm so amazed, I have to catch my breath. Wide-eyed I gaze at the enchanted world that surrounds us, hoarfrost sparkling on straight rows of pruned boxwood trees, tall dark pines, a shimmering, silvery lawn framed by curved flower-beds in which hundreds of snowdrops and crocuses are pushing through the dark soil, a little pond with a fountain.

Then I start to run. I want to jump and dance and skip, but my legs are stiff. I wander on tiptoe among the flower-beds, touch the flowers, dip a finger into the ice-cold water of the pond, and collect little white pebbles. Kneeling at the edge of the water I try to spot the fat red and white fish hiding in the dark depths. I admire each snowdrop, each crocus, touch each tree. Forgetting everything else, I play breathlessly in the magic world of this secret garden until my mother's voice pulls me back to reality.

She's been sitting on a bench, waiting. 'We have to go now,' she says, and draws me close.

I throw my arms around her. 'It was beautiful! Can I come back here to play sometime?'

My mother nods, smiles. She is happy because her surprise worked and because I am happy. The man with the rattling keys lets us out, then locks the gate. My mother puts some money into his hand. All the way home in the cab, I don't say a word, I'm too full of joy. But then when we're back at

the Kierniks' it all comes
bubbling out of me, and I tell
Manuela and the grandmother
about the Secret Garden my
mother found for me.

'What a wonderful idea it
was to take the child to the
Botanical Garden,' Manuela
whispers to my mother. 'Good
thing you knew someone there,
Teofila. I think the excursion
has brought *Poziomka* back to
life. Just look, her cheeks are
quite red.'

'Tell me about long ago,' I ask
my mother. Today is such a
boring day. Not a ray of sun

*A dangerous excursion
(about 1943).*

comes through the clouds. Quite the contrary, it is snowing
even though it's already spring.

'April weather,' Mrs Kiernikowa says gloomily, reminding
herself to take her umbrella when she leaves the house.

My mother and I are sitting in Dudek's room. We often
spend hours at a time here because it's better if nobody sees
us while Mrs Kiernikowa – she is a teacher – is tutoring her
pupils in the kitchen. Dudek is expecting visitors at any
moment, and Manuela and her friends are rehearsing in the
parlour. My mother sits on the bed, sewing, just as my grandmother used to do long ago. Then she puts the things away
and gestures for me to come and sit down beside her. It is
always like a ritual when she tells me about long ago. There's
something festive about it.

Finally, after seven long years Tosia and David were allowed
to get married. That was in the year 1934, the night of the

*A family celebration: father David (third from left), mother
Teofila (fifth from left), Roman Polanski's parents (standing at
the back) and Grandmother Maria (far right) (about 1939/40).*

winter solstice. David was twenty-six years old, Tosia twenty-
three, and they were as deeply in love as on the day they
met. After the wedding ceremony in the Old Synagogue in
Kraków, Jakob and Anna Abrahamer invited all their friends
and acquaintances to a big party at their house. For days
there had been baking and roasting in the kitchen, and the
entire house smelled of cinnamon and chocolate, of roast
goose and raisin wine. Now the tables were bending under
the weight of the delicacies.

Tosia was so excited she couldn't swallow a bite all evening,
but the guests and her brother and younger sisters did full
justice to the magnificent spread. Sabine was especially viv-
acious, and when Tosia asked her whether she was glad that
she would now be the oldest daughter in the Abrahamer
household, Sabine whispered that she wouldn't be staying
much longer either. She had fallen in love again, but this
time, she assured her sister, it was really serious. Tosia
laughed. It was what Sabine said every time.

Anna Abrahamer managed to get through the festivities without letting her feelings show; she played the perfect hostess. Only once, as she was counting the cakes in the pantry, a tear rolled down her cheek. It was very hard for her to lose her eldest daughter who was so much like her, to see her become the wife of a young man she still thought did not come from the right social background. But she had learned to accept fate, and therefore she merely sighed deeply, wiped her eyes with her lace handkerchief, and told the staff to serve dessert.

As a wedding present David gave his wife a small summer-house in the country, in Krynica near Kraków. He named it 'Villa Tosia'.

The young couple moved into a large, beautiful apartment in Kraków's best neighbourhood. It was where one lived in those days. They ate off the finest porcelain dishes, drank from cut-glass goblets, and on the walls of their living room hung paintings by well-known Polish artists from Grandfather Abrahamer's collection. Tosia and David were happy. They were young, healthy and in love. A good-looking pair, with enough money to do what they wanted most, which was to enjoy life.

David bought himself a car, and for Tosia he bought perfume and elegant dresses. They danced the charleston late into the night, went skiing in winter, and drove to the seaside in summer. David loved sports. He was an enthusiastic water-polo and tennis player and an umpire in the Jewish soccer club. He skied like a world champion. He was temperamental and daring, possessive and jealous, and he showered Tosia with jewellery and wrote her ardent poems in which he rhapsodized about her beautiful green-brown eyes. But he did not permit her to go to work. Once when she took a temporary office job, he did everything he could to get her dismissed. It worked.

So Tosia stayed in the apartment and devoted herself to being a spoiled young wife. David came home for lunch every day in order to spend each free minute he had with Tosia. One day he saw her standing in front of the house talking with a strange man. He walked past them without saying a word and went upstairs. There, he opened a window and flung out the tablecloth, with the porcelain, silverware and veal cutlets, into the street. Only then did he ask her with whom she'd been talking. She said she hadn't done anything wrong, and he regretted having flown off the handle. But that didn't prevent him reacting in the same way the next time.

David and Tosia postponed having children. They wanted to have time for each other and, besides, in a few years business would be even better. But some day, when they were ready, they hoped to have at least five children.

My mother stops her story because, she says, her voice has become hoarse. I know that she stopped because it makes her sad to remember the stories of the past. And yet I would like to hear more. I'm especially interested in knowing about the brothers and sisters.

That night there is another inspection.

Three of them enter the apartment shortly before bedtime. I'm already in my nightgown.

KENNKARTE . . . SCHNELL, SCHNELL!

They stand in the hall, their legs spread apart, examining the documents. Something isn't quite right, it seems; they're talking to Mrs Kiernikowa, who has turned pale. My mother trembles, reaches for my hand, holds it tight.

Suddenly the grandmother comes out of her room. She has thrown on a dressing-gown and is still smoothing her tangled hair. She looks like an old lioness ready to pounce.

The grandmother barks at the soldiers, pointing at their boots covered with dirty snow. The snow is dripping off the boots, forming dark puddles on the floor.

'Can't you at least wipe your boots before you come bursting into the homes of respectable citizens at night?' she says loudly. 'Just look at the mess! Now my poor daughter will have to spend hours on her hands and knees scrubbing the floor! Didn't they teach you any manners at home?!'

The German soldiers stare at their feet in embarrassment. They look like schoolboys caught red-handed, being lectured by the teacher. One of them tries to wipe his boots with a handkerchief.

'That won't help!' the grandmother says. 'You need a rag and a pail for that.'

She winks at Manuela, who goes to get a pail.

'Not necessary,' the soldier with the handkerchief stammers. He jabs his comrade in the ribs. 'We were going anyway . . .'

And they leave the apartment quickly.

There's a dark water stain on the floor.

Babcia always stands up for me when they want to force me to eat. Today we're having spinach because they think I look pale. I sit at the table in front of my plate with the green mush on it. It smells of rotten leaves, and I know I can't eat it. They all stand around, watching me. They take turns to scold me, first my mother, then Mrs Kiernikowa, then Manuela.

'Come on, eat! Just think how long I had to queue to get it.'

'Can you imagine what it means to feed six people with only four food-ration cards?'

'How are you ever going to be a famous actress if you starve to death?'

I say nothing and stare stubbornly at my plate. Now I'm going to have to sit here again until evening. The more they nag, the greater my loathing of the food. My cheeks are full of spinach but I can't swallow it.

'Leave the child alone. She won't starve,' the grandmother

calls from her room. She is the only one who can get me to eat because she doesn't force me to. She also understands that children can't stand liver and spinach. 'I didn't like it either when I was your age,' she whispers to me. But in the long run she can't do very much when she's up against the three scolding women.

Finally they leave me alone, and I sit there and think about the Secret Garden and about Maria Rökk, or I imagine what it would be like if Dieter and I were to get married. Sometimes I fall asleep at the table with my mouth full of food.

Spring is here, and the tree in the yard has lots of green leaves. The air smells wonderful – of flowers and fresh soil and sunshine; the birds chirp happily. Now and then the horse-drawn cab pulls up outside our house and drives us to the Botanical Garden. With the exception of Christmas and the rehearsals, the hours I spend there are the most beautiful of my life. In my Secret Garden, time doesn't exist, and there is no fear, there are no Germans, and nothing is forbidden. There's only me and the enchanted trees whispering stories into my ears, the bright flowers that sprout from the dark earth like living jewels, the silent red and white fish in the mysterious pond. Once I even saw a robin. It looked exactly like the one on the cover of *The Secret Garden* book. I was a little bit afraid of it. As I am of all birds, of all animals.

I sit in a shady corner of the garden and use twigs to build little bridges, tiny huts and little gardens. And all the while I'm telling myself stories.

Maybe it has something to do with the sunshine; in any case my mother is more daring now and goes out more often. Sometimes, secretly, we go to visit Ella who brought us Father's ring. Ella is always cheerful. When she laughs she makes the walls shake.

She lives in a small apartment with her fiancé, a Polish engineer. His name is Marian, and he looks German in his long leather coat and boots. At first I was afraid of him, but then I discovered that he was very nice. He and Ella don't have any children, but they have a big, black and white spotted dog. His name is Kazimir and he is a genuine Great Dane. Even though I'm afraid of animals, we immediately take a liking to each other.

Finally my mother has found someone with whom she can talk, and she makes good use of it. As soon as we step into the apartment, she and Ella disappear into the living room. They sit on the sofa for hours on end, telling each other things. While they talk they drink vodka out of little green glasses. Never before have I seen my mother drink alcohol, but whenever she's with Ella that seems to be part of the routine. After a while their laughter gets louder and then they tell each other jokes that have to do with men and women and love. I can only understand half of what they say, but my mother and Ella end up rolling on the floor with laughter. When Ella's fiancé gets home, he too has a few drinks and then he laughs even louder than the two women. He sings 'Your daughter, your daughter, has a sweet little hole . . .' (*'Ihre Tochter, ihre Tochter, hat ein süßes kleines Löchlein . . .'*)

Kazimir and I think it's all very silly. We're quite sober and don't approve of these childish grown-ups. Kazimir curls up like a pretzel, and I lie in the hollow formed by his legs. His snoring is nice. If I didn't have him I couldn't stand all that chattering and loud laughter.

Later, we have to hurry home to avoid getting caught by the curfew, and I have to pay close attention to my mother. Sometimes she's unsteady on the stairs or sings to herself, and I worry that someone might notice us. It is very dangerous. But so far we've been lucky.

Summer has arrived. The door to the balcony is slightly ajar; it's hot outside. The tree now has many heavy white blossoms; they look almost like the candles on the Christmas

Rescued memories: Teofila (right) with her family (about 1928).

tree. Children are playing down in the courtyard. I hear them laughing and calling to each other, and again I feel that longing ache in my tummy.

I'm drawing pictures on a piece of paper. This has been one of my favourite pastimes lately, especially when I feel sad. I draw pictures of Kazimir, Maria Rökk, Tadeusz, the flowers in the Secret Garden, and my grandparents' house.

'Please tell me about your brothers and sisters,' I ask my mother.

'Which one? Jakob? Sabine? Irene?'

Whenever she mentions Irene she looks sad. I quickly say, 'Sabine.'

She sits down next to me. 'In those days I was much younger than you,' she says, smiling at me, and then she begins her story.

Tosia was only about two years old when Nana told her she would have a little sister. Nana was the nanny. She had a big soft bosom, always wore a white apron, and sang beautiful

Polish songs. Tosia liked her a lot. In those days the Abrahamer children were raised by the staff; they saw their parents only rarely.

Tosia was very happy with the news about the new baby because she felt lonely in the big house. She kept asking her nanny, 'When is my little sister coming?' She asked so often that it got on Nana's nerves. And one day Nana said, 'Look, Tosia, the baby has finally arrived!' She pointed to a little bundle on the bed. Tosia was overjoyed. She lifted up the bundle carefully and held it in her arms. Then she looked inside. It wasn't a little sister, only her old doll that Nana had put there. Everybody laughed, except Tosia, who was disappointed and angry. Nana played the same trick on her a few more times, and Tosia got angrier and angrier.

One day another little bundle was lying on the bed, and everyone was smiling mysteriously at Tosia, saying that at last her little sister had arrived, she really had. But Tosia didn't believe them any more. They had lied to her too many times and then they had made fun of her. 'I don't believe it!' she screamed, and in a fury she grabbed the bundle and threw it on the floor.

For a moment it was deathly still in the room. Then the bundle began to scream. Anna Abrahamer rushed over and picked it up. She was so upset she couldn't say a word. Luckily nothing had happened to the baby.

They named the child Sabine, and Tosia, who was terribly ashamed of what she had done, developed a special closeness with her little sister. Even though they were quite different, the two girls were inseparable. In contrast to her rather quiet, reserved older sister, Sabine was jolly, straightforward and stubborn. She always managed to get her own way.

My mother looks at me thoughtfully. 'Just like you,' she says, 'you are very much like Sabine. Did you know that your birthday is on the same day as hers?'

I shake my head. No, I didn't know that. 'Is my birthday soon?' I ask. I would like to get a doll for my birthday. If I get one, I'll call it Jacek, like Manuela's doll.

'In a few months,' my mother says, 'not much longer. Then you'll be six years old.'

It's a rainy summer day, and once again we are walking through the city. I hold on tightly to my mother's hand, which is cold and damp, and that doesn't make me feel safe. On the contrary, through her cold hand her fear flows directly into me and then it has no way out.

In spite of that it's an adventure to be allowed out of the apartment, to feel the wind and the rain on my skin, to see the people queuing in the market square, waiting to buy something to eat. We're probably not particularly conspicuous, a tall blonde woman leading a little blonde girl by the hand. No one is particularly conspicuous except the uniformed men, sauntering through the streets or standing on street corners watching everything. What if they notice that I have dark eyes? I keep my face lowered all the time. I can feel how their eyes follow my mother and me even when they're standing with their backs to us. That's when I try to make myself as invisible as possible. None of them has ever spoken to us, but I expect it to happen any moment. Whenever we pass one of them my heart pounds so loud, I'm sure they can hear it.

And then it happens. We are walking along Karmelicka, the long street from which Manuela's street branches off. A man comes towards us. He is wearing a sand-coloured raincoat, looking down at the pavement. His hat is pulled down over his face. Just as he passes us, he looks up, directly into my mother's face. There is a flash of recognition in his eyes. My heart stops beating. We've been found out. It's all over.

But the man keeps going. My mother, who had stopped for just a fraction of a second, also continues walking. She pulls me into our side-street, into the hallway of our house, up the stairs, into Manuela's apartment. 'Who was that man?' I ask, still frightened. 'Why didn't he arrest us?'

My mother is silent, bites her lips. She doesn't want to tell me.

Some time later we meet the man again, and then again. By now I'm quite sure that he won't arrest us, but still I sense the danger that surrounds him. This is confusing. Who is this man? Is he on our side or on theirs? Anyway, I'd rather we didn't run into him again. I wish the earth would open up and swallow him, or something like that. But here he comes again, walking along in his light-coloured coat. He stops in front of the Carmelite Church. It's where we've recently been going to Sunday mass. Instead of hurrying past, my mother also stops in front of the church. I want to pull her away, but she simply stands there. Can't she see how dangerous it is? I tug on her coat, but she pays no attention to me. In front of a saint's statue, she crosses herself and pretends to pray. Actually she exchanges a few words with the sinister-looking man. She even slips him some money. Then to my great relief she quickly walks on.

We see the man one more time. I spot him among a group of people at the end of the long street. A man in uniform and another man in a long leather coat grab him and drag him into the hallway of a nearby house. My mother freezes. Then she runs into a side-street with me. I feel her fear like a huge wave pulling me along. After a while she drags me back on to the main street and walks on as though nothing has happened. The man in uniform and the one in the leather coat are coming towards us; I feel the coldness that surrounds them as they walk by. The leather coat brushes against my arm. One of the men says to the other, 'One less Jew.' He sounds satisfied.

A couple of houses away I see the feet of the man in the sand-coloured coat. He is lying in the dirty hallway of a house and his trousers are open. He is dead. The earth really has swallowed him. I feel guilty. My mother's hand clasps mine even tighter. She walks faster, and tears are running down her face.

Once we're back in the apartment I again ask, 'Who was that man, Mama? How did you know him?'

She wipes away her tears with a corner of her apron and begins peeling potatoes.

'That was Leo,' she says, in a flat voice. 'He was my brother Jakob's best friend.'

After that we are both silent.

Today, years later, I know that Leo was probably hiding out somewhere near our apartment. Someone must have given him away for a few złoty. The secret police made short shrift of suspicious males in those days: they opened their trousers and looked to see whether they were circumcised. If they were, they shot them.

For days the city has been enveloped in humid, sweltering heat; our clothes stick to our skin.

The Kierniks have turned us out again because there has been another wave of night-time raids. This time we really have nowhere to go. 'We'll go to Warsaw,' my mother says suddenly, with determination. 'Nobody knows us there. I'm sure we'll find a place to stay somewhere.'

Gripping my suitcase, I follow her to the railway station. I am sad. Will I ever see Manuela again? The grandmother, my friends the actors? Warsaw is far away; that much I know.

The station is noisy and full of people in a hurry, carrying their baggage. There's a roaring in my ears. In this milling mass of people nobody notices us. We search for the right track. The train and its huge black locomotive, groaning and steaming, is already in the station. Terrified, I stare at the monster.

'We only have a few minutes before it leaves,' my mother says, walking energetically towards the train. But then she stops abruptly.

'I feel dizzy,' she mumbles. Her face is wet and has turned white, her skin shiny with sweat. It's frightening to see her like this.

I make her sit down on a bench. She leans back exhausted, looks as if she's dead, collapsed into herself. Her eyes are closed.

To keep people from noticing, I stand in front of her and take her hand, like a doctor. Her hand is very cold, but this time it's not from fear. My mother is sick. What should I do? I know I can't ask anyone for help. That would be much too dangerous.

'Is something the matter?' a fat woman wearing a hat asks. She has just plumped herself down on our bench. Her little dog barks and barks.

'No, no,' I reply quickly, and push myself down on the bench between my mother and the fat woman, 'everything's all right. My mother is just a little tired.'

'She looks sick,' the fat woman says, and looks at my mother suspiciously. 'Somebody should get a doctor.'

'Not necessary,' I say instantly, and give my mother a furtive prod in the ribs while I help her to get up. 'We were going to the doctor anyway, weren't we, Mama?'

My mother opens her eyes and nods weakly. 'Yes, yes,' she mumbles.

I take her arm and drag her away from the bench.

'Goodbye,' I say to the fat woman. She looks more and more mistrustful. Her little dog keeps barking.

I know she's watching us as I pull my mother towards the exit of the station. My mother follows me with staggering, uncertain steps. We merge with the crowd and I breathe a sigh of relief when I see that no one is following us.

Finally we're back on the street.

My mother sways back and forth. She is going to fall! I have to hurry.

Each step is torture. I drag her along, one hand clamped around her arm, the other clutching my suitcase, pursued by fear. Has someone seen us? Are we now going to be arrested? Will my mother collapse? Or will I manage to get her home in time?

The way seems endless, but at last we've made it. We're standing in front of Manuela's house. My mother refuses to go in. 'But they threw us out,' she says. For the first time I realize how humiliating this has been for her. I also know we have no choice. We've never had a choice.

'We *have* to go in, Mama. You're sick. They *have* to help us.'

After a while she gives in. Her pride collapses like a house of cards. She allows me to pull her up the stairs without resisting. I push the bell button.

Mrs Kiernikowa opens the door. *'Poziomka!'* she cries in surprise. Then she sees my mother. 'For heaven's sake, Teofila . . .' She takes my mother by the arm and pulls us into the apartment.

'You can thank your lucky stars you got sick, Teofila. If you'd gone to Warsaw, you'd be dead by now,' Dudek says, as he dumps a bucketful of coal into the kitchen stove. 'Here, read this.'

He slides a thin sheet of paper across the table to my mother. It's a newspaper printed by the Underground. It's called *Polska Walczy*, 'Poland Fights'.

I'm relieved to see that my mother looks better today; she slept a long time the night before. She skims the headlines.

'The Day of Judgement for the Germans approaches. They will stand before the tribunal of the nations and of human conscience . . .' she reads. 'What does that mean?' she asks Dudek.

'There has been an uprising in Warsaw!' he explains, his eyes sparkling. 'There's fighting everywhere! On every street, in every house. Lots of people have been killed, many women and children . . . The Germans are burning them alive—' He breaks off in mid-sentence, grimly silent.

'Those gangsters,' my mother says, her eyes wide with horror. 'Those gangsters!'

Ella has an idea. 'Listen, Teofila,' she says one day, a glass of vodka in her hand. 'How would it be if we rented an apartment together? Marian can take care of the details. He'll do the lease and everything, and you two simply move in with us. Things just can't go on like this, you being constantly thrown out by the Kierniks. After all, you've been there for a year and a half already, and neither of you can stand this continual tension any more. What do you think?'

My mother gulps down her vodka and nods. 'That's nice of you, Ella,' she says, 'but it will put you in even greater danger, and your fiancé, too.'

'You can pass as my sister!' Ella says. 'Either we're lucky and the war will soon be over, or we're unlucky. And up to now we've been lucky – haven't we? We're still alive! Besides, the inspections have slackened a little recently. A lot of Germans have left or they've been called away. The situation is getting steadily tighter for them. They've had some serious defeats at the front. You can't impose on the Kierniks for ever. You know that as well as I.'

Ella is right. We really can't stay at the Kierniks' any longer. My mother nods her agreement, and they clink their green glasses.

Now the drinking starts again. The dog Kazimir and I look at each other. Then we trot off to the kitchen and settle down under the table. I tell him that my birthday is coming soon and that I'm hoping to get a doll. Kazimir is a good listener.

*　　*　　*

A few weeks later, with no elaborate leave-taking from the Kierniks, we move into a small two-room apartment with Kazimir, Ella, and her fiancé. You can see the relief on Mrs Kiernikowa's face as we stand in the hall with our suitcases. Dudek, who never said much, must have been happy to move back into his room with the weapons cache under the bed. Only *Babcia* hugs me for a long time. 'Come and visit me soon, little one,' she says, pulling her crocheted shawl tighter around her thin shoulders. I know she'll miss me.

Manuela flutters through the hall and gives me a brief kiss. 'See you soon, *Poziomka*!' she says, and disappears into the parlour to rehearse a new play with her friends.

Life was never complicated for Manuela.

I had spent my entire childhood at the Kierniks, always on tiptoe – so it seems to me today. There were dolls and plays, books, music, crayons and paper, and it was like having a home except that none of it belonged to me. It was a borrowed life, a borrowed childhood with a borrowed family, even a borrowed grandmother. After that my childhood was over, and nothing in the months before the war ended or during the rough post-war time could make up for that. I did not get a doll for my sixth birthday – you couldn't buy dolls anywhere in those days. But I was now six years old, and had finally grown up.

4

January 18, 1945. The Russians arrived in Kraków during the night. They stole into the city with the snow, almost noiselessly. We didn't even notice. And now they're everywhere. They wear shiny black boots, like the ones I have always known. And though their language is different from the Germans', their shouting sounds just as hoarse, imperious and harsh.

But on this snowy January morning I have no inkling of any of this, not yet. For I'm sitting peacefully under the kitchen table with Kazimir, stealthily feeding him my breakfast.

My mother and Ella know that the Russians have occupied Kraków. Ella just heard about it at the bakery. They are tremendously excited, fearful and hopeful at the same time. 'Will the war be over soon? Maybe Poland will be free again.' They worry about what will become of us. The Russians are gruesome, they say. They rape women. They're rowdy, they drink a lot and they steal. Ella says the Russians all wear lots of stolen wristwatches, one on top of the other.

My mother buttons me into my coat, and we walk through the snowy city to the market square, curious, but careful, too, of course. Jews always have to be careful. The market square is full of people and lots of Russian soldiers are standing around. I look at their wrists and I'm disappointed. Not one of them is wearing more than one wristwatch. The Russian uniforms are different from the ones the Germans wore, but they, too, have gold buttons. And the Russians wear a red star. It reminds me of the yellow star we used to have to wear.

'Why do the soldiers wear a red star?' I ask my mother once we're back in the apartment, warming our frozen hands at the kitchen stove.

'Because they're Russians,' she replies.

That doesn't explain anything. 'But why do Russians wear a red star?'

My mother thinks it over. 'It's very hard to explain,' she says finally, and that means she doesn't really want to talk about it any more.

'But didn't we once have to wear a star too?' I prod, remembering my grandmother sitting on a kitchen chair, sewing yellow stars on our jackets and coats.

'Yes.' My mother sighs. 'That was how it all started. That was the Star of David the Germans used to stigmatize us . . .'

Another word I don't know. 'Tell me about it,' I beg her. 'Was I already born by then?'

When David and Tosia returned from their skiing holiday in March 1938 – that was almost seven years ago – Tosia realized she was pregnant. 'It was a skiing accident,' she told her sister Sabine, beaming with happiness. Sabine, who was on one of her frequent visits, embraced Tosia and congratulated her. By now she, too, was happily married. Her husband was an engineer, a respectable young Jewish man named Krautwirth.

Later, while they were in the living room having tea, they discussed the worrying events taking place in Germany. Distant relatives of the Abrahamers who lived in Berlin had written to them recently. They told of Jews being dismissed from their jobs, being abused on the streets, and of the many new regulations that made life increasingly difficult for them. Some of their acquaintances had vanished without a trace. Suddenly Tosia had a vague presentiment of something unknown, of something terrible that was in store for them. 'When I hear stories like that I am really afraid for my child!' she said. 'What if the same thing were to happen here?'

Sabine reassured her, 'You can't take this Hitler seriously,' she said. 'He's crazy, anyone can see that. After all, the Germans are a sensible people – think of the nuns who taught in our school. The German people will get rid of him as fast as he came in.'

David, who had just come home from work, agreed. 'You shouldn't be thinking of such things now,' he said to his wife, trying to calm her. 'Sabine is right. This Adolf is just a clown. That's why I named our dog after him.' Having said that, he petted the head of the young German shepherd they had recently acquired. Tosia laughed. David was right, of course.

David didn't mention that many of his friends had recently emigrated to Brazil. He himself had thought of leaving Poland. But there was his pregnant wife, his old mother and the firm he had built up with much effort. And, after all, his family had lived here for generations. Kraków was his home.

As a boy he had stolen apples from other people's gardens, had played truant from school, had secretly kissed Tosia in the Abrahamers' gazebo. His roots as well as Tosia's were here. In her parents' home German was spoken as often as Polish, and they valued and respected German culture as much as he did. They considered the Germans a civilized people; really, there was nothing to be afraid of. And besides – should he run away from a clown like Adolf Hitler?

No, he couldn't leave his homeland, nor did he want to.

'What happened to Adolf?' I interrupt my mother.

She looks at me in confusion. I have pulled her out of her memories too abruptly. 'But you know that . . .' she says.

'I mean the dog!' I say.

'Oh, him,' she says. 'Yes, you would have liked him – when the Germans came your father took him to a peasant farmer and asked that he take care of him. But the dog walked all the way back to the city, eighteen miles, to be with us. His paws were all sore and bleeding. Soon after that your father had to give him up anyway.'

'Why?' I ask.

'Because they issued all these regulations against Jews . . . But that was long after you were born.'

I think about what she has said.

'What was it like when I was born?' I ask.

David and Tosia had been longing for a child, but when the baby was born it was at the wrong time. David took his wife to a Kraków hospital on 9 November 1938 – *Kristallnacht*, the night when the synagogues were burning in Berlin. But baby Roma took her time, and didn't see the light of day until 13 November, after many long and painful hours of labour.

As happy as they were with their healthy little girl, the young parents were also in despair. The first German Jews had already been deported to Poland. Shocking rumours and frightful premonitions were circulating. The mood among the Jewish populace was heavy and dark as if a terrible thunderstorm were approaching. Nobody knew if and when it would break, or what to expect. Many Jews still felt safe in Kraków; others had already fled to the rural areas or abroad. But David still could not make up his mind to leave.

When the Germans invaded Poland in September 1939, he decided to escape. David and his family, together with Jakob and Anna Abrahamer, Tosia's younger siblings, and a lot of luggage, left Kraków in two horse-drawn carriages. They were taken in by some poor Polish peasants who lived far out in the country under the same roof with their farm animals. It was a simple hut with a clay floor and no hot water. Tosia had never seen such poverty and so much dirt. There were lice and vermin, and after a while she couldn't stand it any longer.

'The baby will fall ill,' she said to David. 'There's no way to keep her clean here. I can't bathe her, can't take care of her properly. I want to go home again.'

She was right: little Roma was weak and sickly. David looked at his daughter, her dark eyes, the dark fuzz on her head, and his heart was heavy. She looked very much like him, like a little Jewish girl. But Tosia was so worried that David gave in. They couldn't head further east because that's was where the Russians were. So they harnessed the horses again and went back. Back into the ghetto.

At first, my mother is silent. Then she says, 'I'm going to make us some tea now. Wouldn't you like something to eat, Roma?'

I shake my head.

'What about the star?' I ask.

In the meantime the Germans had seized Kraków. In early September the narrow streets echoed with the goose steps of marching German soldiers. And then came the decrees, the regulations.

Jews were not allowed to have any money or jobs, no houses and no pets, no jewellery and no furs. They weren't allowed to ride on trams or go shopping on the main street or eat in restaurants. Entire sections of the city were suddenly off limits to them. Signs were posted: 'No dogs or Jews allowed.'

David had to give up his dog, his firm, his car, his money, his apartment. The Germans came and packed the beautiful porcelain, the cut-glass goblets and the paintings into boxes. The things they didn't like they just threw out of the window.

For a while David and his family lived in a little room on the outskirts of the city. Tosia's parents also lost everything and were thrown out of their beautiful house with the big garden. The Abrahamer bakery downtown was taken over

by a German who simply added his own name in small letters
to the sign, and continued the business under the old name.
After all, Abrahamer's wholewheat rolls were known
throughout the city and it was a fine business.

Roma was one year and two weeks old when the order
was issued for all Jews to wear a yellow star on their clothes.

My mother looks at me and hugs me.

'You must have known why you didn't want to be born
into this world,' she says.

One day, there's a stranger standing at our door. He looks
terrible, wild and dangerous. He's not even wearing shoes!
His clothes are torn and dirty, his cheeks are sunken, his hair
is grey and straggly, he has an unkempt beard and deep
shadows under his dark eyes. He's emaciated, probably wants
a piece of bread. Kazimir growls; he's afraid of the stranger
too. I want to close the door again quickly, but just then my
mother calls from the kitchen, 'Who is it, Roma?' She runs
over and stands behind me, tries to close the door.

'Tosia!' the man says. My mother gasps; it's hard to tell
whether from shock or joy. For a moment she stands there
as though rooted to the spot. Then she throws her arms
around the stranger.

I back away, terrified. This is not the quiet, calm mother
I know. She shouts and sobs with joy, she covers the beggar's
dirty face with kisses, and he kisses her. It's a weird scene
and it frightens me. What does this man want from my
mother? Finally he releases her and bends down to where
I'm standing. He stinks of sweat and damp rags. 'Rominka!
Don't you recognize me?' Now his face is very close to mine.
'My precious little daughter.'

I stare in horror. I'm furious at this sinister stranger who
has kissed my mother. Now he probably wants to kiss me
too.

Before and after the war: Roma's father David in 1928 and in 1946.

I turn away quickly, run off, and hide under the bed. Behind me I hear my mother say, 'She's still very young, David. And after all, she hasn't seen you for such a long time.'

My father has come back.

He escaped from the camp. Fled. 'Just in the nick of time,' he says, 'otherwise I'd be dead, like the others.' The name of the camp is Auschwitz, and it must be horrible there because my father is crying while he tells about it. They are sitting on the sofa – my father, my mother, and Ella – drinking vodka out of the little green glasses. My parents are holding each other tight. Then my father tries to take me on his lap, but I pull away.

'Come on, Kazimir,' I whisper in the dog's ear, 'let's lie down under the kitchen table. All they do here is cry and drink.'

Kazimir understands. We lie down under the table and I lean my head against his warm, silky soft belly. His warmth and his regular breathing make me feel safe. From here I can see the upper left corner of the kitchen window. I can see a blue patch of sky, turning night-blue as it gets darker, and I can hear the long drawn-out wailing of an air-raid siren far away.

This man isn't my father. He can't be! David Liebling is young and good-looking, a handsome man, an adventurer who kissed girls in the garden and skis like a world champion. I think of the photo my mother always carries with her. It shows him sun-tanned and laughing, wearing a white suit and a straw hat. On the back it says:

Dear Mami,
The handsome young man in the photo, smiling at you, is your loving son David.

Suddenly a scene from the ghetto flashes through my mind. They have picked up my grandmother, and my father is sitting on the edge of the bed in the dark, stuffy room, rocking back and forth with pain and sorrow – the same way as now while he tells about the camp.

The same way as now? What if he really is my father?

No. I don't want this to be my father. My real father is dead.

The stranger sleeps in our bed at night. I slide as close to the edge as I can, so close I have to be careful not to fall off. Now that he's had a bath and has shaved, he doesn't smell bad any more, but still I don't want to have anything to do with him. Whenever he tries to touch me, I run away. When he talks to me, his powerful voice scares me.

Now my mother cares only about him. She tries to find food to buy and then she stands at the stove for hours. 'So that you'll get some flesh back on your bones,' she says, and sets a full plate before him. He devours the food as though he hasn't eaten for years. 'Come,' he says to me, when he has finished, 'come, sit on my lap.' But I don't want to. I run away and hide under the table again.

They talk and talk. I don't listen to them. I sit around and draw, or I tell Kazimir about my troubles. Sometimes I miss Manuela and *Babcia*.

'Oh, we'll visit them soon,' my mother says, and resumes her conversation with the stranger.

'I'll kill him!' shouts the stranger, who is supposed to be my father. 'I'll find him, Tosia, you'll see. And then he's going to pay for cheating us.' Suddenly he looks like a wild man; his eyes flash as he puts a pistol into his pocket. I'm afraid of him.

'Don't, David,' my mother pleads. 'Please don't. What's done is done, and no one can turn back the clock. You'll only put us in danger.'

The stranger doesn't reply immediately, he looks at my mother for a long time. 'I have to do it,' he says. 'You've got to understand, Tosia, I must. It's the right thing to do.' Then, with firm, determined steps, he strides out of the apartment slamming the door behind him. I breathe a sigh of relief. My mother covers her face with her hands. 'If only I hadn't told him,' she says, almost to herself. 'It's all my fault.'

'Whom does he want to kill?' I ask.

'The policeman. Remember that time when we escaped from the ghetto and were looking for a certain address? We paid a lot of money for that address, and we were supposed to be safe there. It was a trap, a trap to catch Jews. And that man, the policeman, took the money and betrayed all those people to the Germans!'

Now I remember: Glittering diamonds sparkling in the damp gutter; my arms around the policeman's boots, begging him to let us go . . . Yes, I remember it clearly.

The stranger returns late that night.

He takes off his clothes and sits down on the edge of the bed. He is breathing heavily.

'David?' my mother asks still half asleep. Then she sits up with a start. 'David! You're alive!' She throws her arms around his neck.

I move as far away from her as I can.

'What happened? Did you kill him? Tell me, David, did you kill him?' My mother has grabbed the stranger by the shoulders, is shaking him.

'No,' his voice sounds forced, 'I couldn't.'

'Oh, David, I knew you could never do something like that. I knew it!' My mother's voice is shrill with relief and joy.

'I couldn't,' the stranger repeats in a flat voice, 'because when I found him he was already dead. Someone else had just shot him.'

Occasionally the air-raid alarm sounds. The yowling of the sirens hurts my ears. Then we have to sit in the cellar for hours and hours with the other people who live in the house. But the stranger refuses to go down into the cellar. He's not afraid. That's something new for me. I admire him for that.

'David, please,' my mother begs.

But he doesn't want to. He is obstinate. 'Nothing can happen to me any more,' he says. 'I've been through worse things.'

Now, in spite of his loud voice, I sometimes listen to what he says. I like him much more, now that he leaves me alone. I've decided that his eyes aren't really dangerous. They are black and shine with an inner light.

Gradually I begin to believe that he may indeed be my father. In any case, I am getting used to him.

It's spring again. The windows of our apartment are wide open and the sun shines in. Outside, on the street people are shouting, there is laughter, an unusual excitement is in the air. It feels like sparkling soda water or as though you were being gently tickled. Holding hands, my mother, my father and I walk to the market square, the place to go if you want to find out what's going on. That's the way it is in Kraków.

From far off I can hear people yelling and shouting joyfully. I've never seen the market square so crowded. I have to be careful not to get lost, and I stick close to my mother. But then two strong arms lift me up and my father puts me on his shoulders.

It's wonderful to be sitting up here. Now I'm taller than anyone else. I can see everything, the market stalls around the fountain, and all the people pushing and jostling and dancing, and because my father is carrying me, I'm safe.

'The war is over!' people yell. 'The war is over!'

They toss their hats into the air and scream and shout nonstop. The crowd below me surges back and forth, celebrating, singing, happy. I'm amazed that people can be so boisterous and so happy. But suddenly I am laughing and singing and shouting along with them: 'The war is over!' I yell too, even though I don't quite know what that means.

Hours later, we're back in our apartment, exhausted and happy, and my mother is preparing supper. I ask her why the people in the market square were so happy today. She laughs. 'Because the war is over.'

I don't understand. 'What does that mean?'

'It means that we are safe now,' she replies.

Safe? I stare at her. 'Does that mean that nothing can happen to us any more?'

She kneels down in front of me and holds me tight. Her eyes shine. She looks so happy. I have never seen her like this. 'Exactly,' she says, and beams. 'It means that we'll never have to hide again.'

'You promise?' I ask.

'Yes, I promise,' she replies.

'But for how long?' I just can't grasp this.

'We're free now, you understand?' she says. 'The war is over. Hitler is dead. There is peace. And now we're just people like everyone else.'

'For how long?' I ask again.

'For always.'

'Always? But how long is that?' I shake my head in disbelief, almost angry that she doesn't understand my question.

It can't be. How casually she says it: Always.

Now we're just like everyone else. It's hard to believe, but our life has really changed. We don't have to hide. We can go anywhere, anytime, without fear. Yet, I can't get rid of the feeling that we could be arrested at any time. I feel uneasy when we're going somewhere, and on the street I don't dare look directly into people's faces.

News about missing relatives and friends spreads through the city like wildfire, passed from one person to the next, day and night. The word I hear constantly is 'SURVIVE'. Did she, did he SURVIVE? people ask one another. They're not always told the truth, but as long as there is hope, they hope. At the synagogue people have put up lots of pieces of paper with brief messages:

> Has anyone seen my sister Rosa Seelenfreund?
> She is twenty-one years old, has long brown hair, wears glasses. The last time we heard from her she was in the ghetto in early March 1943.
> Please contact Miriam Seelenfreund.

Some people turn up again; most are dead.

Aunt Sabine is alive! My mother heard that she was liberated from Auschwitz. We're all overjoyed. Of course my mother sets out immediately to pick her up. It was a long and arduous trip because no trains were running. So she went as far as she could by hitching rides on trucks, and then she walked the rest of the way.

By the time she got there, Sabine was dead. There was a typhus epidemic raging in the camp, and she must have been very sick. It's hard for my mother to talk about it. She isn't even able to cry. Not until one evening when my father tells how Sabine had to watch as her husband, the engineer Krautwirth, was sentenced to death in the Płaszów camp because he had tried to protect a little boy. Now she can finally cry again. Krautwirth had tried to kill himself but didn't succeed. With his cut wrists bleeding, they hanged him until not a drop of blood was left in his body. And all the prisoners had to watch.

And yet later, after they sent her to Auschwitz, Sabine fell in love again. She even got married secretly. A rabbi married her and her new husband behind the barbed wire.

'She was always in love. And so stubborn.' My mother sobs. I think of the last time I saw my aunt Sabine, cheerful and pretty, with a colourful kerchief tied around her head.

The weeping is endless, because gradually we hear about what happened to the rest of our family. Grandmother and Grandfather Abrahamer and Irene were killed in the gas chamber of the Bełżec death camp. Jakob, my mother's younger brother, lost his life when the Germans blew up the munitions factory where he was working. My other grandmother, Maria Liebling, disappeared and no trace of her has ever been found; she, too, was probably murdered in one of the gas chambers.

I don't want to believe all the things I hear and pull the bedcovers over my head, the way I did back in the ghetto. But there is no escape. These are just the first of the horrendous stories I will have to listen to from now on.

Suddenly Kraków is full of people. That's because so many bombs fell on Warsaw that hardly any houses are left standing there. Almost none of the little Jewish towns still exist. Finding an apartment in Kraków is now very difficult. My mother says we're lucky that we already have an apartment. Ella and her fiancé Marian have gone to their room. I think they took the bottle of vodka with them because after that I never saw my mother drunk again.

She has no time for that anyway because people keep turning up. More and more strangers come to our house, almost the way it used to be long ago. As more and more people are crammed into our small apartment, it gets to be

Roma Ligocka

too much for my mother and she almost goes to pieces. Eventually there are fourteen of us.

I have a little 'brother' now. My father brought him home one day. His name is Ryszard Horowitz, and he is six months

Sąd Grodzki w Krakowie O.I.
Sygn.L.1.Zg.1348/46
dnia 30 grudnia 1947 r.

P o s t a n o w i e n i e.

Sąd Grodzki w Krakowie w osobie Sędziego Dr.E.Regnierzicza po rozpoznaniu wniosku Teofili Liebling,zam. w Krakowie przy ul.Mazowieckiej Nr.8 - o stwierdzenie zgonu

1/ Dawida Abrahamera,syna Jakuba i Ryfki,ur.dnia 15 maja 1885 r. w Krakowie

2/ Henczy vel Anny Abrahamerowej,córki Izraela i Tauby Seelenfreundów,ur. dnia 10 lipca 1889 r. w Myślenicach,

3/ Ireny Abrahamer,córki Dawida i Henczy vel Anny z d.Seelenfreund Abrahamerów,ur.dnia 22 listopada 1925 r. w Krakowie

4/ Sabiny Abrahamer Kreutwirthowej, córki Dawida i Henczy vel Anny z d. Seelenfreund Abrahamerów,ur.dnia 13 listopada 1913 r. w Krakowie

5/ Jakuba Abrahamera,syna Dawida i Henczy vel Anny z d. Seelenfreund Abrahamerów,ur. dnia 4 lutego 1918 r. w Krakowie -

wszystkich zam. ostatnio w Krakowie przy ul.Warszawskiej Nr.69 - po przeprowadzeniu dochodzeń urzędowych i ogłoszeniu o wszczęciu postępowania

p o s t a n a w i a :

uznać za stwierdzone,że:

1/ Dawid Abrahamer, syn Jakuba i Ryfki,ur.dnia 15 maja 1885 r. w Krakowie,

2/ Hencze vel Anna Abrahamerowa, córka Izraela i Tauby Seelenfreundów,ur. dnia 10 lipca 1889 r. w Myślenicach,oraz
/vel
3/ Irena Abrahamer, córka Dawida i Henczy/Anny z d. Seelenfreund Abrahamerów, ur.dnia 22 listopada 1925 r. w Krakowie, - zginęli w dniu 31 marca 1943 r. w obozie śmierci w Bełżcu,

4/ Sabina Abrahamer Kreutwirthowa,córka Dawida i Henczy vel Anny z d. Seelenfreund Abrahamerów, ur. dnia 13 listopada 1913 w Krakowie, - zmarła dnia 9 maja 1945 r. w obozie Bersen Belgen,

5/ Jakub Abrahamer,syn Dawida i Henczy vel Anny z d. Seelenfreund Abrahamerów,ur. dnia 4 lutego 1913 r. w Krakowie, zmarł śmiercią naturalną w dniu 9 maja 1945 r. w obozie w Flossenburgu.

This document from 1947 lists some of Roma's family members who were killed during the German occupation.

younger than me. From the moment I saw him I loved him, his big eyes, his wild black curls, and his thin little body. One by one his entire family comes to stay with us: his parents, grandparents, and twelve-year-old Bronia, his sister. The whole family was saved by a man named Oskar Schindler.

For a time the Rosner brothers, Mrs Horowitz's brothers, also stay with us. They are musicians and survived only because they performed for the camp commandant while he ate his meals. Then my father's two brothers turn up. I already know Szymon – he's the one who hid behind the armoire in Dieter's apartment. His wife had hidden on a farm somewhere, and she comes to stay with us too. I didn't know the other brother before: Moshe. I'm afraid of him. He is small but strong and he gets angry quickly. That's because he was in so many camps; that makes you crazy.

Ryszard is a little crazy too. He has a number on his arm, just like all the grown-ups. A blue number that starts with 144. I sometimes touch the number when we're sitting in the bath together. Then he pulls back his arm. At mealtimes he becomes quite wild, grabs his piece of bread and hides it under his pillow. He never eats it then and there, only at night, in the dark. Sometimes I can hear him chewing, because we sleep in the same bed. I don't know why he does that.

The grown-ups don't understand it either. They don't seem to realize that he's mad. They scold him when he hides his bread. They want him to sit at the table with everyone else and behave himself.

Now that the war is over, the grown-ups still don't have much time to spend with us. It's as though we were never affected by the war. Children have to be good. Children have to behave. Grown-ups can't be expected to take children's feelings into account. Everyone has to cope with the war's after-effects. The grown-ups think they're having a hard enough time putting up with everything and feeding us all.

Sometimes when I'm frightened at night I ask them to leave the light on a little longer. But lately my mother has become very strict.

'Close your eyes and turn over on your side!' she says, and turns off the lamp.

Then I lie there in the dark and hear Ryszard who is lying next to me secretly gnawing on his bread crust while the grown-ups sit around the kitchen table, talking and sobbing. All they talk about is death.

Every morning my father leaves and doesn't come back till late in the evening. He is looking after what is left of his company and brings home money and food. From time to time he picks up lost or abandoned Jewish children wandering in the streets and puts them into an orphanage that he and some other Jews have founded.

One day he comes home with a boy who is a few years older than me. He looks angry and neglected. I can't take my eyes off him, can't help admiring him for his anger.

'Roma, guess who this is?' my mother says, as she puts a plate of soup before the boy. 'It's your cousin Roman!'

'I recognized him immediately,' my father tells my mother. 'I knew right away that he was my brother's son. Having him here won't be easy on you, Tosia. I literally pulled him out of the gutter. He must have had a terrible time after he was smuggled out of the ghetto. But he's alive!'

Little Ryszard and I now share our mattress with Roman. Under the covers he tells us exciting, eerie stories.

I can also still hear the stories the grown-ups told. I won't ever be able to forget them. It didn't help putting my hands over my ears, creeping under the bed, or pulling the blanket over my head. There was no escape for us children; they had no pity on us. We were turned into involuntary witnesses by those who were bearing witness. As soon as it got dark outside, the grown-ups would begin to talk about all they had lived through, about death, about unimaginable atrocities, unbelievable tortures – the agonies human beings are capable of inflicting on fellow human beings and that their victims are able to endure. This was the time for lamentation and for grief, the time for anger and bitterness. After that the voices of the survivors fell silent, many of them for all time. And our generation, the generation of their children, we too no longer spoke of it.

During those endless nights the word 'Auschwitz' was indelibly burned into my soul. The grown-ups talked about the camp, almost as though they felt a terrible, sick desire to describe every single horrible detail. How people were shot and strangled, how their veins were cut open, how they were sent naked into the gas chambers. How corpses were hung on the Auschwitz Christmas tree. How those doomed to die had to sort their clothes and shoes before they took their last steps, and how a little boy was forced to stand there handing out little pieces of shoelaces for them to tie their shoes together.

They told about being forced to count the whiplashes as they cut through the flesh on their backs, of being deprived of their names and having blue numbers tattooed on their skin instead. Of almost freezing to death when they were made to stand naked outside for many hours, forced to recite their camp inmate numbers, while they were doused with ice-cold water. They described dogs ripping open the bodies of the prisoners. How hunger and fear nearly drove them out of their minds. And over and over again they described, quite matter-of-factly, the banal details of everyday life in the camp: the best place to hide bread, what to do when your shoes were stolen, how to make yourself look healthy by pricking your finger and rubbing the blood on your cheeks, how to drink your own urine, and how to wash with it – such things could mean the difference between life and death. Their whispering, weary voices didn't even sound indignant. They were only reporting facts, events, things they took for granted. And this went on hour after hour, night after night, month after month.

It often seems to me that I can't stand it any more. Why won't they stop? Why are they torturing themselves and us all over again? If only I could yell like Roman, or sleep through it as peacefully as little Ryszard, who takes it all in stride because he himself lived through it. But I'm not allowed to yell, not allowed to be noisy; I have to behave and be quiet, lie there in bed, listening to their stories. I have to be a good girl. Always and for ever I have to be a good girl.

Although the nights in our apartment are full of madness, during the day the grown-ups try frantically to present a picture of normality. As always, it is very difficult to find enough food for everyone. But now there are food packages labelled 'UNRRA' in large letters. My father brought one home, very proud that he succeeded in obtaining such a wondrous treasure. The package is full of all kinds of things. My mother cries out with joy as she inspects the contents: several cans, some of them containing syrupy sweetened milk that tastes wonderful; others had a yellow liquid in them. 'Orange juice,' my father says in triumph. Orange juice? I sniff the open can. It has a pleasant smell. I take a sip. It is sweet and cold. I've never tasted anything so good!

Then, with shining eyes, my mother hands me a flat, round box. 'Roma, look,' she says reverently, 'this is chocolate.' A tingling sensation runs down my back. Chocolate! How long have I dreamed about it? And now, at last, I'll be able to taste the real thing. Taking off the lid, I see something dark brown and hard inside. I break off a little piece and put it into my mouth. It is very hard and breaks apart when I chew it. It is sweet, but also bitter. Actually it tastes awful.

'This is chocolate?' I ask. They all nod, and I feel as though Paradise has turned into an allotment garden.

I still have a photograph from that time. It was taken on Mother's Day in 1946 and shows Roman, the Horowitz children and me. That day in May my father came home with a bunch of lilac he had picked in the park. He presented it to my mother and then he took us all on an excursion to Kraków's Wawel Castle. We looked just like an ordinary family. A father, his little daughter, his nephew and two of their young friends.

I still remember we were told to smile for that photo. My smile looks a little shy. But I was happy and proud.

'Children have to go to school,' my mother says, and before we know it she sews a sailor suit for Ryszard and a little sailor dress for me using the old striped prison clothes she has dyed blue.

A small Jewish school has reopened in Kraków. It is located in a shabby dark building with tiny rooms. I am put into the second form because I already know how to read and write and because I'm almost seven years old. There are eleven children in our class. They come from all over, from the countryside, from Warsaw, even from Russia.

I sit down on my school bench and fall silent. I had looked forward to starting school, but now it leaves me speechless. The atmosphere in the classroom is so tense. Hardly a minute passes when someone doesn't break down in tears. The teachers and the pupils cry at almost anything. Everyone is nervous, almost hysterical. All that's needed is for someone to raise his voice, and the teacher, a woman who was also in one of the camps, flinches and begins to sob. When she wipes away her tears you can see the blue number tattooed on her arm. Sometimes classes turn into communal crying sessions.

I don't want to cry, and I don't want to learn anything. I don't want to eat. I don't want to listen. I don't want to say anything.

An outing to Wawel Castle (1946): seven-year-old Roma (right front), her thirteen-year-old cousin Roman Polanski behind her, next to him Bronislawa Horowitz, also thirteen, and in front, her six-year-old brother Ryszard Horowitz.

We are supposed to be learning Yiddish and Hebrew. But I am silent. I put my notebook under my desk and scribble little pictures into it.

At break I take my coat and go home.

Everyone here is crazy. This isn't a school; it's a ghetto.

My mother doesn't know what to do. 'Are you sick again, Roma? Why don't you want to go to school?'

I hang my head. I can't explain to her why I've been coming home early the last few days, and I can't stand being at that school.

'But you have to go,' my mother says, and I can tell she's as unhappy with this situation as I am. She takes me back to school. I hear her talking with the teacher.

'She just sits there,' the teacher says reproachfully. 'She doesn't want to learn anything. She doesn't answer questions. She stares at the wall and scribbles in her notebook.'

'It's the war, you know,' replies my mother. She sighs.

'But we all have to pull ourselves together . . .' I can't hear the rest of what the teacher says because I have to go into the classroom.

From then on my mother sees to it that Roman walks Ryszard and me to school in the morning. And he does. But only as far as the nearest street corner. There, the two boys leave me and run off. I can't run with them: my legs are as stiff and heavy as lead. The boys catch up with a tram, grab on to the doors, and in no time at all they've disappeared from view.

I stare after them longingly, but I never tell on them. Slowly I walk down the street, daydreaming. Usually by the time I reach the classroom the first hour of lessons has already passed.

For a long time no one has any idea that I'm the only one of the three children who regularly goes to school, even if it's with great reluctance.

* * *

One day we visit Manuela.

It's all so familiar, yet I scarcely recognize it: the sofa in the living room seems not as high, the hall not as long, the tree in the yard not as tall.

'How you've grown, *Poziomka*!' Manuela says and gives me a kiss. She's as blonde and beautiful as ever.

As usual *Babcia* is in bed. She is very happy to see us. We give each other a hug and play a game of cards together.

Everything is as it was before.

When I walk into the kitchen, Mrs Kiernikowa is standing at the stove. She looks me up and down. Instantly I shrink a bit.

As before.

'And what about Dudek?' my mother asks Manuela. They are all sitting at the kitchen table, drinking tea.

'We don't know,' Manuela replies. 'We haven't heard from him since the end of the war.'

Mrs Kiernikowa takes a deep breath. 'I hear you're going to school now, Roma,' she says pleasantly. 'Do you like it?'

I nod. Mrs Kiernikowa is the last person on earth I would pour my heart out to. There isn't anyone I can talk to about school, no one I can tell what that school is really like. And how terribly lonely I feel.

As before.

It's the first time I have had the chance to be with other children, and I'm lonelier than ever. Yet no one notices my loneliness, because everybody is on his own in that school. Nobody talks to anybody. During break we take a walk in pairs, but nobody says a word. In class some of the children just sit there, rocking back and forth. Some wet their pants. Each is trapped in his or her own story and his or her own fear, the teachers, too. Hardly any of the children play together or make friends. Now and then they fight. The boys hit each other over the head with their wooden pencil boxes; the girls scratch and bite. Sometimes a child gets hurt; there are black and blue marks, even bloody wounds. We are like frightened wild animals.

I no longer try to leave and go home because my mother only brings me back. Other children keep running away during the lessons; one jumps up and hides every time there's a noise. For a time the teacher runs after the children to bring them back, but eventually she gives up. We are all exhausted and stupefied by the constant tension.

A tall, thin black-haired boy sits on the bench next to me. If you touch him, his body feels strange, not hard and bony like the other boys, but very soft. His gestures are girlish and graceful. When he sits down, his hands move as if he were smoothing an invisible skirt. During the lessons his fingers move as though they were making braids.

He is weird.

One day during break while I'm watching him out of the corner of my eye, he smiles shyly and gestures for me to come closer. He rummages in his pocket and pulls out a photo. It shows a little girl with long black plaits. She is wearing a flowered dress and looks a lot like him.

'Your sister?' I ask.

He shakes his head. 'Me,' he says. There is pride in his voice. The photo is something like a testimonial, a justification for him. 'I had to pretend to be a girl,' he says, blushing, 'so that the Germans wouldn't check' – he points at his crotch – 'down there.'

I look into his eyes. Does he long to be a girl again?

There's no school today, and Roman and Ryszard have taken me along on one of their secret expeditions. Roman knows the town like the back of his hand. He knows how to hitch a ride by jumping up on trams or trucks, where to get something to eat, where the best places to hide are, and who is willing to pay a boy a few złoty for doing some odd jobs.

Confusion has reigned in Kraków since the end of the war. The city teems with people. On every street corner there's someone who has something to sell: vodka, buttons, fresh mushrooms from the nearby forests, hand-knitted wool socks, old books, laundry soap. Nobody has any money, and everybody wants to earn some. There isn't a thing that isn't being traded on these pavements.

We discover a deserted shoe shop on a small side-street. The door has been boarded up, but Roman finds a window in the courtyard through which one can climb into the back room of the shop. The boys give me a boost, and I squeeze through the little window. Down below, the room is dark. A memory comes back and takes my breath away. I don't want to jump.

'Go on, jump!' Roman hisses. It's an order. Still, I hesitate, pull myself together and jump. I land on a pile of shoeboxes. Soon Ryszard's pale face appears in the window opening, and then Roman and his jug ears.

It's quiet in the room, we hear only our own panting breaths. My heart is beating very loud, very fast.

'Come on!' Roman urges in a whisper. 'Let's see what kind of treasures we can find.'

We steal into the shop. If it weren't so dark and dusty, one might think the people who worked here had just left for the day. A big shiny cash register stands on the counter, over there a row of chairs and little stools, and shoeboxes neatly stacked on the shelves. There's a ladder in one corner. The place smells of leather.

'Let's go,' Roman says. He climbs up the ladder like a monkey and throws down shoeboxes. Ryszard and I catch them and inspect the contents.

Empty. Empty. Empty . . .

The packages form a pile on the floor, but there's not a single shoe in any of the boxes. Roman climbs down again.

'No loot,' he says bitterly.

Then he spots a stack of smaller boxes on the shelf behind the cash register.

We rummage through them and find real treasures. Shoelaces in various lengths, widths, and colours, a few cans of shoe polish, even two shoebrushes. 'This is good stuff for us to sell,' Roman says. He's very practical.

Ryszard nods enthusiastically. 'We're going to be rich!'

We gather up our booty and disappear back out through the window.

A few blocks away we set up our stand.

'Shoelaces for sale! The very best shoe polish. Top quality!'

Roman is the barker. Ryszard hands the merchandise to the customers. I count the money. But not everybody needs shoelaces, and a few people even ask us where we got them. Our prices are suspiciously low. When things get awkward, Roman points at Ryszard and me and pleads, 'These two little children will starve if you don't buy something from us.'

This gambit is especially effective when people look at Ryszard. As soon as they see his pale little face, dark eyes and long eyelashes, they buy something.

It isn't long before we've sold everything. We proudly count the money we've earned.

It's quite a lot.

'Enough to go to America.' Roman announces. 'Let's take a trip round the world.'

Ryszard nods, and I'm for it too. America – that sounds good. But then something occurs to me: 'We're going to need provisions.' It's something to consider.

The boys think about it. It's true. We can't go on a trip without provisions.

'All right. First we'll buy some food and then we'll start our trip,' Roman decides.

We go into one of the few sweet shops still open on the market square and lay in a supply of sugar canes, raspberry whipped-cream cake, and white nougat bars – things we've never eaten before. At home we only have disgustingly sticky, flavourless jam.

We watch, shiny-eyed, as the assistant puts everything into a paper bag. Then it's time to pay. Roman puts our money on the countertop. The assistant counts it and puts it into the cash register. She gives him one coin in change.

'But where's the rest?' he asks.

The assistant shrugs. 'Sorry, children,' she smiles, 'there is no rest. You spent it all.'

We slip out of the shop, deeply disappointed because our trip abroad will have to be cancelled.

The candy canes and the raspberry cream cakes are a consolation of sorts, and right now we need a lot of consolation. Only after the last crumb has been devoured do we drag ourselves home, feeling as though we had stones in our stomachs.

'Where have you been all this time?' my mother scolds, when she sees how dirty and sticky we are. But then she runs to get a pail when she sees how green around the gills we look.

I'm the first to throw up, then it's Ryszard's turn. Only Roman wins the battle against his stomach.

In the Jewish school we often sing songs by Mordechaj Gebirtig, a carpenter and a poet who was born in Kraków. The Germans shot him while he was being taken from the ghetto to a concentration camp. His songs are terribly sad, but I love them, even though we all cry when we sing them.

I still remember one of those songs, '*Es Brent*' (Our Shtetl Is Burning):

> *S'brent! Briderlekh, s'brent!*
> *Oy, undzer orem shtetl nebekh brent!*
> *Beyze vintn mit yirgozn*

The Girl In The Red Coat

Raysn, brekhn un tseblozn
Shtarker nokh di vilde flamen,
Alts arum shoyn brent.
Un ir shteyt un kukt azoy zikh
Mit farleygte hent
Un ir shteyt un kukt azoy zikh –
Undzer shtetl brent!

It's burning, brothers, it's on fire!
Oh, our poor shtetl, God forbid, is burning!
Worse than the wild flames,
are the angry winds
that rip, break, and churn things up.
All around, everything is burning!
And you stand there looking on
with your hands clasped behind your backs
and you stand there looking on –
Our shtetl is burning!

The song touches something deep inside me. I'm able to put up with school only because we sing these songs. Otherwise I'm not really there, even though I sit on the bench, next to the boy who is a girl.

There's only one girl I like in that school and with whom I'd want to be friends. But it won't work because she is as crazy as all the rest. Her name is Janina, and she has beautiful long hair. Every day after school, the same thing happens, and I always get goose pimples watching it. It's like a scene in a play performed over and over.

A pale, somewhat plump woman is waiting at the school entrance to pick up Janina. She approaches her, smiles, tries to put her arms around her, but Janina pushes her away. 'I don't know you,' she shouts. 'Go away! Leave me alone!'

The woman starts to cry. 'But I'm your *mama*! Please, Janina, come to your *mama*. Please.' And she runs after Janina.

'Leave me alone! You're not my mother!' Janina yells angrily, walking faster.

The woman grabs her sleeve, holds on to her. Now both of them are crying. 'Forgive me,' the woman says sobbing, 'please forgive me.'

One day during break I pluck up courage to ask Janina about the pale woman. Janina's face instantly turns sombre. 'She says she's my mother,' she says angrily, and clenches her fists, 'but she's lying. I grew up on a farm in a Polish peasant family. They are my parents! Then after the war, this strange woman suddenly turns up and says she's my mother! She looked terrible. She didn't even have any hair, and she wanted to take me with her. I cried and screamed, but my parents gave me away. They sold me to her. Really. I saw how this woman gave them money. And that's why I can't run away, I can't go back home. They sold me!'

Janina started sobbing; I just stand there, thunderstruck. I can't understand how parents could sell their own child. But now I see why Janina doesn't want to have anything to do with that woman.

Then I think of my father and how I didn't want to recognize him when he came back. What if the woman is telling the truth? What if she really is Janina's mother?

The thought hurts. No, I'd rather not know about any of this. If only I hadn't asked.

It's great to have Roman and Ryszard around. Sometimes we sing naughty songs at the top of our voices. Songs like:

> *Kusine, Rosine,*
> *Silbertaler,*
> *Krieg verlor*
> *der dumme Maler*

> *Kusine, Rosine,*
> *hartes Brot,*

hat verloren
und ist tot . . .

Cousin, buzzin',
silver dollar,
stupid painter
lost the war

Cousin, buzzin',
crust of bread
lost the war
and now he's dead . . .

Gradually we become an inseparable little gang of three. Whenever we can we prowl through the streets looking for adventures. The grown-ups know nothing of the mischief we're up to, and it's just as well, because most of the time it's something forbidden. Roman's favourite game is throwing firecrackers in front of people's front doors then watching their frightened faces. They think it's a bomb.

These wild pranks give me something like a real childhood. And I have Roman to thank for that.

I admire him without reservation. He seems to know everything about everything and is always eager to learn more. But not school. He wants nothing to do with school.

One day Roman says to me, 'Come on, Roma, let's get out of here. I have something great to show you!' He drags me to a rear courtyard and pushes me through a half-open iron door into a completely dark little room. I hold my breath in suspense. After a few seconds my eyes get used to the dark and I can see that we're sitting in front of a stage, just like in a theatre. When the curtain is pulled open I expect to see actors, but instead lights flicker across a white wall, on which there are huge letters that read:

Roma Ligocka

BIA Y MURZYN (THE WHITE NEGRO)

Suddenly moving pictures appear, people are running across the wall, they're talking, a car drives across the stage, there's even a barking dog. I can't understand what's going on because everything is so loud, is happening so quickly, but one thing is clear: this is a story about being in love.

I get quite dizzy. It's as if I were in a fog. I try to follow what's happening when suddenly there's the sound of a fanfare, the pictures vanish in a flash, and the word KONIEC, 'The End', appears in big letters. I rub my eyes and grope my way along behind Roman until we're back on the street.

'Well, what do you think?' His face is glowing with enthusiasm; his small bright eyes gleam.

'What was it?' I ask, still dumbfounded.

'That,' Roman announces solemnly, 'was moving pictures.'

For my seventh birthday I get Jacek.

Who knows where my mother found him? There still aren't any toy shops in Kraków. I have been wishing for Jacek for such a long time, have kept talking about a doll, a baby, have even rolled up a piece of old material and rocked it back and forth in my arms. And then, suddenly, here he is! Jacek has a soft body made of fabric and a porcelain head. He has blond hair and blue eyes, and he's the most beautiful baby in the world.

I am overwhelmed with joy. Gently I put him into the doll's pram a neighbour gave me, and then I carefully spread a pink blanket over him. Roman and Ryszard laugh at me, but I pay no attention to them. I drag the pram out to the street and push it to the park.

It's a grey November day and fairly cool, but for me the sun is shining and the birds are chirping, the flowers are in bloom, and everything is beautiful because I am taking my baby out for some fresh air. I hum a song, straighten his blanket, and look into his little face. He is sleeping peacefully, his eyelids with the long, thick lashes closed over his blue eyes.

I sit down on a park bench, like the young mothers always do, and take him out of the pram to cuddle him.

Suddenly there's a little girl standing before me, thin, hungry-looking and angry as a wasp. 'Can I hold your doll?'

I know instinctively what's going to happen next. I can see it passing before my mind's eye, just as if it were in the moving pictures that Roman calls the movies.

'No.'

The girl gives me a menacing look. 'Just for a second!' She tugs my sleeve. I say nothing and press Jacek close to my chest. She gets angrier and angrier, and my 'no' gets weaker and weaker. She just won't stop.

So I give him to her, wrapped in his pink blanket.

'Please be careful.'

And, just as I feared, she drops Jacek. His head breaks into four pieces, his empty eye sockets blink sightlessly until they are finally still. I think of the baby in the ghetto. How it lay there on the ground.

The birds no longer twitter, no flowers bloom, no ray of sunshine pierces the dense grey clouds. The girl runs away. I collect the porcelain shards and put them into the doll's pram. Then I slowly push it home.

'Something's the matter with the child,' Uncle Szymon says one day. I'm sitting in the corner with a book and look up in surprise at his words.

'What do you mean, Szymon?' my mother asks.

'Well, just look at her, Tosia. She looks like a little adult, not like a child.' My mother nods. It's true. Jokingly, they often call me 'the little old woman'.

'I think it has something to do with the school,' my mother says. 'It isn't good for her. Maybe I should send her to a different one.'

It's strange, the way they talk about me as if I weren't there. It never stops amazing me. But that's what grown-ups are like. They make decisions about our lives, about allowances and punishment, about our clothes, school, food. They decide what's good or bad for us, what's right or wrong. They never ask us what we think.

These days I still sit at the table for hours, my mouth full of food, unable to eat.

Then Roman pokes my full cheek.

'Ouch!' I can't help laughing, and out comes the spinach. My mother scolds us.

'These children,' the grown-ups say, shaking their heads and sighing. We're a burden to them.

Roman has a secret.

One evening when just the two of us are sitting on the stairs in the hallway, he tells me what it is. 'I'm going to buy a bicycle,' he announces proudly.

A bicycle? I can't believe it. Bicycles are hard to get, and terribly expensive. I don't know anybody who has one.

'But *I'm* going to have one!' Roman insists. 'Tomorrow night, I'm meeting a man in the park, and he's going to give me the bicycle. Look how much money I've saved up for it.'

He takes a dirty little pouch out of his trouser pocket and allows me to look into it. It's full of coins. I've never seen so much money at one time, and I'm deeply impressed. 'Where did you get it?' I ask him, full of admiration.

'I earned it,' he replies nonchalantly, and puts the pouch back in his pocket. 'I bet my father's going to be surprised! But don't you dare tell anybody about it. It's our secret. Understand?'

I give him my triple word of honour, even though that really isn't necessary because I always do what Roman says.

The following evening, straight after supper, Roman slips off to pick up his bicycle. I'm incredibly excited, wondering what it will look like and what the grown-ups will say when they see it. I wait and wait, but Roman doesn't come back.

'He'll be back,' my mother says, as she takes the dishes off the table. I don't say anything.

But Roman doesn't come back. Not that evening, or the next day. That night I can't sleep because I keep thinking of Roman and his bicycle. If only it weren't a secret! What if something has happened to him? But maybe he ran away to America with his new bicycle – he always dreamed of doing that.

I don't waver. I say nothing.

In the meantime the grown-ups start to worry too. Although Roman has disappeared before, he has never stayed away for such a long time.

They search everywhere for him.

Another night passes and I have awful nightmares. My triple word of honour weighs on my heart like a rock. Should I break my promise? With every passing hour, my fear for Roman grows.

Finally I can't stand it any longer and I tell my mother about the bicycle. 'Don't tell Uncle Moshe,' I beg her. When they find him at last Roman is seriously hurt. He has a head injury and is terribly weak because he's been lying in an underground bunker in the park for the last two days, more or less unconscious. His money is gone, and there's no bicycle.

'Did you break your triple word of honour?' he whispers, when I'm finally allowed to visit him in the hospital.

I nod, ashamed.

'It's all right,' he growls, and grins crookedly, 'If you hadn't, I think I would have died. But don't ever let it happen again!'

I give Roman my triple word of honour that I'll never break my triple word of honour again.

All the talk about the atrocities has stopped, and the apartment has emptied. One by one, they have left us to start new lives. Uncle Szymon and his pregnant wife emigrated to

Australia. The Horowitz family found an apartment of their own. I miss little Ryszard, but luckily I still have Roman.

Recently he has been spending all his evenings in our kitchen practising knot-tying with a piece of rope. That's because he has joined the Boy Scouts and has to know how to do such things. 'When you know how to tie all the knots, you get a badge,' he explains.

The Boy Scouts give out twenty-four badges, and Roman has them all, except for this last one. I'm sure he'll get that one too. When he makes up his mind to do something, he always manages to do it.

And one day he'll manage to get to America. When the Horowitzes said goodbye, Roman and Ryszard swore to each other that they would meet there. What is it with boys? They always want to go to America.

5

We're going on holiday as if we were just an ordinary family.
One day my father surprises me. 'We're going to Zakopane,'
he says, smiling. 'It's a little village in the mountains not far
from here. We're going there for a few days to relax. Just
imagine, we're going on a *real* trip. And Roman can come
too.'

I'm delighted and throw my arms around his neck. Then
I run off to tell Roman.

It's spring, and Zakopane is the most beautiful place in the
world. Flowers are blooming in the meadows; there is a
silvery, bubbling mountain stream, leafy forests, twittering
birds, even a little wild rabbit with long ears. I never knew
anything as beautiful as this existed. Now for the first time
I get to touch damp warm soil, smell the perfume of little
blue violets, hear the rustling of the wind in the leaves, feel
the rich warmth of the sun on my skin. In the country I have
a sense of security and at the same time of freedom.

We are staying in a little boarding-house and every morning
there are fresh rolls and home-made strawberry jam for breakfast.

At night we sleep under thick, soft, clean feather quilts.

I'm hungry and eat my fill. I sleep soundly all night, no
nightmares. I feel free and lighthearted.

And so are my parents. My father and mother look like
the couples you see in the movies. They giggle, hold hands
and kiss as though they have just fallen in love. My father,
pointing at my mother sitting in the grass, laughing and

The only family holiday (1946).

holding her face to the sun, keeps saying, 'How beautiful she is, look at those raspberry lips.' I nod. What am I supposed to say? It's nice to see my parents so happy, but they're acting like silly children.

Roman thinks so too. He and I build dams in the little brook and sail little ships made of bark. Sometimes my father helps us. Often he lifts me up on his shoulders and carries me through the countryside. And we sing songs, cheerful children's songs, not like those sad songs at school. Roman whistles along and tries to teach me to whistle too. For a while I walk around with pursed lips, trying to make the right sound. Finally I produce a thin whistle. Everyone applauds, and I'm proud.

In those days it seemed the world was full of sunshine. The dark shadows had dissolved.

But then something terrible happens.

We had gone on a glorious hike and now, sweaty and hungry, we are on our way back to the boarding-house.

I can already see them from far away – two men in raincoats, carrying briefcases. They are wearing hats even though the sun is hot, their faces immobile, like the faces of soldiers. I know straight away that they are policemen and that this spells danger.

'I hope you haven't got sunstroke, Roma,' my mother says. 'You suddenly look so pale.'

One of the men steps towards us. Gruffly he asks, 'David Liebling?'

My father nods. Again I feel the icy cold, the fear, flowing into me from my mother's trembling hand. Icier than ever before. The sun so hot, her hand so cold, the immobile faces of the policemen. Standing next to me, Roman is breathing heavily. He's afraid too. 'You are under arrest,' says one of the men in the raincoats. 'Come with us.'

My father is silent, lowers his head. He is thinking. Should he do as they ask? Should he let them take him away without resisting? Should he fight? Seconds pass. Then he glances at me, and he smiles just a bit. 'Don't be afraid, little one,' he says. 'I'll be back soon. I'm sure it's just a mistake. And, Tosia . . .' he looks into my mother's eyes '. . . don't worry about me.'

And now they're getting into the black car parked in front of the boarding-house and now they're driving off. We stare after them in silence. For a while a little cloud of dust the car has raised hangs in the air. Then it's gone.

Again my mother and I are alone.

When I come home from school my mother is usually still wearing her hat and coat, having returned only minutes before me. I'm not supposed to be in the apartment by myself. Roman is usually off on one of his expeditions. Day and night my mother tries to find out where my father is being held. So far, even though we've been back in Kraków for several weeks, we haven't been able to learn a thing. We left Zakopane right after that terrible day. My mother has done everything possible to find him, but he has vanished.

'Why did they arrest him?' she sobs, over and over again. She has gone to pieces since my father was picked up. I don't know why. After all, she ought to know that any of us can be arrested at any time.

She keeps running to the post office to make telephone calls. Finally, she finds out where he is.

In Montelupich.

I flinch when I hear the word. Montelupich – that's what the policeman said back then. For me Montelupich is the worst place in the world. Montelupich means certain death.

My mother sighs and wipes away the tears. 'I couldn't find

out anything definite,' she explains. 'Apparently they claim that he's a traitor. But isn't everybody nowadays? The people they're persecuting now are the very same people who were in the resistance, who risked their lives. Poor Dudek is probably in Montelupich too . . . I've got to find somebody who's on the take!'

I know that a person 'on the take' is someone who will help you if you give him jewellery or money. Now my mother runs from one government office to another trying to find out who is in charge of my father. I don't know whether she has been successful. In any case my father has not come back. She often takes me along when she goes to see an old man who is a lawyer. They talk for a long time about how to get my father out of jail, but when we leave, neither of them has figured out what to do.

Finally, in September, in time for the Jewish New Year, my father manages to send us a message on a little piece of cardboard: 'To my beloved wife and Rominka – All good wishes for the New Year.' I still have it today.

Now my mother has to provide for us because the little money we have isn't enough to make ends meet. 'If David doesn't come back soon, I'll have to find a job,' she says. She looks worried and her forehead has recently become more wrinkled.

But then something happens that none of us expected. My father comes home! They released him because he had been taken seriously ill in Montelupich. His hair has turned even greyer than before. He had a stroke, and for a while he was in the prison hospital, but finally they sent him home. Can it be that my mother had at last found somebody who was 'on the take'?

She knows a lot about medical things, and now she's beside herself because of father's stroke. 'Things like that only happen to old people, not to someone who's only thirty-nine,' she cries.

It doesn't surprise me that he had a stroke. I'm sure they beat him in Montelupich. Now he lies in bed; he is paralysed, can't move, can hardly speak. Only his black eyes are as alive as ever, and they follow everything going on around him.

During this time I am closer to my father than ever before. In fact, I get to know him for the first time. As soon as I come home from school I run to his room and sit down on the edge of his bed. I whistle tunes for him or tell him about everything that happened to me that day at the Jewish school. I recite poems and act out plays for him. He listens to me the way *Babcia* did; she was always in bed too. People in bed have a lot of time on their hands.

I have time, too, and I have a lot of patience. My mother's eyes always redden when she looks at him lying there, speechless. Her nerves are shot. But I don't mind seeing him so weak. On the contrary.

Now I am the grown-up and he is the child. It's weird, but it's nice too. I teach him to talk again. He points at an object and I say its name, slowly and clearly. Then with a lot of effort he repeats the word. He has to relearn everything – his own name, our names. It's all new for him.

'You are David Liebling,' I say and take his hand. 'And I' – I point at myself – 'I am your daughter Roma . . . and this is your wife, my mama. Her name is Tosia.'

'Tosia,' he whispers indistinctly, and his eyes flash as though he suddenly remembers everything.

I know how hard it is for him to learn and that he is aware of what has happened to his brain. My mother explained it to me, but I didn't understand all of it, except that something burst in his head and that is why he can't think properly any more. I can tell how hard he is struggling to teach himself to think again, and both of us glow with pride when he manages to learn a new word. He is also beginning to write. I show him how. He writes *Mama, Papa, Roma* . . .

Now that my father is weak and needs me, now that he is no longer the strong hero who carried me on his shoulders – now I love him more than ever.

Six days before my eighth birthday, on a grey November morning, my father dies.

I remember it as though it were yesterday. It was pouring, and by the time I got home from school I was soaked. As I rang the downstairs bell I already had a peculiar feeling in my belly. I raced up the stairs and stormed, dripping wet, into the apartment. My mother, who usually scolds me if I don't immediately take off my wet shoes, is sitting on a low stool in the kitchen. There's a little box on the floor in front of her. She gives me an odd look. 'Father is gone,' she whispers in a husky voice.

I stare at her in horror, run into the bedroom. The bed is empty; he is gone.

'Where is Papa? What happened?'

'He was running a high fever the last few days,' she says slowly. Her voice sounds hollow, cracked. 'This morning he suddenly had to be taken to the hospital. But it was too late. The doctors couldn't save him. His heart became inflamed, he was weak from having often been sick in the camp, and the medicine that could have made him well wasn't available.' I open the box. In it are a shaving brush, a razor, a wristwatch with a worn band, and the beautiful blue fountain pen with which he had only a little while ago written my name.

That's all that's left of my father. Afterwards, my mother says that only a few weeks later it would have been possible to buy penicillin on the black market. It might have saved his life.

For seven days my mother sits on the stool in the kitchen and mourns my father. All the mirrors in the apartment are covered. Life has suddenly come to a standstill.

I tiptoe through the apartment, bringing my mother food,

making tea. I sit in a corner and make myself invisible.

Then my mother puts on the black veil that she will wear for a year, and life goes on.

There were many things about my father I found out only later, some very recently. During the war he worked secretly for the Jewish resistance group in Kraków. He belonged to that small band of young idealists who distributed leaflets, dismantled railways, blew up military barracks and trucks, then set off a bomb in Café Cyganeria on the market square.

While he was in Płaszów, he volunteered for a construction gang, which allowed him to leave the camp during the day. That's when the 'connections' he had made in his wild days as a youth on the city streets paid off. Through underworld contacts, he was able to obtain explosives and weapons for the resistance fighters.

Once or twice, while we were still staying with the Kierniks, my mother thought she saw him doing street-repair work. But maybe she only imagined it.

How I wish I had had more time with my father.

Since his death my mother and I are entirely dependent on each other. When she cries at night I console her. She holds me close when I come home despondent from the Jewish school. I can only fall asleep when she is holding my hand. She takes care of me and I take care of her. I feel what she feels. We are almost like one being with two heads, a big one and a small one.

Sometimes I feel overwhelmed by all this responsibility. Then I wish my father were still here to take the burden off my shoulders. I often miss him, but not as much as my mother does. She doesn't eat, she can't sleep, doesn't even cry, just lies in bed silent, motionless. I worry about her.

'You have to eat something,' I say, bringing tea and zwieback to her bedside.

'Go to sleep now,' I whisper, and cover her.

She needs my help, as though she were a child. We just couldn't live without each other.

Little by little my mother tries to organize our life. The first thing she does is go to the municipal register office for permission to legally keep the name Ligocka. She wants to forget the name Liebling. Perhaps she also thinks that this would be better for me.

I don't ever want to hear my old name again. Back in the ghetto days it was buried in the lowest layer of my memory. I had to recite the little speech with the new name so often that eventually I came to believe it myself. I can't say the name Liebling any more, even if I wanted to.

After that's done, my mother tackles the money problem. She gets an office job in the firm that once belonged to my father, it is now being run by a friend. Then she goes about the nearly hopeless search for a smaller apartment because we are not allowed to keep the large one any longer.

Like many others, she also hopes to get a portion of her inheritance. Her parents' house had been expropriated by the Germans then confiscated by the Communists. Once again she runs from one government office to another.

'We'll manage,' she says, and I'm glad she isn't crying so much any more.

It is spring again and we are in a carriage driving along Warszawska Street towards the Abrahamer house. Remembering all the things my mother told me about life in my grandparents' house fills me with happy anticipation. I'm looking forward to exploring the wonderful garden with the fruit trees and bushes, and I'm planning to sit in the garden house in the sunshine the way Tosia did when she first met my father. Inside the main house I'll tiptoe on the thick carpets in the drawing room, and go into the blue-tiled kitchen, which smells of raisin rolls and roast turkey. Then in the bedroom I'll sink down into the white bed with the carved lilies and admire the lace-trimmed sheets and pillowcases with their embroidered monograms. If the musical box with the porcelain dancers is still in my mother's room, I'll take that with me.

But nothing is left. No fruit trees, no garden house, no garden. Instead we find gravestones in an unkempt cemetery. In the centre, a dilapidated old wooden house. The carved balcony balustrade is half torn off. Laundry hangs out of the open windows.

There must be some mistake. I turn round, look up at my mother's face. It appears to be carved of grey stone. Slowly I realize there has been no mistake. My mother hasn't been back here, hasn't seen her parents' home since the war started. This run-down house in a cemetery is it. A small cemetery nearby had been enlarged until it finally reached my grandfather's garden. Now the entire neighbourhood has become a cemetery. So many graves were needed for all the dead.

We make no attempt to get into the house, which is full of strangers. My mother takes my hand and we return home. We have never gone back there together.

'After all,' she says wearily, 'I can't live in a cemetery.'

She never received a single złoty of compensation for her parents' house.

Walking through the city with my mother is like calling up old ghosts. 'Look,' she says, 'look, this is where such-and-such a store used to be, here they sold fine fabrics, there you could buy the most stylish hats, and over there was the jeweller from whom one bought one's jewellery, there one bought lingerie . . .'

I point at an empty shop window on which old flaking letters are still legible. 'And there,' I ask, 'wasn't that a jeweller too?'

Roma Ligocka

'Yes,' she replies, 'but one didn't go *there* to buy jewellery.'

Now there's practically nothing to buy. No fabrics, no jewellery, no hats. We pass a shop window and I look inside. The walls and floor are covered in beautiful blue and white tiles. It is empty. 'Look at the beautiful tiles!' I say.

My mother sighs. 'In the old days that was a butcher's shop,' she murmurs. 'He was the best butcher in the city. You should have seen his liver pâté! Just thinking of it makes my mouth water.'

Little by little I find out more about what life was like in those days. How easy and beautiful it must have been, how colourful, how elegant! Sometimes I long for that kind of life; my mother also yearns for it, though she never talks about her feelings.

Those days are gone for ever. Everything has become grey. People try hard to lead normal lives again – we do, too – but everyone is poor. There's hardly anything to buy; only the black market is flourishing. And, as always, the city is bursting, teeming with intellectuals, artists, journalists, professors and literary figures, people who were either born in Kraków or who have come here to make a new home.

At any rate, the coffee-houses have reopened, the trams circle the market square just as they used to, newspapers and magazines are being published, plays are again being performed in the theatre. Manuela and her friends sometimes appear on stage and naturally my mother and I attend the opening. I applaud till my hands hurt, and afterwards I'm allowed to visit Manuela in her dressing room.

On Sundays, after church and a walk, those who can afford it go to one of the elegant bakery cafés. This is an old tradition in Kraków. There you can have *Napoleonki*, a kind of whipped-cream torte with raspberry syrup, or one of their famous éclairs.

Every Sunday we go for a walk on the avenue that runs around the Old City. It is the city's salon. You stroll up and down, politely greeting one another, just as in the old days. The men have little parcels of cake dangling from their coat buttons, and after the promenade people go home to drink tea and eat cake. That's the custom, and my mother insists that we also observe it.

She has decided it's time to teach me etiquette. 'We may not have any money, but at least you should have good manners.' She shows me how to conduct myself at the table, how to curtsy, and other things like that, all of which I think are pretty useless. When I ask her why people do all this, she says, not brooking any backchat, 'That's how we always did it at home.'

Therefore, on Sundays I always have to wear white stockings, high button shoes, a bow in my hair and gloves. I feel stiff and silly, but my mother is unyielding. Roman laughs at me. 'Aunt Tosia, why do you dress Roma to look like an idiot?' he asks.

'That is how one dresses to go into town,' she answers curtly, pressing her lips together.

Roman isn't spared my mother's rules of conduct either, but they run off him like water off a duck's back. By now he pretty well lives his own life. Part of the time he stays with us and part of the time with his father.

'I have a surprise for you, Roma,' my mother one day announces. 'When we come back, we're going to move into a new apartment and you'll be going to a different school.'

I'm ecstatic and pelt her with questions.

Where will our new apartment be? What does it look like? Will there finally be enough room for me to get a dog? And what about Roman? What is the new school like? Is it a Jewish school? And wait – what do you mean 'come back'? Are we going away? Maybe to Zakopane again?

'No,' my mother says, 'we're not going to Zakopane. We're going much further than that. We're taking the train to the Czech border. To Upper Silesia, to the Riesengebirge, the

Giant Mountains. We're going to take a week's holiday there, in a real hotel.'

I jump off her lap and immediately begin to pack my suit-case.

A few weeks later we are on the train. I'm terribly excited. This is the first time I've ever sat in a train. And I'm not really sitting, I'm running around, skipping through the corridor, looking at the people in the other compartments, craning my neck to look out of the window. The train clatters; it huffs and puffs and whistles and makes a hellish racket. The landscape flies by – sometimes hilly, sometimes flat; the trees and meadows are an intense green, the sky a cloudless blue. It is summer-time.

'Mama, look!' I tug at her sleeve. I want to show her all the things I see, a red car on a road, horses, an old ruined castle . . .

Her eyes are closed. Groaning, she turns away from me. Her hands suddenly feel very damp, and cold perspiration covers her face. Is she afraid? Is she sick?

I remember the time we were going to go to Warsaw and she was ill in the station. Maybe train rides aren't good for her?

'Mama, what's the matter?'

'It's all right, Roma . . . Let me be . . .'

She is shivering. I hear her teeth chattering. She feels terribly cold. I cover her with her coat and sit down beside her. Finally she falls asleep. An old woman next to us watches sus-piciously.

'That woman is ill, and it might be catching,' she says indignantly. She takes her suitcase and leaves the crowded compartment. I'm glad because that gives us more room.

Mama really *is* sick. I'm worried about her, but what can I do? I don't know anyone who can help me. And so I wait. I sit there for hours while my mother sleeps and the landscape flies by. Gradually the countryside becomes more hilly; then we're in the mountains. The locomotive whistles and puffs.

The train stops at a small white building with bright window boxes.

I shake my mother. 'Mama, wake up. I think we're here!' She looks out of the window, gets unsteadily to her feet and then, as if in a daze, follows me. The conductor hands down our suitcases.

I don't recall how we got to the hotel, a dark menacing old box of a place. Someone leads us through endless musty corridors to our room. It has a large window with heavy green velvet curtains, from which you can see a dense forest. A table covered with a fringed green plush cloth stands under the window. I don't like this dark room. I don't like the hotel. The people here aren't friendly, and I think they don't like Jews. They speak German to each other.

My mother lies in the huge dark wooden bed, which looks like a coffin. She is in pain and has a fever. She mumbles confused phrases. Luckily there's a wash-basin in the room. I give her sips of water and cool her hot forehead with a damp towel, the way she always did when I had a fever. Then I try to give her some of the food we brought with us, but she won't even look at it. I feel as though we are all alone in the world. Eventually I undress, curl up next to her, and fall asleep.

Somebody is shaking me, pulling me out of a dream. Is it the Germans? The light in our room is on. I rub my eyes. My mother is bending over me. It was she who woke me. Her face is red and swollen and she is wheezing in a strange way. I stare at her. She scares me.

'Get a doctor,' she says, in a hoarse whisper. 'I'm dying.'

I run as fast as my legs will carry me. 'She's going to die!' a voice in my head screams. 'She's going to die!' I'm still in my nightgown and slippers, running into the dense forest.

Where should I run? Where can I get help? My mother didn't answer when I asked her how I should go about getting a doctor. She only lifted her hands and let them drop again. The light was on in the hotel lobby, but there was no one about. So I ran out into the forest. I know I've got to hurry, I can't just wait till someone comes. 'She's dying!' I gasp, panting so noisily that I can't hear my heart beating. I run very fast to avoid the black shadows behind the dark pine trees. They follow me. The voice in my head is screaming louder and louder. I am scared, scared, scared.

I come to a crossing. One path leads to the right; the path on which I came goes on straight ahead. Or is it the other way round? On which path did I come? And where should I run now? I'm lost.

I stand there, alone, in the middle of the dark forest, wearing my thin nightgown, and for a moment I think I'm going to die from fear and cold.

But I don't die; the voice won't let me. 'She's dying!' it cries. I run on, heedless of losing my slippers, my nightgown getting tangled in the undergrowth. I run on and on.

Suddenly I see a light in the darkness, far away. I run towards it; it gets brighter and brighter. I can see a street-lamp, the outlines of houses. It's a village.

A doctor! Maybe there's a doctor in the village!

The windows of the houses are dark, but I pound on the first door I come to. Someone inside mutters angrily. A woman opens the door a crack and peers out at me.

'She's dying!' I pant. 'I need a doctor . . . a doctor . . . Mama!'

The woman nods, understands, points to another house, then says something in German.

I run over to the other house, and pound on the door with both fists. 'Doctor! I need a doctor!'

On an upper floor a light goes on, a window opens, and a man sticks his head out.

'She's dying,' I say, barely able to speak, completely exhausted. I am crying, talking confusedly. He seems to understand because he closes the window and I hear him coming down the stairs.

He opens the front door, I rush in, and clasp his legs with both arms. 'She's dying!'

'At least let me get dressed,' he grumbles, in broken Polish. He's wearing striped pyjamas. I wait for him, each second an eternity. Finally he's ready, carrying his little bag. We walk back to the hotel along a road rather than the forest. It's much faster this way. In no time we're there and the doctor is standing by my mother's bed, listening to her heartbeat, feeling her pulse. She's still alive. She's still alive!

But she is very, very sick, the doctor says. She has to go to the hospital, immediately. An ambulance arrives. Two of the hotel staff are there too. No one says anything to me. They carry my mother out on a stretcher. Her eyes are closed; she does not see me. No one sees me. I sit down in a corner of our room and my throat tightens with stifled tears.

Finally in the early-morning hours I fall asleep.

I wake up because it is hot – terribly hot. It takes me a while to realize where I am. I see the table with the plush green cloth; there's a tray on it. The bed next to mine is empty. In a flash I remember it all.

I crawl out of bed, pull back the heavy curtains, and open the window. The noonday heat floods the room. The sun is high in the sky. Could it already be afternoon? I don't know; I no longer have a feeling for the passage of time, and I have no watch.

The food on the tray looks disgusting so I don't touch it. I have a sip of tea and plait my hair. Then I get dressed and go out into the hall, down the stairs, and out into the garden. I sit down on a bench.

None of it seems real to me. It's like a play in the theatre. I dangle my legs. The sun beats down on me and I can hear my mother saying, 'Careful you don't get sunstroke, Roma.'

A young girl sits down next to me and stares at me curiously.

'Are you here all by yourself?' she asks. I nod.

'Where's your mother?'

For some reason I feel I have to lie. 'She's asleep,' I say.

'Want to come with us? We're going for a walk.' The girl is nice. She wants to cheer me up; maybe she can sense how forlorn I feel. I nod again.

We walk through the forest – the girl, her mother and I.

Now that it's daytime, the forest seems light and cool. The ground is soft and the air is scented with the smell of resin and pine needles. I hop around a little and run into the undergrowth because I've seen some juicy fat blackberries and I want to pick them.

Suddenly the air is filled with the humming and buzzing of wild bees. What have I done to harm them? They attack me, pursue me. I lash out at them, but there are too many and they are everywhere – in my hair, my ears, my mouth and on my throat. They sting; I scream and cry and run out of the forest.

As if through a fog, I hear the calls and the footsteps of the girl and her mother behind me. They want to help me, but I can't stand still. I'm almost frantic with fear and pain. Finally the bees stop and the buzzing moves away. I stand there, trembling, my arms and legs red and swollen. The pain is intense. Carefully I touch my face. It feels thick, puffed up. One bee is still caught in my hair; I pull it out carefully. The girl and her mother catch up with me. 'You poor child!'

the mother cries. 'Quick, run to your room and have your mother put some cold wet towels on the stings.'

I nod as if in a trance, stumble back to the hotel, along the corridors, into the big dark room. I get undressed and wrap myself in wet towels, just as the woman said and this lessens the pain a little, but only for a short while. I can feel the poison raging through my body. So this is what it's like when you swallow poison.

With my last bit of strength I drag myself into bed, pull the sheet over me, and sink into a world that lies between sleeping and waking, a place where reality has no meaning.

My grandmother comes to my bed and puts her dry hand on my forehead. 'You'll be all right,' she whispers. 'I'm here with you.'

I'm glad she's here. I'm so alone.

'You have to drink something . . . You've got to pull through . . .'

I take a drink. I feel so hot, so terribly hot.

At last I fall asleep.

I can't open my eyes because my eyelids are swollen shut. And my mouth feels thick . . .

Time doesn't exist any more, only the feeling that my body is being consumed and no longer belongs to me. But my thoughts still belong to me. I know things will get better, as Grandmother said. I just have to hang on.

The days and nights I spend in the dark hotel room seem endless.

Now and then the door opens, I hear footsteps, a muted clatter. Someone enters the room noiselessly, removes the tray of food I haven't touched and puts down a new one. Never is a word spoken. I just lie there and my body pounds, hammers, pulses, fighting the poison. That takes all the strength I have.

I manage to pull through.

Suddenly a stranger with a walrus moustache appears in my room. He says he is a taxi driver. 'Is your name Roma Ligocka?' he asks.

I nod weakly.

'Get dressed. I'm taking you to your uncle's house.'

He carries my suitcase to his car; I follow him on shaky legs.

I don't look back.

I like Uncle Mittelmann immediately. He's a doctor. A small, friendly man, he tells funny jokes but he takes me seriously, and that's rare for grown-ups.

'You must have been terribly worried, Roma,' he says. 'A little girl, all alone in that big hotel. That can't have been nice for you. Your mother was unconscious for three days. She had a serious case of septic angina. But as soon as she regained consciousness she asked about you and called on me to help. You'll stay with us until she is back on her feet again. Is that all right with you?'

It's fine with me. Uncle Mittelmann lives in a nice house that has a small garden. He's married to one of my father's great-aunts. Aunt Berta is tall and fat and has a pointy nose. She is loud and exuberant; he is quiet and doesn't talk much, especially when he is with her. Maybe he's afraid of her. But she is kind to me. I am glad to have these nice relatives I've never heard about before.

During the war they were in a camp too – I can tell this from the blue numbers on their arms – but they don't talk about it. They have a grown-up daughter; but their son, Janek, is dead. In the living room there's a photo of him. He's wearing his school cap. Whenever they speak of him their voices grow soft.

My aunt lets me help her water the plants in the garden. The garden is wonderful. There are gooseberry bushes, just like those in my grandfather's garden long ago, and flowers, and a small bed of vegetables with radishes and carrots. Aunt Berta buys me a little duck. I call her Kasia and I love her more than anything else in the world. She follows me everywhere like a little dog, quacking incessantly. I'm even permitted to take her up to my room.

Whenever he can, Uncle Mittelmann takes time to be with me. He plays the piano for me, lots of popular old songs. They sound a little odd, for the piano and his voice are out of tune. Everybody loves Uncle Mittelmann. His patients come to the house day and night. Aunt Berta scolds him about that. They leave cakes, eggs and honey on the stairs. Once they even left a live chicken. But in the drawer where he keeps the money he has earned, in the room he uses as his office, there are only small banknotes. In the evenings he counts them and hands them to Aunt Berta. Then she scolds him again because he doesn't make his patients pay.

'But they don't have any money,' he says, winking at me.

'If things go on this way, soon we won't have any either,' Aunt Berta replies.

When we're by ourselves my uncle and I have long conversations. He explains all sorts of things to me. I learn about illnesses and about life. He knows a lot of short sayings and poems and they seem to fit every situation. We laugh a lot together. The only thing he doesn't explain to me, in spite of my many questions, is where babies come from.

For the first time in my life I see what it really means to have a family and to feel safe. And yet it is in this house that I first experience one of those strange episodes that will return for years. It happens while I'm sitting on the bed, thinking of my mother in the hospital. I become so completely absorbed in the ticking of the clock that I can't move, as though held by invisible chains. Tick tock, tick tock. Even Kasia's quacking doesn't rouse me, and I don't hear Aunt Berta calling me to come to dinner. I am like a stone.

I didn't talk about it with anyone, not even Uncle Mittelmann. Perhaps I should have – he might have helped me. Today I know there is a name for this condition: depression.

6

Our new home is a dark little ground-floor apartment in the old part of Kraków, not far from the market. The building has a gloomy entrance where drunks often loiter.

The apartment consists of one large room, which is a combined kitchen and living room, and a narrow hall. We have to keep the lights on almost all the time because it's so dark. Looking out of the barred window I have a view of the rear courtyard. I can see the feet of people who walk by and the concierge when she raises her skirts in the semi-darkness to pee on the cobblestone pavement directly outside my window. She uses a big rusty key to unlock the front door for people coming home late at night. She disgusts me.

My mother has redone the apartment as nicely as possible. I sleep in the big room in my own bed. There's also a desk for me and a glass cabinet with books. A big green tile stove stands in one corner.

My mother sleeps on the couch in the kitchen-living room. The apartment is terribly cramped, but it's all ours.

Roman has gone to live with his father. Sometimes I miss him.

Shortly after we moved in, a wizened creature wrapped in shawls appeared on our doorstep – short, bony and ugly. Marynia.

She fell on her knees at my mother's feet and kissed her hand. I was so embarrassed I escaped to the living room. But I could hear them talking. My mother was deeply touched that Marynia, who was a servant in her parents' house, had found us.

'But I can't afford to pay you anything, Marynia!' I heard my mother say. Even though she now goes to the office every day, she doesn't earn much.

'That don't matter, madam,' Marynia replied, in her rural dialect. 'I'll stay with you anyway. You can't do all the housework by yourself. It wouldn't be proper.'

And so Marynia has been with us ever since. She sleeps on a camp-bed in the hall. Every morning she comes into my room and starts the fire in the tile stove, muttering to herself all the while.

'Some people are allowed to lie in bed and sleep as long as they want. Oh, yes, some people take it easy and do nothing while other people have to work hard,' she says, in a voice just loud enough for me to hear. She keeps it up until I can't bear to stay in bed any longer.

Marynia can't read or write. She's been a servant since she was nine years old – the same age I am now. After breakfast she wraps her shawl around her shoulders, takes the market basket, plants herself in front of my mother and asks, 'What would Madam like for dinner today?'

At first my mother tried to explain to her that we would have whatever we could afford, but Marynia would have none of that. In the end my mother went along with the game.

'As a first course I'd like to have . . . umm . . . sorrel soup, then veal meatballs with rice, and for dessert, apple strudel,' she says. Marynia nods, satisfied. She takes the money and goes shopping. A few hours later she is back, carefully adding up what she's spent. Naturally they never have what she's looking for. She brings back whatever happens to be available. But nobody complains when, instead of veal meatballs, we're having groats again. That's one of the rules of the game.

I now attend the Catholic school around the corner. There are about forty girls in my class. Everyone stares at me because I'm new. I sit down at one of the wooden desks that stand in neat rows in a classroom much too small for so many pupils and stare at my notebooks. I don't dare look at the other children. I'm afraid of them. When I do pluck up the courage to talk to them, they laugh at me because I don't speak their language, because I speak like a grown-up. For instance, I'd say, 'That's absurd,' and they would double up with laughter. Actually, I don't know how to talk to real children.

These girls are real children, completely different from the ones in the Jewish school. They are noisy and boisterous. During break they play games that are new to me. I stand on the sidelines, a bow in my hair, and watch them silently. They are strange, threatening creatures. And I am from another planet.

At first the other kids just think I'm odd. They are poor and unkempt; some even have lice. Not one of them wears a bow in her hair or a little apron like me. Few are as properly scrubbed and combed. Gradually they no longer consider me simply odd; they begin to hate me for being different.

In spite of all this, I find the school exciting and wonderful, at least at the beginning. There isn't as much crying as there was in the Jewish school. The teacher is a stocky woman with red cheeks. She doesn't run out of the room because her nerves are shot. This normality gives me a feeling of security. I'm finally rid of the Jewish thing.

I do especially well in religion. The subject interests me. I often think about Jesus, and would so much like to believe in him. I can answer every single question the priest asks and I'm very proud of that. But the other girls hold it against me. I am aware of their resentment, yet I'm beginning to feel that I belong. That's a mistake.

One day a girl on the other side of the schoolyard calls out, 'Roma is a Jew! She's a Jew! She killed our Saviour! The Jews did it!'

I stand there thunderstruck. What is she talking about?

Who was I supposed to have killed? After all, the Jews were the ones who were killed. Confused, I try to straighten things out, but I don't have a chance. The other kids pounce on me, pull my hair, scratch and kick me.

That afternoon I come home crying, covered with black-and-blue marks, my bow torn. Sobbing and indignant I tell my mother what happened. 'They-they-they said I killed the Saviour, Mama.'

My mother says nothing. She washes my face and puts a new bow in my hair. I stare at her.

'Is it true? Did the Jews really kill the Saviour?'

She takes a deep breath. 'Well, now . . . that's what the *goyim*, the non-Jews, keep saying . . .'

Marynia, who has been busy at the sink, now joins in. 'It's true,' she says. 'The Jews nailed our Lord Jesus to the cross. But that's the way it had to be.'

I'm bewildered. No one can or wants to explain this monstrous thing to me.

So, it's true: the Jews are to blame.

I am to blame . . .

After that, school isn't wonderful any more. Now, the others either treat me as though I didn't exist or they make fun of me. I still don't quite understand why they hate me, even though I now have an explanation of sorts. The priest who teaches religion, a fat, pale man who smells of sweat and who always had nothing but praise for me, he too has betrayed me. Oh, I'm still allowed to attend his classes, but now he points a fat finger at me and tells the class, 'You see, Roma is of the Mosaic faith so she knows the Old Testament better than the rest of you.' And everybody laughs. I am ashamed to be Jewish. I'd really like to fight the others, but I haven't learned how to fight, and I don't have the courage to learn.

The teacher with the red cheeks doesn't like me either, though she pretends to be fond of me. She's constantly holding me up as an example for the other girls, which makes them hate me even more. 'Just look at Roma,' she says in the biology lesson, when we're discussing hygiene. 'You can tell a cultured person by how well they take care of themselves. Come up here, Roma.' I stand in front of the class. The kids whisper and grin. 'Just look!' the teacher says, with a broad smile and in a sweet tone. 'Her hair is freshly washed, her teeth – open your mouth, please – are brushed every day, she wears an ironed apron and a clean white blouse . . . She smells good, of soap.'

The teacher sniffs, pretends to inhale my smell. A girl in the second row snickers, another bursts out laughing, and then the entire class roars.

I stand there, my face red, and try to make myself invisible, but I can't do that any more. I sense the girls' hatred growing. I'm scared. During break they're going to beat me up again.

And I'm right. In the yard they surround me and taunt me. 'You killed our Saviour!' they chant.

The girl who was the first to snicker confronts me. 'I'm going to scratch your clean face,' she hisses.

Then she leaps at me. The others just stand there, laughing.

My mother doesn't know what to do. 'Maybe it would help if Josef brought you to school.' She sighs. Josef used to work at Father's firm and also did all the heavy work around the house: polished the parquet floors, split firewood, things like that. Now he helps my mother with work she can't do herself. Sometimes he also helps out at the firm. Like Marynia, he doesn't get paid much. He is tall and thin, has a small twirled moustache and wears a cap. There's always a cigarette in the corner of his mouth. His clothes look too small for him.

He plays with me – and gives me piggyback rides. I like him very much but I wonder, Is it really a good idea for him to take me to school? What are the other girls going to say?

*　　*　　*

'Look, the princess is coming with her servant!' they jeer, when they see Josef. But my mother insists that he accompany me each morning. Worst of all are the days when we have gym. I hate gym. Just thinking of it makes me sick. I've never in my life turned a somersault. I've always just sat around, lain in bed, or hidden under the table.

'Ligocka, do a somersault!' the teacher orders. The whole class just sits there, waiting, staring at me. There is a tense silence in the gym. I'm afraid my muscles won't do what I want them to do. I kneel down on the rubber mat, which smells of sweat and feet, and try to turn a somersault. Each time I try, I topple over. Everybody shrieks with laughter.

'How can anyone be so awkward?' the teacher scolds. 'How can anyone always be so stupid?'

Something must be wrong with me. Why is my body so stiff and clumsy? Sometimes I practise at home, but I simply can't do it. I'm afraid my spine is going to break. My mother tries to get me excused from gym as often as possible. 'Roma has a headache,' she writes to the teacher. 'Roma has a stomach-ache, Roma isn't feeling well today . . .'

It's not even a lie.

At weekends we usually go to visit my father's grave in the neglected, overgrown Jewish cemetery. There's a large stone engraved with his name and the name of his father. Each time we go I place a small pebble on top of the stone. My mother always cries during these visits. The tears well up as soon as she reaches the graveside, and the sorrow she never talks about is briefly washed away. Afterwards she blows her nose, takes a little mirror from her handbag, applies lipstick, and takes my hand. 'Come,' she says, 'let's go home.'

I spend long, lonely hours wondering where all the many dead people are now. Nobody can give me a satisfactory explanation. The priest at school can't because his faith cannot be my faith. Nor can my mother, to whom religion doesn't mean much any more, though she sometimes takes me to synagogue.

The synagogue isn't as full as it used to be just after the war. Many Jews have emigrated. I find the services very moving; if only briefly, they ease a deep yearning in my heart. Everyone lights a candle for their dead, and the synagogue gleams in a sea of lights. I am touched when, sobbing and singing, we recite the prayers for the dead. The names Majdanek, Auschwitz, Bergen-Belsen are repeated like an incantation, and I think that we Jews are a people of battered children. Then, for a moment, I feel I belong.

On the other hand, I miss the Catholic services we used to attend as a cover during the war. Kraków is a city of churches. Each street has at least three, and there is a constant ringing of church bells.

The churches are always open; they are filled with incense, flowers and statues. They are almost like living rooms. You can simply go in, sit down in one of the deep armchairs in the side aisles, and feel safe and secure. I like the churches of Kraków, and I like church services in which people don't cry. I love the smell of incense, the singing, the bright colours, the processions and the festivals. At solstice, wreaths with candles are thrown into the river, the bells ring even more beautifully than usual, and there are solstice bonfires down by the Vistula. First Communion is also celebrated in a big way, almost like a wedding. Even the poorest families scrape together everything they have to buy their little girl a white dress.

But the best times are in May, when the festive processions take place. People walk in a procession around the church, wearing traditional folk costumes, singing old songs, and carrying holy pictures and statues. Young girls in long white dresses scatter flowers. They wear wreaths in their hair, which has been curled with curling tongs.

One of my most fervent wishes is to wear a white dress

and scatter flowers in front of the church. I would like to go to First Communion, like other girls my age, except that I haven't been baptized. My mother, who fulfils all my other wishes, remains adamant on this point. 'No, that's for the *goyim*. You're not allowed to do that,' she says. 'You are Jewish, not Catholic.'

I don't see why it should be a sin for Jews to be baptized. And therefore why it's impossible for me to be baptized.

I have this constant, persistent feeling of not belonging – to any place or any group. The feeling never leaves me; nor does my yearning for the Catholic, the normal, the beautiful, the blond world. Everyone is blond and Catholic; only I am a dark-haired Jew.

The next time I feel sad because I haven't been allowed to scatter flowers, my mother sits on my bed and tells me the story of the great-aunt who ran away with a Christian man, and what a terrible scandal it was. This is not the first time I've heard this story.

'Your great-grandfather, my grandfather, had three beautiful daughters,' she begins, 'and he and his wife were proud and happy parents. But one day their youngest daughter fell in love with a dashing young army officer from the neighbouring village. Of course the officer wasn't Jewish, he was Catholic. The girl knew her parents would never permit her to marry him. So she ran off with him. In the dead of night. She even had herself baptized and they were married in church.'

The way my mother tells the story, it sounds as though the girl had committed a serious crime. But I simply don't understand what can be so bad about baptism. This story just strengthens my suspicion that something isn't quite right here, that there's a huge mistake somewhere in all this.

'For your great-grandfather,' my mother continues, 'it was as though his youngest daughter had died. And as you know the Jews have a custom: when someone dies, the relatives mourn by sitting on the floor or on a low stool for seven days. All the mirrors and windows are covered with cloths. So for seven days your great-grandfather sat and mourned. His own daughter was as good as dead.'

I shudder every time she comes to this point in her story, remembering that this is how it was when my father died.

'And later, when your great-grandfather lay dying, his daughter wanted to see him to ask for forgiveness, but he didn't allow her to come near him. I was still a little girl then. I saw her standing on a table so that she could look through a little window into the room where her dying father lay, and I saw her crying because she wasn't allowed to say goodbye to him. This shows you what a great sin it was for her to change her religion.'

My mother sighs.

I think my great-grandfather was cruel.

Marynia, of course, is Catholic. Every Sunday she puts on her best dress and goes to church. When she comes back she always tells us about the sermons in the various churches. Then for the rest of the day she sits in the kitchen, her hands folded on her lap. 'You are supposed to rest on Sundays,' she says.

Marynia also strictly observes the fasting rules. Although she won't permit me to eat meat on Fridays because Catholics are forbidden to do so, and threatens me with terrible punishments, she knows Jewish customs better than my mother. She has always worked for Jewish families and never stops reminding us of that. She corrects my mother when she's cooking. 'In Jewish homes you use onions only for beef. For veal you use garlic,' she says. Or 'You chop the fish for gefillte fish with a knife, you don't put it through a mincer.'

She's also critical of me. 'A lady stands up straight,' she says. 'Stomach in, chest out.' She insists on following certain rules that, of course, apply only to my mother and me, not to her. 'A well-bred lady always wears gloves,' she reminds me whenever I am about to leave the house, so I have to put them on. As soon as I get to the corner I take them off and hide them in my schoolbag.

Marynia is not the only one to insist on good manners: my mother is also trying to turn me into a 'well-bred lady'. A while ago she got the idea that I ought to study German, just as she did when she was a child.

For the first time I stand up to her successfully. 'I'm not going to learn that awful language!' I reply stubbornly, putting my hands over my ears to shut out her arguments. I wonder whether my mother understands why, or whether she gives up because she has no strength left to fight me.

'All right.' She sighs. 'Then you'll learn French.'

Once a week I take French lessons with the old Countess. She lives in a building nearby, in an apartment crammed with antique furniture, curiously patterned carpets, paintings and books. She has partitioned off one room with a curtain; this is her salon. We sit there on the sofa (she calls it a *canapé*) and drink lukewarm tea from delicate porcelain cups brought in by an old manservant who seems to be sleepwalking.

'*Merci*, Jean,' the old Countess says, after he retreats without making a sound. Her pale bony hand is adorned with many rings, and she graciously gestures for me to take one of the biscuits that taste of dust from the little silver platter on the table.

'Jean is such a loyal soul. He stayed with us even after the Bolsheviks drove us out of our castle,' she says, carefully lifting the cup to wrinkled lips made up with a light pink lipstick. It is the one and only time she ever mentions her past life in my presence. The Countess is proud and she is very strict with me – but especially with herself, I think.

Right from the start, I realize that I am here not just to learn French but to be taught good manners. I learn how to greet people properly, how to curtsy, how to sit up straight, knees and legs together, and how long my skirts should be.

The Countess shows me how to take small sips of tea while delicately nibbling a wafer. It must all be restrained, quiet, inconspicuous, polite. Speaking in a loud voice, hearty laughter, sweeping gestures or displaying an obvious appetite are not refined.

It isn't hard for me to be inconspicuous, polite and quiet, and she is pleased with me.

After the lesson in manners, the Countess hands me a French book, her watery eyes staring at me expectantly, and says, 'Lisez, Mademoiselle.' I open the book. Unsure of myself, I stutter my way through while she mechanically corrects my pronunciation. At some point I notice that her eyelids are drooping, I read more and more slowly until she finally dozes off. Then I sneak out of the apartment and walk home.

Luckily no one ever questions my leaving, because the Countess is embarrassed about always falling asleep. When I get home, my mother asks, 'How was your French lesson today?'

'Fine,' I answer casually. 'I keep learning more and more.'

It feels good to be telling the truth.

My mother nods with satisfaction.

In spite of the increasingly difficult living conditions in our tiny dark apartment, my mother does everything in her power to provide us with the trappings of the life she led before the war. There is a glass cabinet in our living room in which she has put precious items from her youth: old silver spoons, a polished wineglass – it has 'Anna' engraved on it – that belonged to her mother, a porcelain vase, all of which she gradually got back from former neighbours or came across in junk shops. Former neighbours no longer remember most of the items the Abrahamer family gave them for safekeeping just before they were sent into the ghetto. The grand piano, the carpets, the paintings – these have vanished and are gone for good. One day my mother finds a white chest of drawers decorated with carved lilies and green tiles in an antique store and has it brought to our apartment. I know immediately that it's the chest of drawers that used to stand in my grand-parents' bedroom. She has told me about it so often.

She runs her hand over the green tiles as though she were caressing a loved one. The chest of drawers gets a place of honour directly under the barred window that faces the court-yard.

Our lives consist of certain rituals.

Sunday, following our visit to the cemetery, we take a midday walk in the market square where one goes to see and meet people. After that we have tea in a café.

Whenever possible my mother takes me to the theatre or to a concert. Every Friday she polishes all the brass door handles. Monday is wash-day. Marynia doesn't cook on Mondays. It's the day the laundry is washed, starched and carefully ironed. My mother and I go out to eat, the way one did in the old days.

I hate mondays because Marynia feels I should help her hang up the washing to dry. I protest with all my might, but my mother is exceptionally firm. 'You don't have to do anything else around the house, so it's only right and proper for you to help Marynia a little,' she says.

Nobody understands why I object. It's not because I'm lazy. It's because I'm afraid. Hanging up the washing means having to go up to the attic with Marynia. And up in the attic there are pigeons.

Marynia sets down the laundry basket. Moaning and groaning she opens the heavy iron door. The attic is empty, dark and dusty. A narrow strip of light streams from the skylight on to the floor, which is covered with feathers and pigeon droppings. I cling to Marynia's lean body.

'Don't make such a fuss,' she snaps. 'Better if you help me.'

Roma with her mother (about 1948).

We carry the basket into the corner where the clothes-lines are, where the wooden washtub stands. Suddenly – over the eerie cooing of the pigeons – I think I can hear the sound of boots and my mother hissing, 'Cyanide. Do what I tell you!'

Marynia grabs my shoulder. 'You're daydreaming again. Go on, get to work.'

I bend down, take the cold, wet towels out of the laundry basket and, fingers trembling, hang them on the line.

What I like best is when my mother, Marynia, Roman, Ryszard and I visit Marynia's family in the country. Roman has been living with us for some time now.

In the country everything is wonderful – not grey, cramped and dark, as in the city. There are no children to laugh at me and beat me up. Nobody forces me to wear gloves and hair bows. There are green meadows and open fields and a barn with cows, goats and horses. Marynia's big family lives in a little farmhouse with a straw roof, an earth floor and low windows. They are poor, but always warm and friendly.

Marynia's brother is a shoemaker and works in his tiny shop till late at night. He tells us stories, such as the one about how once, many years ago, when he was still a young man, he went to Kraków to the cinema.

'What did you see?' Roman asks him.

'*Ben-Hur*,' he replies, pounding on a leather heel.

'So? Don't you want to go to the cinema again?'

Marynia's brother shrugs his shoulders, 'What for? *Ben-Hur* was such a beautiful film, it will last me my whole life!'

In the village I learn about old Polish customs that are still observed in rural areas. For instance, there are the coloured eggs at the Easter festival, and on the second day the boys sprinkle the girls with water. Or the custom of courting, where the young man and his entire family visit the bride's house. This is a long drawn-out ritual during which they sit for an eternity at the table, drinking and not talking.

We children act in the big barn. We do both plays and films. Roman teaches us about how films are made. The barn becomes a film studio. He makes spotlights out of old lamps, turns pieces of scrap into a camera, and we pretend that these things work. We put on shawls and kerchiefs and make believe we're stars. I am Greta Garbo, and Roman is Ramón Navarro. Ryszard is allowed to hold the spotlights.

'Camera! Action!' Roman yells, and I throw back my head and gaze dreamily into the distance, just as he's instructed me to do.

'No! No!' he yells. 'How can anyone be so untalented?' Then, for the hundredth time, he shows me the right way to look dreamily into the distance. By now Roman is absolutely certain that he is going to become a film director. He explains everything in detail. 'A film consists of many little pictures that follow each other rapidly.'

I can't imagine how that works. 'Theatre is nicer,' I say defiantly. 'I'm going into the theatre when I grow up.'

'Ridiculous. The theatre is old-fashioned. Nothing beats film,' he insists, his eyes aglow.

That always leads to an argument.

After we've made up, we sit in the hay and he reads me poems he's written.

At the flea market, my mother has bought a glittering box covered with small pieces of reflective glass. 'It's a radio,' she says proudly. I touch the little pieces of mirror glass reverently and turn the radio on and off, thrilled by the voices and music coming out of the box. It has always been a mystery to me how a thing like that works. There's no phonograph record like the ones in Manuela's living room.

'It's really very simple,' Roman says, superior, and he explains about waves that fly through the air. He even claims he'd have no trouble building one like it himself. Naturally I don't understand any of his explanations, but I'm careful not to let on.

I listen to the radio every free moment I have. My favourite programme is the one where a group of children perform fairy-tales, though I also like the broadcasts for grown-ups – dance music, piano recitals. It doesn't matter what's on. I will listen.

Marynia grumbles even more now that we have the radio. 'Devil's work!' she mutters, when she sees that I'm listening again. 'Some people, of course, have nothing else to do . . .' And she gives the unearthly box a mistrustful look.

Basically, Marynia is at war with modern technology. The telephone we've acquired is spawn of the devil. Whenever it rings she pretends she hasn't heard it. Only when my mother insists will she cautiously take the receiver off the hook, hold it three feet away from her ear as though it were a poisonous snake, and say in a loud voice, 'Yes!' Then she immediately hangs up again. It is useless to explain to her that the telephone is harmless. Even if it isn't ringing, she always gives it a wide berth.

One day when Marynia again won't answer the telephone, though she knows my mother is expecting an important call, my mother scolds her. 'Be sensible, Marynia,' she says. 'From now on you're going to answer the telephone whenever it rings. Do you understand?'

Marynia nods, but her wrinkled goblin face is twisted in a painful grimace.

'I'm leaving,' she says, and puts her house keys on the

table. Then she goes to the kitchen and packs her things.

It takes tears and hours of artful persuasion to get Marynia to put the keys back into her apron pocket. She no longer has to answer the phone.

The phone rings. The director of the Children's Theatre Group is calling. 'Roma Ligocka? Thanks for your letter. About your application to be an actress here – we'd like to see what you can do. Would you come next Wednesday so we can meet you?'

'Of course!' I whisper, so excited I can't talk. I dash into the kitchen where my mother and Marynia are drinking tea. 'Mama, I'm going to be an actress! At long last, an actress! Can I?'

It takes a while for my mother to deduce from my excited stammer that I secretly applied for a job with the theatre group.

She nods. 'Of course you can,' she says, smiling.

Marynia mumbles something about the crazy world of artists, but nobody pays any attention to her.

The Children's Theatre Group hires me, and in their next piece I play a daisy. It's a minor role. Bursting with pride, I tell Roman.

He raises his eyebrows. 'Oh, yeah?' he drawls. 'Do you think they need anyone else – like me, for instance? Not that I want to go into the theatre – film is much better – but it can't hurt to get a little experience.'

On his first try Roman gets the leading role in the new play. He sweeps the theatre people and the audiences off their feet, and in time he wins prize after prize.

That makes me feel pathetic. Sometimes he and I are on stage together. I'll be playing insignificant roles – an elf, a fish or a squirrel – while Roman bellows his heart out, centre stage, to thunderous applause.

I'm beginning to understand that my forte doesn't lie in

having a big voice and that maybe a life on the stage is not for me.

Josef's daughter is getting married, and we're all invited to the wedding.

Strange to think of Josef having a family of his own. For me he's always been simply 'our' Josef. Now suddenly he is a man, even a father, an independent person with a life of his own.

The wedding takes place in the country and is one of the most beautiful events I've ever been invited to attend. For three days the entire village celebrates. The fire-house barn has been turned into a dance-hall, and there's music night and day. I had never seen such mountains of food: whole wagonloads of veal cutlets, sausages, doughnuts and cakes. People eat and drink, they gossip, laugh and dance until they fall asleep, exhausted, in the hay. And as soon as they wake up it starts all over again.

Shortly after the wedding, Josef vanishes from our lives.

'Why is he gone?' I ask my mother.

'I am no longer permitted to employ him,' she says, and smooths the already smooth tablecloth.

No one notices that Josef no longer escorts me to school. Everybody had gradually grown used to the sight of the tall, thin man in trousers too short for him, leading the little girl by the hand.

A few days later, when I walk into the classroom where we have religious instruction, the priest takes me aside. 'You don't have to attend religious instruction any more, Ligocka,' he informs me. 'You are excused because you are of the Mosaic faith.'

I am shocked. Doesn't that mean I am not *allowed* to attend? As I leave I think I see a triumphant look in his eyes.

During break, the others say it serves me right.

* * *

I am in bed, deathly ill, and having feverish dreams. The doctor says I have tuberculosis of the kidneys and lungs.

Sometimes it seems to me that I've been sick for years, that I've always lain in bed here in this dark room, feeling hot and dry and so weak that every movement exhausts all my strength. Shadowy forms move around in the background. My mother and Marynia brings me tea and zwieback. They whisper softly. I feel my mother's cool hand applying cold wet compresses to my forehead. I hear the doctor's concern when he calls from time to time to see how I'm doing. I taste the bitter medicine they spoon into my mouth.

'Will I make it?' I ask my grandmother. She nods. And eventually I do make it. One day I wake up and know that the worst is over. I sit up and even let them talk me into eating a piece of bread. Little by little I regain my strength.

My mother is overjoyed. She brings piles of books and magazines to my bedside. She's borrowed them from Mr Taffet, a Jewish second-hand-book dealer she knew in the old days. She used to take me to his tiny shop in the Old Town. It is always stuffed with books from floor to ceiling. He has a long pale face and knows more about literature than anyone else. And no wonder. His family has been dealing in books for seven generations. No one knows how, or where, he survived the war.

'Mr Taffet sends you his regards and wishes you a speedy recovery,' my mother says, putting a stack of novels and books of poetry on my bed. They are all about love and fate, about princes and poor young maidens, about beautiful women and brave men.

I devour all these books. For hours at a time I leaf through the magazines – years of pre-war illustrated magazines. I look at the same pictures again and again – of elegant balls and perfectly laid tables, of beauty contests and expensive clothes, of wealthy, happy people in their big, beautiful houses, or off on trips and adventures. At last, I have found the bright, colourful world for which I have always longed. The real world is rough, painful, colourless and lonely. Day after day, the same hopelessness, bleakness, the same bread, the same gummy marmalade, the same boring home-made dresses, and in the winter the same warm woollen things that come out of a suitcase under the bed and smell of mothballs.

For days I lie in bed, escaping into my glittering world of daydreams; without knowing it I am laying the foundation for my future profession.

I don't have to go back to the hated school for the rest of the year.

7

While I was ill the world from which I was escaping changed. The desolate greyness spread, creeping into every corner and taking on a darker hue. Paralysis turned into menace. Religious instruction in the schools is now forbidden to everyone, not simply those of the 'Mosaic faith'. The name 'Stalin' enters my consciousness and gradually assumes a distinct form.

My mother and Marynia are glued to the radio, which blares out military music and bellowing voices. I no longer like to listen. The sounds are the same as back then. But the language is Polish now, not German.

How can Polish sound like this?

Marynia has folded her large, rough hands and her lips are moving. She is praying. 'JesusMaryMotherofGodhelpus . . .'

A priest is on trial. He has been accused of high treason. Why?

My mother shrugs helplessly. Then she says, 'Because religion is too important to the people. The Communists have no religion. Those gangsters.'

A few days ago we visited the Kierniks again. Manuela wasn't there; she was at a theatre rehearsal. After playing cards with *Babcia*, who is always happy to see me, I ambled into the kitchen. The door to the balcony was open, and sunlight streamed in. My mother and Mrs Kiernikowa were sitting at the table, drinking tea.

As I walked in, they suddenly stopped talking. It was obvious they were talking about me.

'Roma,' Mrs Kiernikowa said, gesturing for me to come

closer. 'How would it be if you went to a different school? The school where I teach is really very nice. I'm sure you'd like it. And if you have any problems, well, I'd be there to help you. What do you think?'

I was stunned. A new school. Yes, oh, yes. Anything rather than having to go back to those horrible girls in the school round the corner. But the school where Mrs Kiernikowa works?

'Would you be my teacher?' I asked her.

Mrs Kiernikowa smiled. 'Oh, no. You'd be in a different class – the fifth or the sixth.'

My mother cleared her throat. 'I think this is a good solution for you, Roma,' she said. I could tell she had already decided. 'Please thank Mrs Kiernikowa for her kind offer.'

Like a good girl I thanked Mrs Kiernikowa and shook her hand. For the first time I noticed her eyes.

They are grey, and under their sternness there is sorrow.

The new school is located at the other end of town. Every day I take the tram, with its jangling bell, around the market square. 'Be careful crossing the street!' my mother warns me each morning.

The school building is big, light and ugly. It's teeming with children, none of whom I know.

All Polish schools have been put under state control, so I am now going to be educated to become a young Communist. For hours we are told about the lives of Lenin and Marx and the childhood of dear Stalin. Instead of religion we learn about the exploited peasants, whose children had nothing to eat and who were so poor they couldn't afford to buy matches and had to split each match into four pieces. These stories have the same effect on me as a fairy-tale.

We no longer pray before class begins, no longer give thanks for the 'light of knowledge'. Instead we simply say, 'Good morning, Teacher.'

'Good morning, girls,' the teacher replies.

Purges are taking place in the schools – their purpose is to remove all enemies of the working class.

It's a grey day. I am sitting in the classroom, wearily watching wet twigs tap against the window-pane, listening to the teacher with only half an ear, when the door opens suddenly.

In walk two women, one of them a pretty blonde. They are followed by the principal. The women offer us a friendly hello, then disappear into the conference room.

All the teachers have been asked to assemble there. In the middle of the school day!

Then the five best pupils in each class are called into the conference room. Since I am the second best in my class, I join them. This has never happened before. My heart is pounding with excitement. And with elation – because anything is better than maths.

The teachers are sitting around the long conference table. We are told to line up behind them.

The rain drums against the windows, and it seems as though the room has suddenly grown darker. The pretty blonde woman takes charge. She has a beautiful voice – firm and melodious. I take an instant liking to her. She is wearing a smart green jacket and her eyes are bright green.

The other woman is even younger and looks emaciated. She is wearing an olive-coloured shirt and a red scarf, the uniform of the Socialist Youth Group.

Our principal is sitting in a corner at the back of the room.

The pretty woman talks to us, but it's a little while before I understand what she is saying.

'. . . Mrs Nowakowa has failed as principal of this school. She has not managed to turn the school into a socialist educational institution that measures up to the requirements of the new order. Moreover, she has expressed critical opinions about our worker and peasant state. We cannot, we will not tolerate this. Therefore she is suspended from her position, effective immediately. Anna Nowakowa, please pack up your things and leave the school at once.'

We watch, shaken, as Mrs Nowakowa packs her things, tears in her eyes. This woman, who noted down in her little black book every little misdeed, every tardiness, every forgotten school cap. How afraid we were of that little black book. How afraid we were of her.

We look on in silence as she stuffs her files into her brief-case. She drops a few pages, bends down to pick them up. Her hands tremble. No one helps her. Then she takes her coat and her scarf off the hook.

At the door she turns towards us, tries to say something. 'But I never . . . I only did . . .' Her voice falters, she breaks off in mid-sentence, leaves the room, slowly closing the door behind her. It is deathly still.

The pretty blonde woman continues, 'We have also heard that there is a teacher in this school who must be considered an enemy of the working class. She has repeatedly criticized our new socialist order and spread subversive propaganda. Among other things she has told pupils that people were better off before the war in capitalist Poland and that the working class earned considerably more in those days than now. Under no circumstances will such lies be tolerated in a socialist school. Therefore, Mrs Helene-Janina Kiernikowa, please take your things and leave this school immediately.'

Again, total silence. The rain continues drumming against the window-panes.

I stand there and I know I should do something, that I should say something. I ought to defend her. I ought to yell out that she is a good person – that's what my mother has so often said. That she most certainly is a good teacher and that she will never again do the bad things she has done. I ought to ask them to forgive her. But I say nothing. I press my lips together, like my mother, and say nothing. I stand there petrified and watch as Mrs Kiernikowa packs her things. Her face has turned ashen.

She shoves everything into her shabby old briefcase. Then, without a backward look, she puts on her grey winter coat with the worn fur collar, and leaves.

'Starting today I will take over the administration of this school,' the blonde woman says, as though it were the most natural thing in the world. 'My name is Irene Ratan. Comrade Maja' – she points at her skinny companion – 'will assist me in matters having to do with socialist education. You can trust her to answer all your questions. Together we shall turn this school into a modern, progressive educational institution – taking as our model the excellent socialist school system in the great Soviet Union.'

There is a brief pause. Her green eyes rest on us. Then she adds, 'Now go back to your classrooms. The top pupil in each class will explain what has happened to her classmates.'

Since the top pupil in my class is absent, I will have to do it.

I go back to my classroom, climbing an endless flight of stairs. Each step seems to be a yard high.

I stop at the window in the hall, press my hot face against the cool glass, and watch as Mrs Kiernikowa crosses the schoolyard. She wades through the puddles in her flimsy shoes. Her back is bent, her head lowered; the rain beats down on her shoulders. Where is her umbrella? She probably left it at school. I ought to run and take it to her . . .

Suddenly I sense the presence of my grandmother behind me, her cold hand on my shoulder. 'Aren't you ashamed of yourself?' she asks.

I want to push open the window and yell down, 'Please, please stay! Please don't leave, Mrs Kiernikowa. Don't go, I was wrong. Take me with you, please!'

But I don't move. Mrs Kiernikowa disappears behind the garden gate, leaving me alone with my shame and disgrace.

Later I stand in front of my class. My voice is hoarse: 'Today we removed two enemies of the working class from our community so that our school will become even greater, as great as the great schools in the great Soviet Union.'

My voice grows firmer; I am almost shouting. Then I return to my desk and sit down.

My face glows. But in my heart a strange, cold contentment is spreading.

Communism is simple, convincing and inspiring. In Communism there is room for everyone, including me, the little Jewish girl with the dark eyes.

It's as though a ray of sunlight has suddenly illuminated my grey life. New cheerful teachers come to our school. They sing with us and are always pleasant and friendly. They radiate the enthusiasm of new beginnings and tell us about a splendid future in which there is only sunshine and where all of us will be rich and happy.

For the first time in my life I feel instantly accepted as a person.

I am now a member of the Young Pioneers. I have plaits, wear a white blouse, a blue pleated skirt, white knee socks, and a red kerchief around my neck. I am proud to be a Young Pioneer. At official events and ceremonies I am one of three children selected to march in the first row of the procession. I play a drum, another girl a trumpet, a third carries the red flag. The others are jealous of me. Again, I sense the old foreignness that separates me from them. I'm still an outsider. The difference is it no longer hurts; I have come to terms with it. After my experiences in the Catholic school I have come to realize that I shall never really belong anywhere.

My mother says nothing about my enthusiasm for Communism. She remains silent when, excited and indignant, I tell her what they taught us at school about enemies of the working class and spies. She bites her lip when I proudly report that I received a special award from the blonde teacher. Her silence gets on my nerves. They've told us at school that parents can be enemies of the working class too, that we must keep an eye on them.

I don't even want to think of such a thing.

My mother works hard now, even at weekends, because she is afraid of losing her job with the firm. She says there are constant State inspections. She has to go over things a thousand times to make sure that all the bookkeeping is one hundred per cent correct.

Apart from that, she and a few of her friends try to distance themselves from the system and go on as best they can with their capitalistic way of life. Meanwhile, she has got to know a few people who have survived the war and formed warm personal relationships with them. Only many years later did I find out from some of these friends that they are Jews. One doesn't talk about these things any more.

Fewer and fewer people attend synagogue.

Several of our acquaintances have managed to emigrate. My mother has put in an application to leave for Israel. It is rejected. No one can tell her why. One person is lucky, another isn't. It is all purely arbitrary, my mother says – the approval or rejection of one's application depends on the mood of the official who's handling it.

Friends come to see us; we go to visit them. Roman has again moved in with his father but turns up now and then at our house.

Recently my mother has been bringing home marvellous art books that I simply devour. I sense something very important in the pictures in these books, something I can't put into words.

In spite of all this, life would be pretty boring if it weren't for the theatre.

*   *   *

Kraków has two theatres. One is art nouveau in architecture. The other, where concerts and operas are performed, resembles a round baroque jewel case upholstered in red plush. Giant crystal chandeliers hang from the ceiling and the boxes are supported by plaster statuary; going there is entering a sweet shop. The curtain, on which a famous Polish artist has painted a scene from classical antiquity, is ceremoniously lowered during the intermission.

We go to the theatre regularly and always have box seats. I enjoy this luxury despite my enthusiasm for the class struggle. I love to dress in beautiful clothes, and for such occasions I even put up with the hated gloves.

After the performance we often eat in the best restaurant in Kraków. It is called Wierzynek and is located right on the market square. The new regime maintains it just as they do the theatres, so that they can show them off to foreigners. The restaurant dates back to the Renaissance. The food is served in a refined and elegant manner; it's the one place where I can overcome my disgust for eating and work up something like an appetite. My favourite dish is poached salmon. My mother, who keeps an anxious eye on me, looks happy when I swallow a few mouthfuls.

Naturally we run into Manuela, Tadeusz and their actor friends at the theatre. A few of them have already become quite famous, and I am proud and happy to be their friend. I haven't stopped dreaming of a career as an actress.

The theatre is always sold out. People feel a great hunger to make up for all that they missed during the war.

Not until much later do I understand that for many Poles the theatre was also an answer to Communist greyness, a place of resistance. The Communists could not ban the theatre. On the stage what people thought and felt could be expressed, if only in code. The churches, too, were a place of resistance. But, then, it has always been like that. Even though priests were put on trial, the churches remained open.

Life for ordinary people is getting more and more difficult. Food and necessities are harder to find; there's scarcely
anything left to buy. Marynia often has to queue for hours
just to get a small piece of meat.

Then, on 1 May – a big Communist holiday – sausage
suddenly appears in the shops. It's also my chance to march
in the parade with the other kids, wearing my smart uniform
and beating my drum.

I'm eleven years old now, and Irene Ratan, our blonde
young principal, is still my role model. With her shining hair
and bright green eyes she looks great. But it's her aggressive
manner and her smart, well-cut clothes that most impress
me. I am not the only one for whom she has become an
instant heroine. We all idolize her. Rather than scold, she
praises us, and if you recite a nice poem about Stalin, you
immediately get two good marks. She is cheerful and light-
hearted, not quiet and serious all the time like my mother.
And she treats us like adults.

I do everything I can to make her like me. Every day I
zealously prepare the noticeboard on which the heroes of the
working class are celebrated. In exchange for doing that I
don't have to take maths, and I'm even a sort of heroine
myself. Communism offers nothing but advantages.

People think I'm sweet, what with my long plaits, big eyes,
and my drum. When foreign dignitaries come to Kraków, I am
one of the children in the honour guard. On those occasions
I'm excused from class so I can present the visitors with bouquets
and receive kisses. The visitors give me presents: a fountain pen,
sometimes foreign chocolate – things one can't buy in Kraków.

I beat my drum with great zeal. For the new order. I've
managed to prove both to myself and to others that I'm
special, lovable.

Once Nehru, the Indian prime minister, arrives on a state
visit. In his bright light-coloured jacket he looks like a prince
from the Orient. He drives by very slowly in an open car,

then leans down and gives me a huge bouquet of pink roses. Giddy with joy I run home and proudly hand the bouquet to my mother. 'For you, Mama! From Nehru himself!'

I know she loves roses. Why isn't she happy? She sniffs them, then puts them in a big vase and places them in the centre of the table. Their fragrance spreads throughout the apartment. Even Marynia is impressed by their splendur when she comes home with her almost-empty market basket.

My mother strokes my hair. 'Thank you,' she says softly. But I have the feeling that she isn't very proud of me.

Every day the radio carries reports of arrests and trials. I pretend not to listen, but it gives me goose pimples. My mother and Marynia still spend all their time in front of the radio. The devout Marynia cries when priests and others who had heroically resisted the German occupation and fought in the underground are subjected to show trials. The Communists consider them enemies. The underground fighters of the Armia Krajowa, the Polish resistance movement, are also put on trial. I wonder if Dudek is among them.

It is said that since the end of the war bands of thieves have been roaming in the forests, but everybody knows they are freedom fighters of the underground army. These men are heroes. Most of them are shot in their prison cells without a trial, and often their families don't find out until much later. Writers, artists and poets who speak out publicly are branded as traitors. After that they can't find work.

The show trials cause widespread terror. When you hear the voices of the defendants on the radio, it's obvious that they've been tortured. Shouting prosecutors accuse them of being spies, enemies of the people, plotting to overthrow the government, collaborating with American agents, selling their fatherland for dirty dollars. The priests are accused of having used their position to reveal State secrets, enriching themselves, and inciting a third world war. Many are even accused of child abuse.

A friend of my mother is arrested for telling a political joke in a bar. He is sentenced to ten years in prison.

The radio drones on and on. Marynia sobs. 'Those gangsters,' my mother says.

I can't listen to it any longer. I've become deaf and callous. The coldness in my heart has spread and I feel no compassion, even though among the accused are people I know. I just don't want to know about these things.

I'm not shocked by what's going on around me. None of this is new to me: uniformed men, familiar faces disappearing, the dread, the terror. I feel sad, old and discouraged. How can I be proud of being a Young Communist when I know what all this means? I am leading a double life. Shame and pride are tearing me apart.

Today I know that the perversion of the Communist leaders lay in their accusing others of crimes they themselves were committing, day in and day out. They handed Poland over to the Russians and charged those who tried to defend the country with having betrayed it.

The only members of our family still left in Kraków are my mother and me, and Roman and Uncle Polanski. Uncle Mittelmann, Aunt Berta and their daughter have emigrated to Israel. When my mother's last surviving cousin was killed in a pogrom in Kielce after the war, there was no one left on her side of the family.

One day, by sheer chance, my mother runs into Malwina, a distant relative. She is about my mother's age, has large black eyes and is married to a Communist who was a Party member even before the war. The two women hug each other, overjoyed because suddenly they've found a family connection.

'You have to visit us, Tosia. Why don't you come this weekend?' Malwina says, over and over again. My mother hesitates. 'I don't know . . .' But Malwina insists until she finally gives in.

'Well, if you like, we'd be happy to come for a visit,' she says, with a sigh.

Malwina's husband is a big shot in the government. An elegant black car picks us up at our house and, accompanied by two uniformed soldiers, we drive for what seems for ever through fields and forests. Finally we stop at a large old house.

Servants open the door for us, take our luggage and show us to our room. They're all military men. Not a word is said. They are everywhere, like shadows. A ghostly silence pervades the villa. I feel nervous and cold, and I can tell that my mother does too. It's as though we were visiting a lion in its den.

The house is elegantly furnished – expensive carpets, furniture, silver. Even with all these lovely things everywhere it's not really beautiful; it's too cluttered, too full of stuff. Malwina takes us on a tour. She looks pale and tense. She talks a little too much, laughs a little too loudly.

In the evening we put on our best dresses and go to dinner. Malwina, her husband, Mother and I, and lots of strange men in grey suits and brightly coloured ties are all seated at a long table groaning with delicacies. Guests spoon up Russian caviar in huge silver cups as if it was mashed potatoes. There are oranges, ham, sparkling champagne in tall crystal glasses, and large quantities of Cognac and liqueurs. Never have I seen so much fabulous food at one time. Where did they get it all? You can't buy anything like this at the market.

For three days the uniformed men wait on us, and we do practically nothing but eat. Between meals the guests play cards, sing, smoke and drink. My mother is growing increasingly quiet. When I ask her where all the food comes from, she looks about her apprehensively and puts a finger on my lips. I feel as though we're trapped in a robbers' den. When we're not eating, I take walks in the woods. I sit down in the grass and breathe deeply, enjoying a brief feeling of freedom. I have never met people like these men in grey suits.

On the third evening, after sunset, the black car comes to take us home again. My mother and Malwina are standing by the fence that surrounds the villa, talking quietly. Suddenly both begin to cry; then, still sobbing, they embrace. Finally my mother frees herself and we climb into the car. Malwina calls out something after the car starts up, but I can't hear what she says. We never see her again.

Whenever I feel sad I go to a concert by myself. Mother has no time for that, but she gives me money to buy a ticket. Somehow, there's always enough for that. She doesn't want to admit that she is short of money. She would rather cut back even further on her own needs. And she's glad I have discovered music.

I sit in Philharmonic Hall for hours listening, to Chopin, the *Stabat Mater* by Szymanowski, or Mozart. No one in school knows my secret. I suspect it wouldn't fit in with the new order.

When I listen to music, my restlessness is easier to bear. I am in that other world I always dream about.

Once, when I am out with my mother, I see an old doll's house in a shop window. It is two storeys high, has two bedrooms, a kitchen, and a living room furnished with an embroidered couch and velvet tablecloths on little tables. It reminds me of my grandfather's house, although I've never been there and know it only from my mother's stories. 'That's what I'd like for my birthday,' I tell my mother.

She sighs. The doll's house is beyond her means. The next time I pass the shop it is no longer in the window.

During the summer holidays a few children are chosen to go to the Young Socialists' camp. I am one of those selected and

I'm excited. Three weeks in the outdoors, in the heart of a forest near a lake, far from the city, far from home. The summer camp is one of the privileges accorded active Young Communists. There you get lots to eat, live in tents and play games.

As a teenager (about 1952/3).

But no sooner do I arrive at camp than I feel terribly homesick. I write long letters to my mother every day. Things are better in the evenings. We sit around the campfire under the stars, roast hot dogs and sing songs. Children from all over Poland have come here: workers' children, farmers' children and Young Communists like me.

One evening something happens that shakes my view of things. We are sitting around the campfire, bellowing out a revolutionary song. The refrain goes: 'We despise death, we despise your God. Our God is the people, the working class.'

Suddenly a little girl stands up. She's the child of farmers from the Tatra Range. She has long blonde plaits and wears a colourful traditional costume with flowers and ribbons. She stands as though turned to stone, with light from the campfire illuminating her serious little face. She does not join in the singing.

'Why didn't you sing?' our youth leader asks, when we finish the song.

There are tears in her eyes. 'I can't sing against God,' she replies, in a thin, yet firm voice.

There is deathly silence. Then the leader quickly begins a

new song. For the next few days no one mentions the incident. But I realize that something happened that evening, something beyond my experience, something even beyond my understanding: there are people who have the courage to stand up and say 'no'.

I make friends with the girl – the others have been snubbing her since that incident – and I learn a lot from her. She tells me legends and stories from her native region about heroes and bandits. The mountain farmers are a proud and religious people with a very old way of life that no government has ever been able to corrupt.

I return home from summer camp knowing that there are other people beside me who don't 'belong'. And that many of them are not ashamed of it. They're even proud of it.

Why hadn't my mother ever talked to me about this? I have known that she doesn't approve of my drummer-girl existence, that there are things she'd like to say to me. She says nothing, however. She lets me do what I want to do and rarely puts her foot down. Inexorably we are drifting apart, and I feel guilty about it.

Her disappointment and my guilt surface during our fights over food. I reject the food she sets before me. I become bitter, obstinate. In this way I gradually separate myself inwardly from her. Where once we were one, there are now two.

When we meet Manuela at the theatre, and Manuela puts her arms around me and kisses me, whispers to me and takes me to her dressing room, I can see the pain in my mother's eyes. It is more than envy: it is the recognition that I am moving away from her.

She is suffering because of me, and also because her family is gone. Yet I don't want to be a family substitute for her, and the more I feel her pain, the more desperately I turn away.

If only she had said, 'You're hurting me,' how much easier it might have been for both of us. Perhaps I wouldn't have had to be so horrible to her later. But she suffered in silence, mute and unprotesting. This intensified my feelings of guilt, and I anaesthetized my conscience by being hard and stubborn.

'*Poziomka*,' Manuela says, after the performance, 'if you like, I'll read to you a little and then I'll take you home later.' She looks questioningly at my mother and me.

I nod enthusiastically. My mother agrees reluctantly. 'Just don't be too late.'

My mother has left. Manuela and I are sitting in her dressing room. It's already dark outside. I feel quite grown-up being out so late, and being allowed to sit here, and having Manuela read to me.

I love being backstage with Manuela. It's both exciting and cosy here. There are two plush armchairs, one in the corner for visitors, the other at the dressing-table in front of a large mirror. Manuela has clipped photos of her favourite stars and many cards from her many admirers to the mirror. They send her flowers and chocolates, and they all want to marry her. She often tells me about them. I hang on her every word. 'Which one would *you* go out with, Stefan or Jerzy?' she asks coquettishly, wiping the makeup off her face with cotton-wool and cold cream.

'Oh, with Stefan!' I reply without hesitation, because he has just sent her a huge box of sweets.

Manuela laughs, offers me a chocolate and pops one into her own mouth. She asks me to help her with her zip, and slips into a silk dressing-gown that's hanging on a rack next to the costumes. Then she drops back into her chair and reaches for the book.

'Shall we read?' She takes pleasure in the sound of her own voice. I enjoy it too. Of course, I could read the book myself, but that wouldn't be the same. When Manuela reads, it's like a performance. My mother never reads to me. Frequently Manuela and I sit like that for hours, absorbed in a world of romance and tragic love.

The name of the book is *Tristan and Isolde*. The story centres around a dark secret and is deeply moving. The hero and heroine die of love. Isn't that the most beautiful thing – to die of love?

And then there were the letters.

We had gone to the mountains for the weekend and were sitting in our hotel room drinking tea. Suddenly my mother is called to the telephone, and as she jumps up she drops her handbag, a small brown bag with a gold frame and clasp. It lies open on the rug. It is full of letters. I pick it up and take out the letters. They all bear the same flowing, powerful handwriting in black ink – a handwriting I don't recognize. Who wrote all these letters to my mother? I know I shouldn't, but my curiosity is too strong. I take one of the letters out of its envelope. It is from someone I know well, a nice older man. All the letters are from him.

I start to read. 'My beloved Tosia, I cannot live without you and your love . . .'

Terrified, I stop. I feel my face flush. My mouth is suddenly dry. I shouldn't be reading these. They are full of physical longing. For the first time in my life I become aware of sexual desire, and it confuses and frightens me. I read on and think of my dead father, and I feel sickened by this betrayal of him, of us both. The realization that love is more than just a word makes me ill.

I hear my mother's footsteps approaching. Quickly I stuff the letters into the handbag, put it on the table, and cross my legs, trying to look as though nothing has happened.

'Is something wrong?' my mother asks. 'You're so pale, Roma . . . I hope you're not ill again.'

She puts her hand on my forehead to see whether I have a fever. I want to push her hand away, this hand that has touched a man's body, this strange, cool hand that no longer belongs to me.

I feel sick to my stomach but let her touch me. No one is ever going to know. My mother is never going to find out that I now know she has betrayed me.

8

It is a cold day in March, in 1953, and Stalin is dead. Solemn music drones out of the loudspeaker in the classroom, interrupted occasionally by the sombre, quavering voices of the announcers. It's like being in the theatre. We sit at our desks, quiet and motionless. We have to mourn.

For six months now I have been attending school in a dark pre-war building diagonally across the street from the old Kraków synagogue. Like the other girls, I wear the school uniform: a white-collared blue smock with the school emblem and a blue beret with the school's number.

Irene Ratan is forgotten. My days as a drummer-girl are over. My Communist ideal developed cracks long ago.

Now I sit here and am supposed to mourn Stalin. The sweet baby Stalin, the all-powerful adult Stalin, Stalin the god whose picture hangs everywhere. Can gods die? It seems unimaginable that Stalin could die.

I know I was supposed to love him, but I was never able to do that, because I knew of the terror that lay behind the veneration. However, I'm a good actress. I lower my eyes.

My head gets heavier and heavier; the music weighs like lead on my shoulders. The hours pass. It starts getting dark outside. The tragic speeches are repetitive, again and again the same phrases, the same words: Stalin is dead. Dead, dead, dead.

My head sinks down on my arms.

Suddenly one of the girls starts to laugh hysterically. I join in. The music, the tension, sitting still for such a long time, the compulsory grief – they have simply become unbearable.

The laughter is liberating. It is also a serious offence. They write down our names, and threaten us with dire consequences. We are sent home.

The entire city is in mourning. People carry huge pictures of Stalin through the streets. Loudspeakers have been set up in the market square and are booming out the same radio programme we heard at school. No one dares to talk.

When I turn into our street I can see from afar that a policeman is standing in front of our house.

They've come to pick me up.

I'm trembling as I approach our front door, and try to squeeze past him.

'Stalin has died!' he says in a gruff voice, and looks me up and down.

'Yes, I know,' I stutter. I'm not going to say any more than that. He probably wants to sound me out, wants to find out whether I really loved Stalin.

But he lets me go.

At school there is a disciplinary action against me and the girl who laughed. They threaten to expel us. My mother puts on her best coat and goes to see the principal, a woman.

Much later, when she returns home and is hanging up her coat, I ask her, 'What did she say?'

'You'll be allowed to stay,' she replies. 'I was able to persuade her to give you a second chance. I told her that your father is dead and that you have a delicate constitution.'

I am astonished. Evidently my mother isn't such a bad actress after all.

'And besides,' my mother adds drily, 'she's on the take.'

I now have girlfriends who are different, like me. You can talk to them as though they're grown-ups. My mother says it's because they come from intellectual homes. This is all new to me. I form friendships cautiously, and when I do it's as though I were discovering a beautiful, strange and warm country. There really are people who think I matter. Their names are Marynia, Renata, Bogusia and Barbara.

I like Barbara best of all. She has a calm, gentle, understanding nature. Finally someone who doesn't frighten me and doesn't try to dominate me. Her mother is a librarian. She has an older sister who is so beautiful she draws everyone's attention. Barbara herself has a pleasant, friendly face with slightly slanting eyes. She is shy but very bright, always the best pupil in class. There isn't a question she can't answer.

Her family lives in a gracious old-fashioned six-room apartment that they owned before the war, and from now on that's where I find refuge. Because Barbara's mother doesn't earn much money at her job, she rents rooms to artists. This creates a unique atmosphere.

After school I often go home with Barbara, glad not to have to be in our dark, cramped apartment with the constantly scolding Marynia and my taciturn mother. Barbara and I talk about everything – except the war, the Holocaust and her father, whom she has never seen. When we're together we forget the oppressiveness of Communism and our dull, nightmarish lives. It's been drummed into us for years that we mustn't talk to anyone about politics, and that we can never trust anyone because they might be spies. Instead I recite my poems for Barbara; we read books together; we walk around Kraków, go into the churches, take rides out to the country. Now there's someone in my life with whom I can share my dream world, my secret garden. At last I'm not alone any more.

Life changes after Stalin's death, but slowly at first. Everything is still grey, day in and day out. The same hateful music is still played on the radio, the same war films are still shown at the cinema: soldiers marching, shooting, and winning; then a general pins medals on their chests and the film ends. We have to watch a lot of these films at school. There's love in them too, but it's a clean and impersonal kind of love. Love for the fatherland.

Roman doesn't think much of these films either, but of course he can't say that to anyone. He raves about American films, which we hardly ever see here. I keep wondering how he knows about such things. American movies are capitalist movies. The censor controls what we know, so we know practically nothing about the West. Sometimes, as a rare exception, they'll show an Italian or a French film about the working class. When they do there are long lines in front of the cinema.

'At least *they* have pretty women.' Roman sighs. By now he has his own room in town and often comes to dinner at our house. His grades at school are miserable; it's not even certain that he'll pass the final examination.

'Maybe I'll join the circus,' he confides to me one day. 'They have a school of their own that can't possibly be as boring as mine. I could work there as a clown.'

Roman would probably be good at that – he's been annoying people with his clowning for years.

At school, I continue to work on the Communist propaganda for the noticeboard, even though I don't really believe it any more. It's a good excuse to escape maths lessons. The teachers have to give me a good grade; otherwise it would look as though they didn't have any respect for the displays. I do well in the humanities and often write my girlfriends' essays for them. My best subjects are art and literature, thanks in great part to my friendship with old Mr Taffet, the Jewish second-hand-book seller, who can get me any book I need.

More than anything else I would like to have a pet to love and cuddle. But our apartment is too small for that, and only Party members can hope to get a bigger apartment, not someone like my mother who works for a private company. These private companies are called 'leeches that suck the nation's lifeblood'. She sometimes works long into the night because she is afraid the firm might be shut down. Often she isn't home at weekends.

That's fine with me. Since I found the letters I have been avoiding her, trying not to think about them, because whenever I do, it makes me sick.

It seems that I'm gradually turning into a normal teenage girl. At least during the daytime. At night I have strange dreams . . .

I am taking the usual route to school, my schoolbag on my back. I hate the schoolbag – it's too heavy. Soon I'll be fourteen; the thought makes me feel proud and happy. All at once I see a crowd of people on the street. A theatrical performance is about to start – a kind of Nativity or Passion play. But not on the street, it will be performed on the rooftops. The houses here aren't tall – only two or three storeys high – so it will be easy to see everything from the street. People crane their necks, staring up at the roofs. I stand there too. 'But you have to go to school,' someone in the crowd says. I'll be fourteen soon, so I can stay. I stay.

The performance begins. The actors come flying down on to the roofs from above. They are big – bigger than we are – dressed in bright, garish costumes. Their hair is dyed and they wear coloured feathers in their hats. Their loose bright robes flutter in the wind. It's beautiful – I've never seen anything more beautiful! The performers grin at us with their painted faces. Slowly they begin to move, to sing, to dance.

My mother is among the dancers. My father and my grandparents are there too. Even Sabine – or is that my grandmother? I can't tell for sure. My father waves to me. He is trying to tell me something, to warn me about something. But I can't understand him. I grow desperate because I don't know what he wants to tell me. And just then shots are fired from windows across the way. I know that sound: ping, ping, ping, ping.

The figures on the roof freeze. Then the bullets hit them, and they fall down, one by one. They glide like gigantic colourful birds, turning in the wind, then fall to the ground and are merely grey. I drop to my knees beside them – try to see their faces. 'You'll be late for school,' someone says. I run my fingers through my mother's tousled grey hair. 'You have to go to school, Roma,' my mother says. 'It's already late . . .'

'You have to go to school, Roma!' my mother says, shaking me. The dream vanishes. I rub my eyes and jump out of bed.

One day a girl in the schoolyard asks me, 'Did you know that your mother is having an affair with a married man?'

She snickers and walks away. Stunned, I sink down on a stone bench. They all know. The girls at school, the people in town, they're all talking about it.

My mother! My quiet, kind-hearted mother – someone's mistress? Only now, here in the schoolyard do I fully realize the meaning of the letters in her handbag, the meaning of isolated words and sentences that have been pursuing me like a nightmare. But until now they were just words. Suddenly they have become real. They have materialized into something physical.

Something from the past comes back to me, making me suddenly nauseous – pictures, sounds, scenes from the ghetto. Stinking, noisily kissing, moaning, writhing human bodies . . .

All physical things disgust me.

My mother disgusts me.

I disgust myself, because my body, too, has begun to change.

I eat less and less. Whenever my mother touches me I feel sick. She has no idea what's wrong with me because I don't talk about it.

Barbara knows. She tries to console me without mentioning the subject directly. 'Roma,' she says, 'nobody has her feelings under control all the time. A little while ago didn't you read me Leśmian's poems? So you know what love is like.'

But I *don't* know. Love has become something frightening for me, something I'm afraid of.

I'm convinced I'm going to get pregnant. I dream about it at night and wake up bathed in sweat, convinced that I'm pregnant even though no man has touched me. Actually I have only vague ideas about how you get pregnant, and no one ever talks to me about such things, not even my girlfriends. Everything physical is a sin. It's even a sin to wear trousers. In the depths of winter the headmistress stands outside school and checks whether any of the girls are wearing them. And if she spots one who is, that girl is sent home.

Girls who have already developed breasts are harassed and receive bad grades. One of my girlfriends was sent home with a great deal of fuss because she was wearing earrings. The teacher called her a whore. Earrings are immoral; everything is immoral.

I am drawn to the mystery of love while at the same time it repels me.

'Eat!' my mother says, putting a full plate in front of me. But I just shake my head. I can't, I don't want to eat.

Marynia scolds me. 'Food is so hard to get. It's a sin not to eat it.'

Everything is a sin.

Marynia is right, of course. Food is hard to come by, especially meat, sausage and ham. My mother knows someone who smuggles sausage from the country to the city. The woman works in a State-run public bath-house. We go there regularly, take our clothes off, and walk through the steam room to a cubicle at the back. There we buy the sausage she has hidden. Then, carrying our valuable parcels, we work our way back, through thick clouds of steam and get dressed again. In winter the procedure is a nuisance, but when we leave we're pleased with ourselves.

Despite this I can't eat the greasy sausage.

If I don't eat, I can forget that I have a body.

My mother worries about me, but I can't help that. Besides, it serves her right.

Almost all my free time is spent drawing and painting. In art I have finally found the world I have longed for, a world that has nothing to do with our socialist everyday life or with physical bodies. Of course, I have little free time because we have school in the afternoon as well as on Saturday, and at weekends we get tons of homework.

I'm not particularly good in school, except in literature when I always do excellent work. That's because sometimes I know more about literature than the teacher. I read and read and read. And, as always, art is my favourite subject.

We learn Russian, later also French. English isn't taught at all; it is a capitalist language. Some of the girls study it on their own in secret.

The natural sciences are foreign to me and I hate them. Luckily I have Barbara. She pulls me along, tells me what I should study, prepares me for the questions. And she writes down for me everything we don't have to learn by heart. She's explained maths to me at least a thousand times. With her support, I'm not afraid of failing. She helps me through my depressions when they come. And *I* can help *her* when she has problems with shyness.

Helping someone else, I forget myself.

I discuss painting with my physics teacher. His tolerance has saved my school career. Only in Poland can you find such sympathy for the artistic temperament. Though I'm close to failing physics, my marks improve miraculously.

Most of all I love the theatre. I write and stage plays for my school – again getting out of maths lessons.

I'm constantly dragging my girlfriends to art galleries and

to the theatre, introducing them to Manuela and her friends, and of course the girls are impressed. Manuela remains my top role model. I go to see her in drawing-room comedies, Romantic-era Polish plays, and Shakespeare. The plays deal with the things that go on between men and women – but this is art, not reality.

Sitting there in the theatre I mouth Manuela's lines along with her. I picture myself standing on stage one day as Ophelia, or as Natasha in Tolstoy's *War and Peace*. Even today I can still recite entire passages from those plays by heart.

For Manuela I'm something like a substitute daughter, a mascot. She delights in my adulation, and tells me about her various love affairs.

My mother suffers in silence.

'You're clothes-mad!' she says.

It's true. The way I look matters more and more to me. I designed my new school smock and had it made up by a dressmaker. Then I dyed it a dark blue-grey, just a shade lighter than prescribed by the school regulations.

There's hardly anything to buy in the shops. Barbara and I regularly comb through the flea-market, looking for something colourful. Now and then one of the girls in school receives a package from the West, which always creates a sensation. It may contain an interesting necklace, a lace-trimmed slip or a pretty scarf – real treasures for which we all envy the lucky girl. Once, a girl in my class even got permission to visit relatives in Paris. When she returned, the entire class made a pilgrimage to her house to see whether her hair was now blue or green, and whether she was still the same person.

After attending the circus school, Roman passed his final examination. He then went to Paris at the invitation of his half-sister. You're allowed to take only five dollars officially when you go abroad, but people manage to smuggle out more. When he comes back to Kraków everyone gapes. He loves showing off his red Parisian socks. In Poland all socks are grey. Eventually, Roman intends to enter the film academy in Łódź.

It's incredible how the people here yearn for colour. Maybe it explains my longing for stylish clothes. While my body requires only a little food, my spirit hungers for beauty and luxury. In Kraków you can find these in the expensive hotels, where they sell aromatic cigarettes and foreign magazines. Leafing through one of these is like a breath of freedom. Sometimes I just stand open-mouthed, staring at the pictures. In our country, women are fat and worn-out from work, yet in these photos even the older women are slim and good-looking, their dyed hair done up stylishly.

Occasionally Barbara and I pick up a colourful skirt or shoes and costume jewellery on the black market. We spend hours with our girlfriends in front of the mirror, drawing thick lines over our eyes with a black pencil. We have our hair cut in the styles favoured by French and Italian film stars, and after school we try to dress like them. I transform my cheap gym shoes into ballerina slippers with black india

In front of the mirror (1958).

ink and make skirts out of colourful curtain material. This represents the West for us.

My mother disapproves. 'You look like a parrot!' she says, while Marynia nods vehemently in agreement. She thinks the way I dress is immodest and sinful – and that the necklines are much too low.

I'm often aware of men's eyes on me and take pleasure in looking immodest and sinful. It's enough briefly to raise my self-confidence. I don't necessarily want to have any closer dealings with these men; and I don't know any boys my own age. I just want to be admired.

It helps me to forget.

Sometimes I look in the mirror and see an attractive young girl with black, perplexed eyes.

At sunset on Friday evenings my mother always lights two candles and says the blessing, but it's done almost incidentally, furtively, without conviction. For both of us the past has disappeared, vanished permanently.

I paint dark shadows under my eyes with diluted ink and powder my face to make it look pale. My girlfriends always look healthy and robust. The teachers, who are all spinsters, suspect them of having nothing but boys on their minds, of going dancing out at night and of not studying. 'Just look at Ligocka,' they say. 'She studies – you can tell by looking at her; she's so pale and has dark rings under her eyes.'

To be honest, except for art I, too, think of nothing but love. A growing number of men whom I admire are interested in me, mainly artists, painters, actors and poets. But this is just infatuation, nothing more. I often go out at night, sit around in coffee-houses, go to the theatre and concerts, or meet my girlfriends. Sometimes I play truant from school, sneak into one of the many Kraków churches, and burrow into one of the deep armchairs in a side aisle. There I practise my French and Latin vocabulary or simply enjoy the solemn stillness.

I drank my first vodka in a church. And the first time I kissed someone was in a church pew. His name is Piotr. He is my first love.

I met Piotr on a school trip to the museum. He was a young art student conducting guided tours. With his wild curly hair and beautiful big eyes he looked like a gypsy. I also liked his soft voice. It was fascinating to hear him talk about the paintings, explain how light is painted, how to make a picture glow, and the secrets of composition. I was enchanted and was practically floating on air as we left the museum. Never before had I met such a man.

In maths the next day I told Barbara about it; she had been ill when we visited the museum. I told her rapturously that I'd fallen in love with a terrific man who had curly hair and soft dark eyes, who knew more about art than anyone else in the world. I talked and talked, and Barbara listened silently until the teacher gave me a furious look.

When she turned back to the blackboard, Barbara, a little smile playing on her lips, whispered, 'Your meeting Piotr is really great. He's staying at our house.'

I gasped. I had lain awake all night wondering how I could get to know this man – and now it turned out that a few days earlier he had rented a room from Barbara's mother. Naturally, after that I visited Barbara even more often than before.

Although he is married, beautiful gentle love grows between Piotr and me. I write poems for him, he sends me romantic letters. For his birthday Barbara and I decorate his bed with colourful sweet-peas. Although he likes me very much, he is constantly reminding me that he has a wife abroad, that he can't form a permanent relationship. We both know that's just an excuse. He's a decent man and doesn't want to lead an innocent sixteen-year-old into temptation. Our love remains mostly platonic.

We meet secretly in a church. I've brought a little willow basket with a small bottle of vodka in it, and we sit in a pew, drinking vodka and kissing. It is wonderful and sinful.

Piotr never has any money. One day we are all sitting in a café, hungry and thirsty, but none of us has so much as a penny in our pockets. 'Wait a second,' Piotr says. 'I'll be right back.' Off he goes into the windy, damp autumn night. When he comes back he has a pocketful of money. He's sold the lining of his overcoat.

Barbara shares my love for this man and is happy for me. She is the kind of person who is better at living someone else's life than her own.

All this is hard on my mother. I can't understand her excessive worry about me. How can she suddenly forbid me to do something when all along she has treated me like an adult? Now that I've finally grown up, she starts telling me what to do. It's too late.

Sometimes when I come home late at night she is standing at the door in her nightgown. She doesn't say anything, but I sense her fear, as I did back then – except now she is afraid for me. She is afraid to lose me. I am the only thing she has salvaged from the war, the most valuable thing she owns. But I don't want to be owned. I try to explain to her that I'm not doing anything bad. She doesn't believe me.

When I come home late at night again, having promised to be back early – you can't get to a telephone in some places – she blows her top. Then she's silent again. This makes me feel terribly guilty, as if I were the last whore hanging out at the railway station. On these nights I go to bed and hold my doll close. I feel as though I'm choking, and when I can't stand it any more, I become ill. That's one way out for both of us. She's finally released from her vow of silence and can take care of me.

I am ill a lot these days.

Marynia often says aloud what my mother is thinking. As

usual she bangs the stove door shut early in the morning, muttering reproaches: 'Some people can sleep as long as they want to and don't have any consideration for their mothers. Such selfish people. The mother goes to work after she hasn't slept all night. But some people think only of themselves.'

I bury my head in the pillow.

I still can't believe that she has a lover. Not a word about that ever crosses her lips, even though she knows that I know and that the whole town is talking about it. She has tried to end the affair, but she can't. Her friend is a nice, pleasant man; I like him. My disgust and disappointment are never directed at him. He understands me, always finds excuses for my behaviour, and supports me completely. He tries to persuade her to be less strict with me, to see things in a more positive light, not to criticize my colourful clothes. Unfortunately he's not very successful.

For years he has been trying to live a two-family life. He simply can't do otherwise. He loves my mother too much.

And so none of the three parties involved gives up, and he regularly spends all his holidays, including New Year's Eve, first with one and then with the other family.

'Oh, come along!' says the girl. I know her only superficially from school. She's somewhat younger than I, but has already had experience with men. It's early afternoon. We meet two men she knows and go to a bar with them. I down a couple of vodkas without really knowing what the effect will be. When I try to stand, I pass out.

I wake up in a villa at the edge of town. There are strange men and women all around me, all quite drunk. One of the men tries to take off my clothes. I panic, desperately fight him off. He doesn't understand why I'm behaving like this but is too drunk to be abusive or hold on to me. My head is buzzing, but I do know this: I have to get out of there immediately.

I run barefoot down the stairs, out into the street. No one tries to stop me. I wander through the city, finally reach home. Fortunately, my mother isn't there. I have to throw up and I feel terrible. Again there are those pictures in my head, scenes from the ghetto – people and bodies, of being held and touched. And that same feeling of having to save myself. *You lost control,* I tell myself. *But once again you were lucky.*

I make myself new colourful skirts, cut low necklines into my T-shirts, and wear huge earrings. These make me less vulnerable. I look like a gypsy and play the role of a cheerful, flamboyant young woman to perfection.

When I don't go out, I write and paint obsessively. The subjects of my paintings are faces, fearful eyes, fragile bodies, someone sitting in a closed room with small windows. Or I paint the Pietà in all its variations. As always, I feel drawn to Catholicism: the drama, the suffering fascinate me. I experience them almost physically.

If I do go out and flirt with men, it's invariably with a lonely, unhappy poet who reads me his poems. I don't go to wild parties or dance to the point of exhaustion, or drink too much. I refuse to lose control. I want to flirt. I don't want to get involved.

One day I'm sitting in a café, reading. Two tables away an unprepossessing blond man wearing glasses is watching me intently. I'm used to that and pay no attention.

He gets up, comes over to my table, and bows. 'Would you like to marry me?' he asks politely.

I look up from my book. 'Marry you?' I ask. 'Why should I?'

He bows again, excuses himself, and returns to his table.

Later I find out he is the famous science-fiction writer, Stainslaw Lem.

In those days, poets and writers in Krakow were treated like film stars. We met them at friends' homes, where we listened to jazz music from the West that you could buy on the black market if you were lucky and wealthy. Now and then Polish jazz musicians would play in small clubs and bars. But poets were always my world. Often they were surrounded by swarms of pretty young women, fans like me. They were my universities.

Kraków is like an island in Poland.

We are still not allowed to travel. My mother's applications to emigrate are rejected again and again. The artists in Kraków have built themselves a world of their own and that is the one to which I now belong.

For years attempts have been made to erect a giant industrial complex outside the city so that a real workers' class will arise, alongside the ranks of aristocrats, professors, literati and artists. However, no matter how hard they try, the country's rulers are unable to stifle the spirit of artistic freedom that prevails in Kraków.

Meanwhile they have allowed the beautiful old Jewish quarter, where my school, the synagogue and the old cemetery are located, to fall into ruin. Criminals and undesirables have moved in, but the city administration doesn't do anything. They're too busy constructing ugly concrete-block housing on the outskirts of the city.

I get my second lesson in personal courage during my last year of school.

It happens during biology. We are on the subject of evolution, and, since everything is approached from the Marxist viewpoint, the teacher is telling us about something that Soviet scientists allegedly discovered. I'm dozing at my desk.

Suddenly my friend Renata, whose father is a scientist, gets up. 'That's nonsense,' she says firmly. 'None of that is true.'

There is silence in the room, the same sort of silence as, years ago, around the campfire when the little girl refused to sing songs attacking God.

The teacher has turned pale. 'Please, Renata,' she implores her, 'please don't say such a thing ever again. You're destroying your future. You won't pass your exam. I haven't heard a word you said.'

We remain silent. All of us know what a courageous thing Renata and the teacher have done. And now I realize, this time with the understanding of an adult, what having the courage to stand up for your convictions means. I understand that truth can be more important than personal safety.

One day, Piotr excitedly tells Barbara and me that he's discovered a terrific cellar right on the market square and that he's going to open a cabaret there. Would we help him get it ready?

Of course we will! It turns out to have been a former wine cellar, a beautiful old vault in a palace that once belonged to an aristocratic family. The cellar is full of rubble and rocks but by the end of the day we've managed to shovel it all out. Some friends of ours drag down a piano; Barbara and I put candles into empty wine bottles; in the twinkling of an eye Piotr constructs a small stage; and in no time the first performance takes place. Someone makes music, someone else sings or reads aloud.

'What will you call your cabaret?' I ask Piotr.

'Pod Barana-Mi [Under Aries],' he replies, beaming, and gives me a kiss.

Under Aries cabaret becomes a Kraków institution. It is also Piotr's life. In the course of its forty year existence everyone who is anyone performs there; and in a quiet, surrealistic, idiosyncratic way big things happen on the tiny stage in that narrow, stuffy cellar. I never perform there, but in the early years of the cabaret I'm one of the team.

Now I sometimes stay out all night, and my mother no longer stands at the door in her nightgown when I come home, though her fear is still there. I try not to feel it any more. She has gained weight recently – she eats too many sweets and too much of the cake she loves to bake. We live separate lives, almost as though we don't know each other. Yet we know each other very well.

For my eighteenth birthday she gives me a huge house key wrapped in coloured paper. Until then I always had to ask the concierge, the woman with the many skirts, to unlock the front door for me at night. It was a nuisance and always cost me an extra tip.

'Do whatever you can't stop doing,' my mother says, as she hands me the key. We embrace briefly. How fragile she is, I think, then quickly push the thought aside.

Barbara and I are sitting in her apartment, poring over our schoolbooks. It's hot outside and we're sweating – Barbara from the heat and I from panic. The date of the final exam is near, and the closer it gets, the more convinced I become that I won't pass.

'You'll make it,' Barbara says, for the hundredth time, 'once you buckle down and really get to grips with the maths.'

But I don't want to get to grips with it. I only want to paint, draw and write poetry. A few of my poems have already been published in newspapers, and my portfolio for the Art Academy is almost finished.

'But you have to!' Barbara says, and patiently explains all the things I don't understand and never will. She gives me questions to answer, and crams with me. She is determined to get me through the exam.

I know I've got to pass. Everyone in our family has got their diploma – something my mother never neglects to mention. What I really want to do is to run away, or make myself invisible.

Instead I go to the Jewish cemetery. I struggle through the undergrowth, climbing over ancient, toppled, moss-covered tombstones, looking for the grave of the legendary Rabbi Remu who, it is said, could work miracles.

Finally I find it. I scribble my wish on a piece of paper, and reverently I place it on his grave.

'Dear honoured and revered Rabbi, please help so that my wish will be fulfilled,' I murmur softly. Did a gentle breeze rustle through the leaves?

After the last of the final examinations, I leave school feeling in the pit of my stomach that I didn't make it.

I drag myself home, tired and hot.

I lie down in the bath, dip my head in the warm water and start to relax. But the dull feeling of failure remains.

Suddenly my girlfriends come rushing into the room: 'Roma, you passed!'

I can't believe it, but it's true.

I made it.

9

After I left school, my mother announced that she wanted to send me on a grand tour to Israel with stops in Venice, Paris, Rome. First, she had to get me an invitation from abroad, then secretly exchange dollars on the black market because officially you're only allowed to take five dollars with you. The additional money was hidden in a toothpaste tube and in the heel of one of my shoes. She was even able to wheedle me a visa. My girlfriends – who had come to Kraków station to see me off – all gaped at me as though I were a creature from another planet. None of them had been given a trip to the West after graduation. 'Are you definitely coming back?' they ask.

Yes, yes, of course I'm coming back, I assure them. Absolutely.

In Venice, the bright light, the wonderful blue – an intoxication of colour – acts on me like a drug. I existed as if in a delirium, all the days there, hardly sleeping at all.

I walk through the narrow alleys for hours, absorbing the light, the warmth of the sun, the smell – a mix of warm bread, stagnant water, coffee and expensive perfume. I have very little money, but enough to buy myself one of those round, delicious-smelling flat cakes. 'Pizza,' says the woman behind the counter as I take my first bite.

I immediately discover a pair of shoes I absolutely have to have – heavenly, dreamy shoes! They are black and white, with high stiletto heels. All my Venice money goes into buying them. That evening I return to the hotel with my new shoes and an empty stomach, sit down in the dining room and order a glass of mineral water, intending to pay with the few coins I have left. The waiter noticed my new shoes. '*Principessa*,' he says admiringly. '*Mangiare*?' I shake my head. A knot forms in my stomach; I can't take my eyes off the plates heaped with food on nearby tables. Gradually the dining room empties. The waiter must have seen my hungry glances, because suddenly he is standing before me holding a tray on which is a bowl of spaghetti. '*Mangi, Signorina*,' he says, smiling, '*costa niente. Caffè*?' Hardly ever has food tasted as good!

In Venice I board an ocean liner to Haifa, Israel. On unlocking the door of my cabin, I find it's a double. The curtains are already drawn; it's almost dark inside. A shapeless form is lying on one of the beds, asleep – or, at least, trying to sleep. I walk over to the other bed, put down my suitcase, and excuse myself for disturbing her. The form on the bed has her fat behind turned towards me. Then she sits up and looks at me.

I'm amazed. The woman's hair is two different colours, part dark, part light, and it's parted down the middle. Haven't I seen that before? She looks at me angrily from under thick black eyebrows, my voice sticks in my throat.

'What? A child. That's all I needed.'

I remember the exact same words.

Professor! I want to call out. Is it really you? Here, of all places?

But I don't say it, just mumble an apology for disturbing her. She doesn't recognize me. It's been a long time since we first met, in the dirty room with the bedbugs.

On the ship there are rich young men who court me. But I find their concerns so far removed from my everyday life that I'm not interested. An American I meet even wants to marry me. I think of Roman and his longing for America. Maybe I should grab the chance. I look him over carefully.

He is young, healthy, athletic. But what does he know about me? 'I want to have at least five children,' he says, beaming. That does it. No way do I want five children.

In Israel the air smells of oranges, heated dust, and things I can't identify. Uncle Mittelmann and Aunt Berta pick me up in Haifa and take me to Tel Aviv, where they live. She still grumbles as much as ever, but my uncle has changed. He is now old and tired and having difficulty learning Hebrew. Sometimes, though, he's still the jolly man he used to be. They live on the seventh floor of an apartment block at the edge of the desert; they no longer have a garden.

In Tel Aviv the desert begins right behind the downtown area; the city is like an oasis. I can see how modestly and under what difficult conditions my uncle and aunt live, how hard they try to come to terms with their new lives. At the age of sixty-five Uncle Mittelmann now goes out on emergency calls. Every day, in the searing heat, he tramps through the sand to the bus stop carrying his heavy doctor's bag. 'The old man has to go to work,' he says, winking at me.

Tel Aviv is full of life, people bustling about everywhere. I can't get it into my head that all the people here are Jewish. The Jews I know back home look so different: insecure, serious, intimidated.

Aunt Berta has arranged for me to go on a tour with three elderly English ladies because, as yet, there is hardly any organized tourism in Israel. It's hot and cramped in the old taxi we travel around in. The English women photograph everything that pops up in front of their camera lenses. They chatter and constantly drink tea. After a while they really get on my nerves.

Early one morning as we're driving through Beersheba and my companions ask the driver to stop so they can have their tea, I disappear with my little suitcase around the nearest corner.

I decide to look up Josi, a distant relative and former Israeli soldier who I know lives somewhere around here. Josi is both delighted and horrified to see me. Only men live in this town, which is still being built, and they all sleep in one house. What is he supposed to do with me?

He decides to put me in his Jeep and show me the Negev desert. We visit nomads in their tents, squat on a huge carpet, and drink lemonade with a sheik and his sons. I'm utterly delighted. Suddenly Josi laughs and blushes.

'What's the matter?' I ask.

'The sheik has just offered to buy you for two thousand dollars!' he whispers. 'How about it? Would you like that?' I look more closely at the sheik. He has a matted black beard, alert little eyes and a round belly. And, of course, he already has several wives who are standing at the tent entrance. None of them looks especially happy.

'No, thanks,' I say.

Before we leave we are served coffee containing odd little fruits. I suddenly feel as though I were floating on air; I feel like singing and dancing. Josi has great difficulty calming me down. What should he do with me now? Then he remembers that there is a new as yet uninhabited settlement nearby. He takes me to one of the empty houses. Leaving a candle, a blanket and some water for me, he bids me good night and promises to pick me up the following morning. Then he locks the door and goes off, probably feeling relieved.

The house is pitch dark, only my candle flickers fitfully. Out in the desert there is barking and howling, a choked, yapping cough. Jackals? Hyenas? I even imagine I hear footsteps and voices. Yet, this isn't the real sort of fear I know so well: everything here seems as if it were in a film. I stand at the window staring out into the dark. Now and then I think I see moving shadows. I can almost make out laughter. Are these men who have lost their way? What if they find me here, break the door down and rape me?

I crawl under the blanket, close my eyes, and spend the

night between waking and dreaming. Nothing happens.

As he promised, Josi picks me up the next morning. He's glad to find me safe and well, but eager to get rid of me as quickly as possible. 'The best thing would be for you to take the bus back to Tel Aviv,' he suggests. A bus has just arrived. It disgorges about twenty women passengers, wild-looking women in garish, sweat-stained clothes and wearing huge earrings.

'I thought only men lived here,' I say to Josi.

Again he blushes with embarrassment. 'Oh,' he says, 'they're whores. They keep the men company at weekends.' I had no idea there were so many prostitutes in this world. I'm intrigued. I reach out to touch them, but he restrains me. 'They'll kill you!' he says in alarm.

I get on the bus. From the rear window I see the men walking slowly towards the women. Then the dusty street is suddenly empty.

For the rest of my trip I explore Israel on my own, meeting wonderful people, French, Russian and Polish immigrants, pioneers and idealists. I like the life there.

One day an old man gives me a book called *The History of the Jews*. I read it night after night. I had no idea that Jews *had* a history.

'We were a brave, warlike, proud people,' the old man had said. 'Now the young people are ashamed because my generation didn't fight back. As for that older generation, they just want to forget everything that happened.'

I briefly wonder whether I shouldn't stay in Israel. Deep down, however, I know that nothing here has anything to do with my life. I again have the feeling that I don't belong, not even in Israel. This world is far removed from my poor little Polish *shtetl*. It is so different from the tragic Jewish-European culture in which I feel at home.

There is no other home for me.

*   *   *

Paris. I am swept off my feet. The city arouses an unfulfilled, almost metaphysical yearning in me for elegance and beautiful things. I spend evenings at parties and concerts. As a pretty young woman I'm invited everywhere, introduced by one friend to another. The fashions, the colours, the people, the shop windows, the wealth, the West – they all fascinate me. Instead of eating I buy myself beautiful things: a black velvet dress with white dots, a petticoat, shoes. I am determined to come back here some day.

I'm scheduled to fly from Rome via Vienna back to Kraków on Christmas Eve. At Rome airport I'm standing at passport control.

'Identification?'

I show them my passport with the Italian visa.

'This is no longer valid.'

The police say I will not be allowed to continue my flight. My visa has expired and I can't go home.

One of the policemen calls the Polish embassy, but no one is there. They're at home celebrating Christmas.

So I have to spend Christmas Eve at the airport. There's a large Christmas tree in the departure hall. I'm apprehensive and lonely, even though everyone is nice to me. An Italian stewardess is assigned to take care of me. I'm her only charge, and she spends all day with me. Two policemen guard us. We eat in the airport restaurant, and a bed is set up for me in one of the offices. Even when I go to the lavatory, the policemen accompany me, right to the door.

The next day they find an interpreter who works for the Polish embassy. Signor Grigio is a fussy old bachelor of Polish origin and uncertain age. He is as grey as his name and seems a bit ridiculous. He constantly addresses me as 'my esteemed miss' and kisses my hand.

After Christmas he finally arranges the visa details. As a farewell gift the nice stewardess gives me a little golden musical box that plays Mozart. And even the airline gives me a present: two days in Rome with Signor Grigio as my guide.

At the Spanish Steps he suddenly gets down on his knees and proposes marriage. I think it's funny, but not *that* funny. The next day I climb out of the window in my room and leave the hotel. He's down in the lobby, sitting there and waiting for me, hour after hour.

I feel sorry for Signor Grigio, but not sorry enough to marry him. Still, I don't have the heart to rebuff him. When we part, I solemnly promise to consider his proposal and to come back in a year.

Not until I'm home in Poland do I realize that my mother had visualized the purpose of my trip quite differently. For years she had scrimped and saved to buy the necessary dollars for the trip, hoping that I would meet a nice, well-to-do man in Israel and marry him. Like all Jewish mothers she wanted me to have a Jewish husband and an untroubled future – not a hard life in impoverished artists' circles in poor Communist Poland.

She made only one mistake – she never told me that I was, so to speak, being sent to look for a husband. Maybe if she had, I might have at least toyed with the idea of marriage. There were certainly enough men, but even with all their money, their cars and houses they didn't interest me. I longed for someone who needed my help so that I could feel I was worth loving and could love myself.

The socialist veil hangs over Kraków like a fog. But as soon as the sun breaks through and its warm golden light falls on the church spires and old houses, the city becomes luminously beautiful, especially if you see it from one of the bridges spanning the Vistula. The veil gradually dissolves. The light reminds me of Venice. Only the smells are different. In the summer the Polish air smells of wild strawberries, in the autumn of mushrooms and apples.

I am now enrolled at the Art Academy and finally I can do what I like most: paint and draw.

I arrived for my entrance examination carrying a fat portfolio containing hundreds of small drawings. There were only thirty places and about five hundred applicants. The examination lasted for a week. On the evening of the last day the list of those who had passed was posted in the big hall. I started at the bottom of the list, didn't find my name, and was about to leave when Barbara pulled me by the sleeve. 'Why don't you take a better look,' she said. And there was my name. Third on the list. They had found my work 'refreshingly different, original'.

The Academy has many interesting professors who are willing to engage in frequent and lengthy conversations with their students. One of them, Jonas Stern, our drawing teacher, seems a bit weird, although I find him attractive. He is a well-known painter, a quiet, taciturn man. With his long grey beard he seems ancient, but he's probably not even fifty. His black, dark-circled eyes remind me of someone.

One day, looking at my drawings, he says, 'You know, Roma, you can't draw. But don't try to learn. Just stay the way you are. Your pictures speak.'

Later I heard that he came from a small Jewish town whose inhabitants had all been shot. Only he survived. The bullet that hit him in the back didn't kill him, and for days he lay buried under corpses until he was able to escape. He and I never talked about it.

Shortly after I passed the entrance examination, I showed my pictures for the first time at Piotr's cabaret. The opening was a big success.

At the crack of dawn the next day Barbara brought over a newspaper. While still in the entrance hall of our apartment she started to read aloud: 'The heroine of yesterday's big opening is the youthful Roma Ligocka with her pigtails . . . The opening of the exhibition has met with a universally enthusiastic response – especially because of the age and the beautiful eyes of the young painter . . .' Barbara giggled. I tore the paper out of her hands. The review was written in the ironic tone typical of the Kraków papers.

The enchanting artist, wearing a black and white dotted velvet dress and carrying a yellow bouquet, was discovered by our trusty scout, who is always on the lookout for new geniuses . . .

Visitors to the exhibition, who arrived in great numbers, gave the young artist an enthusiastic welcome . . . Among the guests was the painter's mama as well as many well-known academics, artists, journalists, writers and classmates of the young lady . . . After many speeches, and while the last pictures were still being hung, the visitors began to sing. The song was called, 'No night without Roma' . . .

I liked seeing my name in the paper. I liked it very much.

In those years I tried to soak up everything that was beautiful, important and true. I met artists like Tadeusz Kantor, a painter and one of the most important theatre directors in Poland; the writer Marek Hłasko; the director Andrzej Wajda, poets, dramatists, actors and musicians. Also part of the scene were my cousin Roman, and Ryszard Horowitz, who was studying art and playing in jazz bands on the side. Kraków was a real Mecca for artists, comparable in its way to Rome, Paris or London.

I look at their pictures, go to see their plays, read their books and listen to their music. Jazz has conquered Kraków, and the new sounds are streaming from every cellar night spot.

I've been cast in the role of a young muse – artists paint me, poets read to me. I'm on friendly terms with many of them. I like to imagine it's like being in Montmartre at the turn of the last century. But, then, there isn't much of anything else: no elegant dining, no holidays, no stylish clothes. No one has much money. I spend long evenings with friends, candlelight and cheap wine, deep in conversations about life and death, love and loneliness.

I can put up with these feelings when they're expressed in the language of art and literature; then they're not my own life, not my private disgrace. They are more or less transferred to another sphere, transformed into a gentle *Weltschmerz*. And this *Weltschmerz* is the source of my inspiration.

We often sit in someone's apartment all night, listening to jazz, drinking vodka, talking. When things get too intimate, when people start to kiss, to embrace, I simply leave. I'm afraid I'll suffocate.

Sometimes this odd mixture of yearning to be fashionable and audacious, to be a *femme fatale*, and the fear and misery I carry around inside me almost tears me apart.

At night we stroll through the city for hours on end then walk each other home. We make up jokes, and the art consists in telling the joke, acting out one's own part in it, then just walking off. Everyone has a role to play – just as in the theatre.

A friend of mine, a young poet from the cabaret, commits suicide under mysterious circumstances. A short while later an actor and his girlfriend take their lives. It's said they were on drugs, but maybe it was just too much vodka. The girl's father is a well-known Kraków physician who has devoted himself almost fanatically to fighting alcoholism.

There's a curious mood among the students, almost an intoxication with death. Some of them can't deal with the System, some can't cope with their own lives.

Something morbid is in the air, a mood one often finds in old cities. It's easy to be seduced into depression. I can appreciate this yearning for death, though deep inside I know, as though it has been carved there in stone, that I must cherish my life.

The funeral of the young couple is a social event. Jazz is played. As I walk out of the cemetery into the sunlight, I see children selling wild strawberries on the street. How can anyone want to take her own life as long as there are wild strawberries?

'Where have you been?'

Every time I come home I read this mute question in my mother's eyes, and each time it chokes me. I sense her fear, and I see my own fear reflected. I understand her well, much too well. What I'm choking on are my own guilt feelings – from having left her alone, from causing her grief and worry, from going my own way. I avoid her eyes. A wall of reproach rises between us and neither of us is able to break through it.

I want to escape from my past, from my mother.

One evening I meet a man who needs me.

His name is Wiesław and he looks and acts just as I imagine a young English lord would: snow-white shirt, tweed jacket, tie, perfect manners, completely different from the artists in their old turtleneck sweaters. His curly chestnut-brown hair is neatly combed; he is slender, of medium height, and has soft almond-shaped eyes. Wiesław is in his mid-twenties and studying art history. He is descended from an old aristocratic Polish family. Everything about him is right. He's handsome, intelligent, and altogether wonderful.

Roman introduced us. Roman knows all the important people and Wiesław is a personality in Kraków. He gazes into my eyes, kisses my hand, and calls me *ma chère*. That's enough to make my knees wobbly.

We're sitting in a restaurant by candlelight, talking. I'm wearing a red dress with a sophisticated neckline that I made out of old lining material. Now and then he gives my low neckline a furtive glance. His conversation is enthralling; it leaves me speechless. He is witty, clever and cultivated. I like that. I also like his aloofness; he is not like those men who beseech me, try to grope me, then declare that they can't live without me.

I don't know why but I get the feeling, in spite of the elegant and competent impression he makes, that this man is lonely and lost.

And precisely because of that I fall in love with him.

We have arranged to meet on the market square at the statue of the poet Mickiewicz. Wiesław walks towards me, bright and cheerful, holding a flower. He kisses my hand.

'*Bonjour*, Michelle.' He smiles, and I melt. He calls me Michelle, a novel name, much nicer than Roma.

One evening he tells me that he wants to write a book. 'It will be a small, slender volume,' he says. 'And it will get the Nobel Prize, that's for sure!' I believe him implicitly.

I've already brought him home to our small, dark apartment to meet my mother. He kissed her hand and brought her flowers. Just as my father did for my grandmother long ago.

We drink tea.

Marynia is impressed. 'Finally a man with manners!' she says, after he has left. 'He's different from all those shabby, unshaven artists usually running after you!'

My mother doesn't say anything.

'What do you think of him?' I ask her. I had been sure she would like him. But she avoids looking me in the eye.

A few days later she says, 'That man is not for you.' I stare at her, stunned.

'Why? He comes from an old aristocratic family. His grandfather was a famous Kraków architect; they owned a castle—'

'Which his drunkard great-grandfather lost, along with the rest of the family fortune. And his grandmother drank too.'

'So what? I've never seen Wiesław drunk. How can you condemn him on that basis?'

'He's been going to the university for years without getting a degree.'

'He's just taking his time. Why shouldn't he? He's writing a book.'

A thought occurs to me. 'Is it because he's a *goy*?'

My mother sighs, shakes her head. 'No,' she says. 'That's not the reason. He has – how shall I put it? – he has a dubious reputation.'

Now I really want Wiesław.

How can my mother be so narrow-minded? I'll show her. And my girlfriends, always whispering behind my back, I'll show them too.

'Don't rush into anything. Take your time,' Barbara admonishes me gently.

But I don't want to take my time. I'm nineteen years old, and I want to get out of that dark apartment and finally get a life of my own. I want to live with him in his little romantic attic room in the tower of the house his grandfather built . . .

Everyone says he's no good for me. I don't care. I'm good for *him*. I have to save him, and by saving him my troubles, fears and inadequacies will somehow dissolve – in him.

No one has ever told me that it's important for me to find somebody who will be there for *me*, who will be good for *me*. That thought never occurs to me.

Living with someone without a marriage certificate would not be acceptable. So I'm going to marry him.

My mother has been crying a lot recently. Today, however, she is wearing a beautiful pink suit and looks very young and shy, almost as though she had just got married herself. Up to the last minute she had hoped I would change my mind.

The marriage ceremony takes place with only the immediate family present – his mother and sister, my mother and her friend. My new husband has grandiose tastes: for him it's either a ball in the castle with lots of people or an intimate group, and since the castle is no longer available, we're celebrating at Restaurant Wierzynek, eating poached salmon, as in the old days.

I'm wearing a white dress that I designed and, under it, the petticoat from Paris. I look like the little girls who scatter flowers during processions. I, too, have flowers in my hair.

As a wedding present my mother has given us a short trip to the country. By the time we get back, it's hoped our marriage will no longer be a topic of conversation.

Perhaps the happiest one among us is Marynia. She now calls me 'madam'.

We go to a medieval castle in the Tatra Mountains that has been turned into a hotel and is frequented by artists.

The castle is beautiful and we are treated 'in accordance with our social position'. We sleep in an antique, carved four-poster bed. I'm reminded of the old Countess who used to give me French lessons. It's amazing how these aristocrats stick together, even though they've had to give up their titles; they're often related to one another too. The manager of the castle-hotel is a former aristocrat. He's known my husband since Wiesław was little and tries to make our few days there enjoyable.

I like being a bride. But during the night I have a strange dream. We are walking over a green summer meadow. The sky is bright blue. We sink almost up to our knees in the grass among the flowers. It is hot. The sun burns down on us. 'Hurry up!' someone yells. There is a dark forest on the horizon. We walk towards it.

At the edge of the forest we see a young couple, making love. Behind them stand men in uniform, observing them and laughing. They laugh and laugh, almost grunting. The lovers don't seem to notice. Then one of the soldiers picks up a weapon; it gleams in the sun. He polishes it carefully with a rag. We stand there, waiting.

The soldier shoots. First the girl; then the man. Both are dead. 'Who wants to be next? Step forward,' the soldier says.

We don't move until the shouts of the soldiers drive us on. '*Los! Schnell! Vorwärts! Marsch! Schneller!*' they yell. I am afraid. The fear courses through my body. My hands are stiff and cold. I try to lift my suitcase, but it's too heavy. So I drag it along behind me.

And now I know that I am the girl who is lying there, shot dead. And that at the same time I also have to keep going.

We keep walking. On and on in the searing heat.

My husband and I don't discuss my dream; we don't talk about the past, or about our future. Only the present exists for us.

After we get back to Kraków I move into his little tower room, which is stuffed with books from top to bottom. It's all very romantic.

During the day I go to the Academy and paint. When I get home in the evenings Wiesław is sitting at his desk; the waste-paper basket is full of crumpled sheets of paper.

'Are you getting anywhere with your book?' I ask, giving him a kiss.

His skin feels hot and he smells of vodka.

'It's coming along,' he mumbles. 'Hey, let's go out.' We count up our money. If there isn't enough to get something to eat, we just order vodka. As always Wiesław tells jokes and speaks French a lot. I notice that he has a few too many, but almost everyone does, don't they?

Wiesław is a drunkard.

It took me time to admit it. I simply didn't want to believe it, and he tried desperately to keep it from me. Then came the day when once again I found him drunk, almost unconscious, in our apartment, and my illusions were gone.

'I'm sorry,' he said, 'I'll stop. I promise.'

But he can't keep his promise. Barely a day has passed, and again I find empty vodka bottles in his coat pockets.

I have to get him to stop; I just have to try harder.

His drinking is like a third person living with us, trying to drive us apart. We have no money because he isn't working, and I get only a small State grant. He sells book after book from his inherited library. We live on that money. In spite of this we sometimes go on holiday. He knows people with whom we can stay. Maybe he'll drink less there, I tell myself. Why in the world did he marry me?

I ask myself that more and more frequently, these days.

Of course he likes me; he just can't show it. Our case is that of a man who has had lots of adventures and who feels a poetic affection for a young girl, who is completely different and unspoiled. He continues to respect me, never says anything unkind, not even later when things fall apart.

Once again, I'm leading a double life. During the day I'm happy at the Academy; at night either I find my husband drunk at home or I have to run around the city looking for him in bars and restaurants. When I find him his shirt is often torn or he has a black eye. I don't yet understand that alcoholism is a sickness.

I'm now spending more time with my mother than with my husband. The one person from whom I most wanted to escape knows what I'm going through. She says nothing, makes soup for me, is there for me. But she cannot help me.

Only much later do I realize that my attempt to save Wiesław has backfired. He doesn't want to lose me, and the burden of having to stand up to me drives him into even deeper despair. At the time I don't see any of this. I'm convinced he can simply give up drinking, as long as he has someone like me to take care of him. One day he'll simply stop. He'll do it for me.

I wander from bar to bar through night-time Kraków,

looking for my husband. This seems all wrong and yet at the same time it seems right. That's what it was like before and I assume that's how it has to be. Back then, in the ghetto, I never thought that the others, the Germans – the Gestapo – were responsible for our misfortune. They were decent, blond, handsome men, and they wore polished boots – we were at fault. And now it's *my* fault that Wiesław isn't well; I have to cope with his alcoholism and with everything that comes with it. It never occurs to me that my existence is at stake too.

Our life together becomes more and more difficult, and I'm reaching the limits of my physical endurance. There's hardly any time for sleep because I'm out every night looking for him. I've got to know every tavern and bar, no matter how disreputable. The disgusting characters who used to scare me are now my allies. 'Are you looking for your Wiesław, lady?' a scruffy guy in a bar asks, and laughs, showing toothless gums. 'He's in the station restaurant. I wouldn't go there if I were you.' But I do go, and Wiesław doesn't resist as I take him home.

It's the same, night after night. I can't concentrate on my studies any more. In the long hours I spend waiting for him to come home, I write poetry. The poems are sad and impassioned, almost like prayers. When he isn't drunk, he reads them. He likes them. Wiesław is strong as a bear, forever getting into fights, defending his honour as an aristocrat. Sometimes he's picked up by the police, and I have to go down to the station to get him out. In happier moments he begs me to help him, wants us to lock ourselves in our room, wants me to take care of him. But as soon as I'm not watching him, he runs off. Once he shaved off half of his hair so that he wouldn't be able to go out on the street. Sooner or later the alcohol wins.

Before long I have to raise money for us because he needs his liquor.

I'm so exhausted that I can't eat. My stomach feels like

an open wound. I go to a doctor. He asks me some questions; then he looks at me thoughtfully.

'The situation you're in is a hell on earth,' he says. 'Do you deserve to live a life like this? It's like a private Auschwitz.'

I flinch. Auschwitz? Maybe he's right. All the same, I have to keep going, I have to save Wiesław.

Almost two years pass like this. One night I'm out once again searching for him. It's raining, and I'm wet and frozen to the bone, and still I can't find him. I head for my mother's apartment, shivering with cold. She no longer asks questions. I go to sleep in my old bed. The next morning I wake up with a high fever. Pneumonia.

The antibiotics available in Poland don't take hold. I lie there for weeks, seriously ill. In addition, I again develop tuberculosis.

'She'll probably have to stay in a sanitorium for several years,' the doctor whispers to my mother, 'That is, if she pulls through this alive.' My mother bows her head.

My husband wants to see me. My mother shields me from him. He's probably drinking uncontrollably while I'm ill. But I don't care. I feel so weak, so hot . . .

My grandmother has come back and put her hand on my forehead. Whom to believe now? Her ghostly voice, which urges me to stay alive? Or my weariness, my desire to dissolve altogether?

I don't know. One thing I do know: now that it's a matter of my own life or death, I no longer worry about Wiesław. I decide in favour of myself.

My mother has found a lung specialist who just happens to be slightly mad. He never takes money from his patients and treats only poor people. Now he's at my bedside, ragged and shabby, a heavy grey wool scarf wound around his neck, examining me. 'She'll live,' he growls into his scarf, as he hands my mother some medicine. A few weeks later my mother and I both know that I'm going to recover. 'When you're better, the first thing you'll do is to take a holiday,' my mother says. 'In Zakopane.'

There are lots of interesting people in Zakopane, and little by little I summon up the courage to face life again. A photographer friend takes pictures of me. Almost overnight I become a full-fledged photographer's model. My picture appears in a magazine, also in a series called 'Poland's Most Beautiful Women'.

For these photographs I wear a wide skirt and large earrings, my hair in a pony-tail. I gaze into the camera with a sensual look.

I don't even want to think of Wiesław.

KONKURS ZESPOŁÓW AUTORÓW
FILMOWYCH I „FILMU"

„Piękna dziewczęta
— na ekrany!"
IV

'The Prettiest Girls on Screen:' *twenty year old Roma modelling for a competition run by the Polish Association of Screenwriters and the magazine* Film. *(1958).*

I've gone back to live in my mother's apartment. Her friend, who has helped me out of difficult situations before, is there for me this time too. He goes with me to see a lawyer.

I'm twenty-one and divorced. I am free.

10

I have made a decision. I've chosen the bright and beautiful 'other' world. My course at the Art Academy is now just about completed, and I've made up my mind to go into costume and stage design. This combines two fields that have always fascinated me: theatre and fashion.

My mother has moved to Vienna. After all these years her application to emigrate was finally granted. My grandfather owned several properties in Vienna, and she is hoping to receive restitution of at least a small part of the family assets. However, her real reason for leaving was that she wanted to get away from her difficult personal situation in Kraków. It didn't work. 'I can't live without your mother,' her friend said to me, shortly before he followed her to Vienna.

I miss her. From time to time she sends me wonderful parcels: a pretty blouse, cocoa, coffee, some green apples from California. While she's waiting for the money owed her, she lives as frugally as ever, earning a little cash by babysitting. Some days she subsists on free samples from the department stores. We write each other long letters. 'In Vienna there are marvellous cafés where they serve fabulous pastries,' she writes, 'but unfortunately I can't eat too many of these delicious things because I have to watch my weight.'

I see Manuela only infrequently. We don't have much to say to each other any more. She goes her way and I go mine. *Babcia* is dead.

I still live in the basement apartment with Marynia. She does the laundry, cooks, cleans, and takes care of me. But I'm not my mother, not the 'real madam'. It's often hard for her. In the evening she needs someone to talk to, the way she used to with my mother. More and more often I lapse into a state in which I just sit, unable to talk – not to anyone, not even Marynia. Sometimes I take one of the new pills that are now available. They not only allow me to sleep better but also make me cheerful and receptive, and I can have long conversations before I get tired. These pills are just what I need.

Roman, too, has left for the West. He's living in Paris. His first film, *Knife in the Water*, which he took with him when he left Poland, has made him famous in France. The last time I saw him, he told me about a new film he's making. It deals with fear, disgust, escape from physicality, a young woman's loneliness.

Even today I still believe that I was the inspiration for this film.

Ryszard is also gone; he now lives in America. He was lucky enough to get permission to emigrate shortly after he left school because he has relatives there. I'd like to visit him, but I can't get out of Poland.

It is still a police state, although life in recent years has become somewhat more relaxed. There are still knocks on the door before dawn, and people are picked up without explanation. A critical comment or even the fact that one has friends abroad can lead to hours of interrogation. You have constantly to watch whom you talk to and what you talk about. If you're under suspicion, your mail is intercepted as a matter of course. An old writer whose work I often read was recently jailed because his daughter made some critical remarks about the Polish government in letters she sent him from abroad.

I have written a short story called 'Obok' – 'The Outsider, or, On the Other Side of the Wall.' It's about a young woman who can't find her own place in life:

A friendship of more than fifty years: 'Rysio' and Roma in Kraków in 1947, Ryszard Horowitz and Roma Ligocka in New York in 1997.

She was born in the middle of an argument. While her mother was giving birth, her father and the midwife were arguing noisily.

Her crib stood next to the wall that separated her room from her parents' bedroom. Every night her parents would argue on the other side of the wall. And afterwards they would make love. Both sounds made her feel sick. She often had to throw up in the middle of the night.

'She's vomiting again,' her mother would say reproachfully to her father.

'That's because you spoil her,' her father would say.

Years later, wherever the young woman goes she is surrounded by people. She can never be by herself. At last she finds an apartment of her own. Even there she's not alone:

After working in the library for thirty years she finally got a small apartment and spent an entire day furnishing it. In the evening she opened a bottle of red wine. The radio played soft music. She drank a toast to herself.

Then she went to bed.

In the middle of the night she woke up. Through the wall she heard the neighbours arguing; she heard their screams, heard them breathing. At dawn she died.

The story was published in a literary journal.

'What are you doing?' my grandmother asks.

It is late summer. The smell of the hot cobblestone pavement and apple trees comes in through the open window. I'm sitting on the floor pounding the keys of my old typewriter.

'I'm writing a play,' I reply, and go on typing. She nods. That's good. 'The main thing is that you eat enough and that you dress warmly.'

One of my friends is making a lot of money writing plays for the theatre. 'It seems to me writing a play would be easy,' I say to him on impulse, one evening. After all, I've been familiar with the theatre since childhood and still remember all the lines from Manuela's 'acting school'. It can't be that hard to write it all down. The publication of my story and several poems has given me quite a boost in self-confidence.

My friend laughs. 'You'll never pull it off,' he says.

While I was wondering what my play should be about, the news of Hemingway's suicide reached us. And all at once I was back to my old themes – loneliness and death. Why would a man like that, a man who had everything – fame, money, success – why would he kill himself? Why did he place so little value on his life?

My play is called *By the Way, We Must Get Rid of Father* and it is about Hemingway and his children. It's an ironic piece, even though it's about suicide. But, then, irony is the literary language of my generation.

For three weeks I write as if possessed. I don't go out and eat hardly anything. Marynia brings me tea now and then.

I give the manuscript to the secretary at the Municipal Theatre – she makes a little extra money by doing some typing on the side. She thinks my play is extraordinary and passes it to the artistic director.

A few days later I get a call from the theatre.

'Ms Ligocka? The director would like to see you.'

I put on something pretty, do my hair, apply some lipstick and rush off. The director, a huge man in his mid-fifties, is waiting for me at the door to his office.

'Well, my dear girl, which of your lovers wrote this play?' He grins at me.

'You mean you don't think I wrote it myself?' I reply indignantly.

'You don't need to do this sort of thing,' he bellows. 'Surely you have other talents.' With that he smiles at me lasciviously.

I feel tears coming to my eyes; my face is burning. The manuscript is lying on his desk. I grab it and run down the stairs, out into the street.

The secretary comes running after me. 'Wait! Please wait,' she pants. 'He wants to produce your play.'

I refuse to believe her. And I don't want to have anything to do with the play any more. All I did was make a fool of myself.

A couple of days later the telephone rings again. It's the director himself. 'We want to put on your play,' he says. 'Is the third of March all right with you?'

I can scarcely believe it. I grab Marynia and do a dance of joy with her. Then I call my mother in Vienna. She is happy for me, and I can hear that she is proud of me, finally.

They want to hire a young talented director for my play. He has caused a sensation in the Polish theatre. His name is Jan Biczycki, and he's kind of a celebrity. He directs a satirical student cabaret in Warsaw.

A few weeks later he comes to Kraków. We make a date to meet in a café.

*　　*　　*

Through the glass door of the café I can see him sitting in the semi-darkness at one of the tables at the back. A cigarette hangs from the corner of his mouth and he is reading.

I walk slowly towards him. He doesn't even look up, so deeply absorbed is he in what he is reading. It's my play.

He reminds me of James Dean. He's wearing a plaid jacket; his blond hair is tousled and hangs down into his face, making him look as though he hasn't slept for days. He has a beautiful mouth. My heart starts to beat a little faster.

He looks up. 'So you're Roma?' he asks absentmindedly, stubbing out his cigarette. 'Your play isn't bad. But unfortunately I have no time to do it.'

I'm annoyed to feel myself blushing.

Jan Biczycki is hopelessly romantic. He's lovable, absentminded and impractical. His life is in utter chaos. He has no sense of time or distance and absolutely no appreciation of money. All he owns in life are a leather tie from Paris, a grey sweater, the plaid James Dean jacket, a pair of trousers and the shoes he's wearing.

I order a cup of tea and sit down. The entire conversation consists of my clumsy attempts to persuade him to direct my play, even though he has no time.

When we part he looks at me for a long time and brushes a finger over his lips. 'OK,' he says. He sighs. 'I'll do it.'

I get the distinct impression that his consent has more to do with me than with the play.

Dear Mama,
Guess what. I've fallen in love with the man who's directing my play! His name is Jan and he's blond, intelligent, and funny. I think you'd like him. Even though he isn't Jewish. I hope I'll get my passport soon so that I can at last visit you and tell you everything. It's bitterly cold here in Kraków; possibly the coldest winter of the century – on many days it goes down to thirty-two below zero [–40°C]. But don't worry,

I'm in good health and I wear the lovely warm things you sent me.
A thousand kisses, your Roma

Jan and I meet in the tiny room the theatre management has rented for him. We can't stay in my apartment because Marynia wouldn't permit sinful behaviour in her presence.

The room has no heat. The water in the sink is frozen. Because I want to look beautiful, I wear diaphanous dresses and petticoats, trying not to feel the cold.

I am fascinated by Jan.

One side of him is light-hearted and cheerful, the other melancholy and lonely. It is so deeply familiar, and I feel an instinctive need to take care of him.

His life is a terrible mess. He is constantly shuttling back and forth between three apartments in three different cities. He never knows where to find anything, is always losing things: his train tickets, his keys, his money. But his charm is irresistible, his laughter infectious. He has a beautiful voice and sings and dances at every opportunity.

'Another one of those men who's broke,' Marynia says grimly. She still holds it against me that I got divorced. But Jan wins her over in no time, singing church hymns and gypsy love songs with her in the kitchen. And he can cook, too.

Even though we're very much in love, we wouldn't dream of getting married. Jan thinks – and he's right – that he'd be no good as a husband. And for me what matters most is the première of my play, in spite of all the chaos and infatuation. It is Jan's idea that I should do the costumes and stage design. So I often work late into the night on my designs while he's in the kitchen with Marynia making *Kluski*.

Finally, everything is ready: My play opens. It's a big hit.

All the papers cover it. They call me the Polish Françoise Sagan – young women writers are all the rage right now. True, the critics have mixed reactions to this Western-oriented piece, but I get many offers to write; there's even one from the recently formed television company. I see myself in the future alternating between the worlds of painting and writing.

A few months after the première I unexpectedly get permission to visit my mother in Vienna. She lives in a pleasant little furnished apartment: pink bed, kidney-shaped coffee tables, pink plush-upholstered armchairs, and a small balcony. Vienna is old-fashioned but lively and full of temptations. However, we don't stay there long. My mother has resolved to fulfil her lifelong desire to visit Italy.

Rome, Naples, Capri. I still have a photograph taken on this trip; it shows us standing arm in arm in front of the Fontana di Trevi in Rome. My mother has become a bit plump, but she looks happy. I have long hair, heavy dark eyebrows, a tiny waist – like a typical model of the time – and I smile my Audrey Hepburn smile into the camera.

One day, on the Spanish Steps, I think I recognize a grey face in the crowd, but it's gone before I can be certain. Signor Grigio?

Once our Italian trip was over I had intended to go back to Kraków. But Jan has received a grant to work with Herbert von Karajan in Vienna for three months. He has decided to become the world's greatest director of the musical theatre.

With her mother in Rome (1963).

253

A short while later he arrives in Vienna.

Right from the start Jan and my mother get along famously. He wins her heart by singing sentimental pre-war popular songs, and she recognizes in him the little boy who has to be mothered. My mother, who always wanted more children, loves to mother people.

Jan and I sleep on the couch in the living room. He spends most of his time chasing after Karajan but hardly ever sees the famous conductor, much less talk to him. The great maestro, his hair awry, hurries through the Vienna Opera House, followed by a bevy of people whose sole purpose is to protect him from the outside world. A few times Jan takes me along as bait, but we never catch him. Occasionally we're permitted to attend rehearsals, but mostly we're told the maestro is in a bad mood and people with unfamiliar faces must go.

Nevertheless, Jan makes a lot of contacts, and we get tickets for all the opera performances in Vienna. Jan's German is excellent because he spent the war years with his family in Vienna and attended school there. Now and then he reads Rilke to me: 'Listen to this,' he says, 'this is German too,' because I still refuse to learn the hated language.

> *Reiten, reiten, reiten*
> *durch den Tag und durch die Nacht . . .*
>
> *Riding, riding, riding*
> *through the day and through the night . . .*

When I arrived in Vienna, the first thing I saw was a sign: HALTEN VERBOTEN ('No Stopping'). These words have the power to turn me to stone. I find the city and its people are mostly nice, but when they start to talk or when a tram inspector appears, I get panicky. Jan thinks my reactions are ridiculous. 'Don't exaggerate,' he chides me. 'Don't make such a fuss.'

That remark has stayed with my all my life.

One evening we are again at the opera.

We have wonderful box seats. A gaunt old American woman, wearing an elegant pink jacket embroidered with pearls, is sitting in the chair next to us. I love her jacket. I can't take my eyes off it. The house lights go down, the hall is dark, but all I can think of is the jacket. It would look much better on me; she really ought to give it to me.

Suddenly the lights come on, and the artistic director walks out on stage. 'Ladies and gentlemen, we have just received word that President Kennedy has been shot.'

Absolute silence. Then the American woman in our box starts to sob. She throws herself on Jan's shoulder. She seems to be suffocating. He unbuttons the neck of her dress.

Kennedy's death affects me deeply. But as we leave, I see the little jacket thrown carelessly over the back of the woman's chair, and I have to stop myself taking it.

The telephone rings: it's a call from Warsaw.

Jan has been offered the directorship of a musical theatre in the capital. It would make him the youngest artistic director in Poland.

We go back.

In Warsaw we live in a rented furnished room on the sixth floor of a building without a lift. Jan is full of bold plans. He works day and night, paying the actors out of his own salary because there's not enough money in his budget.

It's an exciting time for us. We're part of the world of the *beautiful people* in the Poland of the sixties. We go to parties and premières and get to know lots of interesting men and women: everybody who's anybody. Marlene Dietrich, who is appearing in a play in Warsaw, talks with Jan half the night about music and old hits.

I start to get offers to design costumes and stage sets. My first assignment is a play by Bernard Shaw.

As the girlfriend of the artistic director I'm also busy organizing our lives. On his own Jan would get everything mixed up – he'd lose track of his appointments, misplace the script of the piece he's staging, and again and again forget to take his money. So I take care of him.

I neglect my own career and continually postpone my writing. I still have some of the earnings from my play and can afford to buy nice clothes.

I know we ought to get married. A chief artistic director needs a wife. It's also my mother's fondest wish. But Jan has many doubts about marriage, and even I can see he's not the sort of man to have a family – though he would like one. He had a fairly loveless childhood, one of nine children raised by a strict stepfather, always drawing the short straw. There's been too little security in his life. Jan often brings me flowers and is very kind to me, but he's afraid of commitment.

He goes repeatedly to the government offices to apply for a larger apartment. They urge him to join the Communist Party and suggest he stages fewer Western musicals like *Oh, What a Lovely War* and *My Fair Lady*. But he wouldn't think of letting the authorities dictate which plays he can and can't present.

All in all, it doesn't look as though we could ever lead a normal life. But I don't mind. As always, life is a dress rehearsal – the performance will start later, some day.

'I'm afraid we really have to get married,' Jan says, wrinkling his brow and smiling. He has received an invitation to direct at the Salzburg Festival. Naturally we want to go together. We could earn enough money there to buy an apartment in Warsaw. But will they permit us to leave Poland together? Probably not. The authorities are afraid that people will stay in the West. So, one of the partners has to stay at home – as security, so to speak. But if we were to get married, we could file an official application for a honeymoon trip to Salzburg. Up to now no one has ever done that.

'Should we give it a try?'

I look at Jan sitting there, his blond hair tousled, a cigarette in the corner of his mouth. How could he ever manage without me? He needs me.

'Sure,' I say, 'Let's get married.'

Sitting in a restaurant late one night, I hear that our plan has worked.

Jan had got into a fight with a heavyweight boxer at the bar. The huge man had reached for Jan's spectacles. Jan isn't very strong, but when he's angry he's like a bear. He punched the boxer in the face. Taken by surprise, the guy swayed, then suddenly keeled over and just lay there. Everybody in the place cheered.

Jan came back to our table, casually wiping his hands on his pants. 'By the way,' he says, 'we got permission to travel.' I nearly keel over, too. 'Now we've *got* to travel – with you as my wife.'

Jan is beaming; we kiss. More cheers. Corks pop.

Of course Jan has no time for wedding details. I have to get him a suit and have a dress made for myself. We can't buy wedding rings because you can't buy gold in Poland. A woman I know gives me her old rings.

Eventually we get an appointment at the register office. Because there aren't any flowers to be had for a bridal bouquet, Jan gets up early that day, drives out to the country and picks an armful of wild flowers. Then he disappears into the theatre again.

He's sure to be late, I tell myself. Plagued by a dark foreboding, I phone his secretary and beg her to remind him of the appointment at the register office. But in spite of that Jan is late.

When at last we arrive, our witness, a pop singer, is already there, waiting for us. 'People kept coming up to me, asking if I've been stood up,' she complains. 'I've had to get rid of several reporters.'

We're hot and we're upset, but we get married. After the ceremony a drunken photographer takes some pictures. The blurred wedding photograph still stands on my nighttable.

Afterwards we go to eat at one of the better hotels. From there I call my mother. 'Jan and I just got married, Mama.'

24 June 1965: Roma and Jan Biczycki.

'*Mazel tov*,' she says.

It is a bright, long summer night.

Early the next morning we go to the station, still afraid that at the last minute one of us won't be allowed to leave. A ministry official is supposed to bring our passports to the platform – if they haven't changed their minds. They might have seen through our subterfuge. After all, we have no right to passports; nor do we have the right to complain.

Marynia holds on to my key to the little basement apartment in Kraków. She and her niece will live there, watching over the green-tiled dresser, the bookshelves with the beautiful art books, and the desk on which sits my old typewriter. All I take is one suitcase full of nice dresses and a few photographs. Any more luggage would make us too conspicuous. And, besides, we intend to come back soon.

Time passes slowly while we wait on the platform. The train is almost ready to move when the ministry official we've been waiting for hurries towards us. He hands us our passports and, our hearts pounding, we climb aboard. The doors

are closed, the conductor blows his whistle, and the locomotive begins to chug.

We hug each other. What a relief. Neither of us has an
inkling that our wedding trip will last thirty years.

I I

The West welcomes us with open arms – my mother's. She is at the station in Vienna to meet us.

We have so much to tell her, and only a short time to do it. After a couple of nights on her living-room couch, it's on to Salzburg, where we'll be working on a musical for the next few months. The play isn't particularly good, but we meet some interesting people. Many actors who would later achieve fame in Germany are in the cast. It's summer-time, we're in love, and we're earning a lot of money.

Then it's autumn and the job ends. Like everyone else from the East, we have asked that our salary be paid in cash. For us a cheque is only a piece of paper. Now we're sitting in a café with a lot of cash in our pockets, wondering what to do next. 'I've called Warsaw,' Jan says. 'They say student riots have broken out in Poland. A couple of my friends are involved. The students are demanding reforms and they're being arrested and jailed. Everybody says not to come back right now.' He sounds depressed.

My stomach contracts. Jan has been getting many strange phone calls recently warning him not to go back to Poland. Evidently the authorities believe he's associated with the rebellious elements in Warsaw. Considering his Western-oriented work, he's been a thorn in their side all along.

We don't know what to do. Should we stay or risk going back? *I* would rather go back so I can get on with my writing. Here in Austria, not speaking the language, I feel as though I were deaf and dumb. But what if they put Jan in jail?

'There are wonderful opportunities for you here in the West,' our new friends say. 'We'll help you.'

We decide to wait to see what happens. We put all our cash into a little makeup case and take it and the suitcases to the station. Jan is as restless as ever. We board a crowded train for Vienna.

Not until we're sitting in our seats and the train has rolled out of the station do we realize that we've left the little makeup case containing most of our cash on the platform.

In Vienna the public-address system rips us out of the daze we've been in. 'Last stop. Everyone off.'

Of course, now that we have no money it's impossible for us to go back to Poland.

Again we sleep on my mother's living-room couch, and she feeds us for a while. But she has only a meagre pension, and her place is simply too small for three people.

That winter, we rent a small apartment belonging to an actress who has an out-of-town commitment. Every day in icy weather we walk from there diagonally across the city to eat at my mother's – because for the price of two tram tickets you can buy a couple of breakfast rolls.

In spite of all this Jan and I are happy. We daydream about what we'll do when we finally get some money.

We do not talk about the past. Of course Jan knows what happened to my mother and me during the war.

He is always late. And when he doesn't come home on time I stand at the window, waiting and wondering if something has happened to him and imagining the worst: he's dead, beaten senseless, run over, in hospital . . .

Then, when he finally shows up, there's a fight. He can tell straight away how anxious I've been, and that makes him furious. I try desperately to make him understand that I can't help it.

'You're hysterical,' he says. 'Can't you ever switch off your sick imagination?'

I start to cry, stop eating. Jan is silent and ignores me. He is exhausted and feels guilty. Once, out of spite, he goes off for two days and stays overnight with a friend. During those hours I nearly die of fear and anxiety.

At some point we make up again. I want so much to trust in Jan – in life – but I can't.

On Christmas Eve we go to the market with what money we still have and buy a huge pine tree with cones. It is so big no one else wanted it. We drag it to our tiny apartment and set it up. It fills the entire room. We have to crawl under the branches to get into bed.

That's all we can afford that Christmas. We spend the afternoon at my mother's, and in the evening we go home and make soup with potatoes and bouillon cubes.

Even though we have no money and no work, we get to know lots of other artists who, like us, are having a hard time. We often go to restaurants with these new friends and sit there with rumbling stomachs, not sure whether we've been invited or whether we have to pay for the meal ourselves. Jan explains that I don't eat anything because I'm watching my figure. Actually I'm so thin I'm almost transparent.

Then Zbigniew Herbert comes to Vienna. He is an important Polish poet, almost a legend, and both Jan and I admire him enormously – but we know him only by name. There is to be a literary gathering in one of the cafés, and that evening we are there, waiting for Herbert to arrive. But the famous poet doesn't come. The group breaks up; people leave. Jan and I are practically by ourselves, bitterly disappointed.

'Are you waiting for Zbigniew Herbert too?' Jan asks a small, chubby, unprepossessing man sitting at the next table.

'I *am* Zbigniew Herbert,' he replies.

We had been waiting for a tall, blond, handsome poet in a velvet coat.

When the café closes, the three of us go to a Hungarian restaurant where they play the *czardas*. Jan and Zbigniew end up dead drunk, and I have to bundle them home. The poet sleeps on the floor.

From that night on we remain friends. He often comes to see us and, in a gentle, Platonic way, he falls in love with me. I'm a kind of muse for him. The men drink, talk, recite poetry. Zbigniew writes a poem for me:

Dla Romy
   Mówi kobieta
Zgódi się namnie, bo miesiąc się zmienia
Nie odchodi dalej niżli mitość moja . . .

For Roma
The woman says
The moon is changing
Go no farther away than my love will carry you . . .

One day I realize I'm pregnant. Jan turns ashen when I tell him. 'What are we going to do now?' he stammers, reaching for his cigarettes.

I had hoped, absurdly, that he would be happy – but, of course, I know as well as he that there couldn't be a worse time to have a child than now. We have no money, no work, not even a permanent apartment, and we don't yet know there's public assistance available in the West. Besides, our documents are invalid. Nothing is valid. Whenever Jan goes to Germany to look for work, he has to apply for a visa. We don't even have health insurance.

It is February, I'm almost in my twelfth week and, like two despairing children, we're waiting for a miracle.

We can't keep the child, but abortion is illegal in Austria. We don't tell my mother. She would only have worried, and we want to spare her. After all, she's gone through enough already. Only Zbigniew knows about it. He stared at me long and hard one day and asked why I looked so unwell. And I poured out my heart to him. Shortly thereafter, he surreptitiously pushed a bundle of money towards me, 'For the operation . . .'

Somehow Jan has got the address of a doctor in Hungary, and we take the train to Budapest. It is a dark, grey day. I press my face against the compartment window. *Don't do it, don't do it, don't do it,* the wheels clack. *Don't do it . . .*

We walk through the streets of Budapest looking for the address Jan was given. Once before I walked through the streets of another city, looking for an address . . .

'This way,' Jan says.

We go down a long street. At its end there's a stone portal. Behind it a courtyard with tall, old houses.

'That's it,' Jan whispers. 'Not much further.'

The street seems endless to me, but at last we're there.

Don't do it, don't do it, don't do it . . .

Jan stops, looks at me. He is pale and nervous, the cigarette in the corner of his mouth trembles. 'We're here,' he says, in a flat voice.

Something inside me screams, *No! I don't want to do this. I want to keep my child.*

But I merely nod.

We go through the courtyard, enter a dilapidated house, climb the stairs to the fourth floor. A doctor's office. The man has been expecting us. He looks at me briefly, pushes us quickly into the apartment and closes the door. 'The neighbours,' he whispers. He's wearing a seedy suit, he's balding, and his eyes are small and watery. Jan hands him some money. He slips it into his jacket pocket.

'Come this way,' he says. I sense that he wants to get it over with, wants to get rid of us. We follow him through a large old apartment, through many rooms. He doesn't say much. We go through a doctor's examination room, then a kitchen, and finally to a small room beyond the kitchen. The linoleum floor smells of disinfectant.

A thin older woman wearing glasses arrives. I am instinctively afraid of her. She doesn't look at me.

'It has to be done quickly,' she says to Jan, 'and she must not scream.'

They put me down on a table, undress me—

They put me on my bed, undress me, hold little round glasses over a candle till they're hot and stick them on my naked back . . .

Over there in the corner? My grandmother? What is she saying to me; I can't understand her—

'Run!' my grandmother whispers. 'Run away! Quickly! Don't do it!'

But I just lie there mute, unable to move, as though paralysed. I want to run away, to scream, to explain that I'm sorry, that I've changed my mind, but I don't have the nerve. Because we have already paid them the money, because it has been arranged, and because I don't know how to tell them. If someone had asked me again if I wanted to go through with it, I would have said no. But no one asks. They treat me like an inanimate object. They speak only to Jan.

'She won't be getting anaesthesia,' they tell him. 'It's too dangerous. You have to hold her down.'

Jan takes a deep breath. He puts his hand on my arm, but doesn't look at me.

I try to whisper, 'Jan,' but no sound crosses my lips. I wish he'd say something. After all, he can see that this is horrible, that we can't stay here.

Still he doesn't say anything.

And now it's too late. They take hold of me and tear my child out of me, slowly, piece by piece. The fiery pain flares up to my neck, into my head; my body is full of fire and blood. And just then I know that it's a girl, that they are killing my daughter and that I can't stop them.

Jan and the woman are holding me down.

As soon as I begin to whimper, she hisses at me to be quiet. And once again I'm not allowed to scream.

It takes for ever.

It's dark outside when I'm allowed to get up. I'm unsteady, sway a bit.

'Make sure that she doesn't faint on the stairs going down,' the balding man says sternly to Jan. 'Walk as though nothing has happened.'

We walk as though nothing has happened. The man stands at the top of the stairs, watching us. We take a taxi to the hotel. I get into bed, cover myself. I'm cold. Jan brings another blanket and sits down next to me, pale and perplexed. We don't know what to say to each other.

'I think I'll go out for a bit, if that's all right with you,' he says, after a while, and gets up. 'They're doing *Hamlet* at the theatre here. I ought to see it.'

I say nothing and turn over on my side.

The following day we return to Vienna.

Finally we get work again, staging plays in small basement theatres for people who produce avant-garde pieces in studio theatres, including some Polish theatre of the absurd. Absurd is all the rage just now.

We don't get paid much. Then, while I'm still imagining what we might do with our next pay cheque – a holiday or buying something practical for our apartment – Jan invites everyone to an opening-night party. I sit there and watch our last penny disappearing into the wineglasses of our guests.

I'm learning how to conjure something out of nothing – especially at work. I had lots of practice using cheap ordinary materials in socialist Poland. Without money, without a proper staff, and without knowing the language, I manage to create stage sets and costumes that are received with admiration and praise. I have to be better than the others, or I may not get the next assignment.

But deep down I know I don't have the strength – physical or psychological – for all this. After each première I am ill, often for weeks at a time. 'It's psychosomatic,' the doctor says. 'It'll pass.'

My mother covers me with a blanket and makes soup for me.

We get a job in a theatre on the Ku'damm, and move to West Berlin. There we rent a nice one-room apartment on Kantstrasse. It has old wooden floors that we paint a dark colour; the walls are white. A big bed stands in the centre of the room and there are lots of gramophone records: Maria Callas, the Beatles. Friends from Salzburg arrive with a car full of household equipment for us. Our first real home.

I'm amazed at the bizarre destiny that has driven us to the very place where I never, in my life, wanted to be. Now Jan insists that I learn German. Of course he's right. I can't even go shopping. I try to learn the hated language, but it's difficult. Again and again there are moments when all my old fears suddenly flare up – whenever I see men in uniform, whenever someone shouts. On an escalator an old man yells at me, 'STAND ON THE RIGHT, WALK ON THE LEFT! (RECHTS STEHEN, LINKS GEHEN!)' I promptly answer, 'Sieg Heil!' The shudder of horror and the trembling come later.

'Don't exaggerate so much,' Jan says.

For the first time in my life I'm a housewife. Until then we lived mostly on toasted bread with garlic, but eating only bread is getting on Jan's nerves. So I decide to surprise him with a fabulous meal. I start by going to a grocery store.

What to buy? I stare in confusion at the overwhelming selection. Fruit, vegetables, all sorts of cheeses I've never seen before, huge quantities of cold cuts and meat. I don't have

the vaguest idea how to prepare all these good things. I buy
a little roasted chicken. At home I decorate it lovingly with
parsley and proudly set it on the table.

Jan is delighted. 'You see?' he says. 'Where there's a will
there's a way!' But when he turns the little chicken over to
carve it, he discovers the shop label.

I often drive Jan to despair.

I am homesick for Kraków, especially when I can't sleep
at night. I miss the ringing of the church bells, my books,
my friends. I'm a stranger here in the West. Fortunately we
move in artistic circles and many of our colleagues come from
other countries and, like me, they are strangers here.

I often wander through the ruins in the Kreuzberg section
of Berlin and rummage around in second-hand shops trying
to find things for the stage. For our new play, we are
building a set with movable walls. After standing on a
ladder for weeks, painting it all, I'm sick again, this time
pneumonia.

My recurring illnesses are a nuisance for Jan. But he
mothers me good-naturedly and brings hot soup to my
bedside.

Then we move again. First to Cologne, then back to Vienna,
then once more to Berlin – I seem forever to be packing and
unpacking. Sometimes I don't remember which city we're in.
All theatre cafeterias look the same.

That summer we go on our first holiday together. Finally.
We badly need to unwind a little, to get away from everything, to get away from the theatre. I book us on a cheap
bus tour to Italy: a few days in a small hotel by the sea, and
then a weekend in my beloved Venice.

The heat in Venice is stifling. In spite of that we enjoy
every minute, sitting in small cafés, and strolling through the
city. But one day, just as we turn into a dark narrow alley,
I see a dead pigeon floating in the canal. Gasping for air, I
begin to tremble and grab Jan's arm. 'Let's go somewhere

else,' I whisper. 'I don't want to walk through there.'

Jan doesn't understand what's wrong with me. He thinks I'm just making a silly fuss again. 'Stop that nonsense. This is the shortest way to the Rialto, and we're going to take it – *basta.*'

'But, Jan, I can't . . . the pigeon . . .'

'The pigeon is dead, damn it. And, besides, Venice is full of pigeons. If you can't stand it, then we might as well turn round and go home! Come on, don't be like that.'

He grabs my arm and pulls me along, past the dead pigeon.

Something inside me breaks with a soft shattering sound. Like glass.

We've been hired by the Municipal Theatre in Dortmund. Professionally this is a big step up. Jan is happy. I am, too, because now we move into a beautiful bright apartment. It's in an old villa next to a brewery. We have the entire upper floor, and can wander around from room to room. I've never had so much space before. The only problem is the sweetish smell that drifts over from the brewery. It makes me feel nauseous.

Those days when dark clouds hung over the ghetto. That sweetish smell.

'It's the smell of fermented hops,' Jan explains.

Because we have no furniture I design our apartment like a stage set. Furnishing it is a lot of fun. I buy material and drape it artistically. For fifty marks I pick up an ugly dark bedroom set, which I paint white and gold. The apartment looks like an enchanted castle, like a set for an opera.

But why do I always feel nauseous? Probably from the smell of the paint.

I go to see a doctor.

'You're pregnant,' he says, adding some other words I don't understand.

What will my mother say? And Jan?

*　　*　　*

'We'll manage,' he says, 'trust me.'

Jan is very happy about the baby. Perhaps he wants us both to forget what happened in Budapest. We celebrate with a bottle of wine, by candlelight, at our new white-and-gold painted kitchen table.

I'm a little nervous because my mother is coming next week. She thinks of me as an impractical princess. I wonder if she'll think me capable of being a mother.

When I meet her at the station I don't even want to tell her. But then a little later I feel sick again. She gives me a quick look – her nurse's look – and immediately guesses what's up. 'You're pregnant, Roma!' she cries, and embraces Jan. 'I'm going to be a grandmother! *Mazel tov*, Roma, *mazel tov*.'

I'm relieved and surprised. Only now do I realize I was actually afraid I had done something wrong again. Still, I don't feel happy, not yet.

At dawn every day we take the train to Cologne where we're staging a Broadway-type play. We work all day long and come home late at night. Only then do I start to cook. It doesn't occur to me or Jan that I should be taking it easy. Our work comes first. In Jan's family the women always worked till they dropped.

Gradually my belly gets bigger. I'm mounting a big musical, doing the stage settings and costumes. It's very strenuous work. I sometimes have to crawl through the paint work-shop on all fours when I can't stand upright any more. There's little time to enjoy being pregnant. But I like my fat belly – though I don't quite understand what's happening inside me. How is it possible that another being is alive in there when I myself feel like an embryo?

Sometimes, sitting in our kitchen, I sink into one of my depressions. I feel so tired, so tired all the time.

Jan doesn't understand any of this. 'Why are you sitting there like that?' he asks. I can't explain it to him. Maybe it's because of the pregnancy. I don't want to accept the fact that these depressions keep recurring. I look for their cause in the hard work, the commuting back and forth, keeping house, carrying our child.

'The apartment's a mess,' Jan says. In his family the women always kept their apartments spotless. 'There's not a thing to eat in the house. Shouldn't you get up and go shopping? And what about the meeting tonight?'

Jan always wants a thousand things. But I just sit there.

If it's a boy we'll call him Jakob, the name of my mother's younger brother, who was killed when the Germans blew up the munitions factory. And if it's a girl . . . But it's not going to be a girl. I can feel it.

It's 11 April. The baby is due on 20 April, Hitler's birthday. 'Don't you dare have it on that date!' Jan threatens jokingly.

That day our landlady gives us notice. She has probably found someone who will pay her more rent. We still don't know that we have certain legal rights, that we could fight back. But we're foreigners, immigrants – it would never occur to us to protest. Quite the opposite. Jan even has to stop me packing our suitcases that same evening.

'We'll go to the police,' he says.

'I don't want to,' I say. I'm afraid.

'Don't always be like that,' Jan says. 'Where else can we go now?'

The next morning we go to the police. The officers are quite friendly. They notice my belly, make some phone calls, then tell us that we can stay in the apartment two more weeks.

But we stay only a few more days. A week before I'm supposed to give birth, Jan unexpectedly receives an offer from the Municipal Theatre in Kiel. It doesn't take us long to pack our things.

On the way to Kiel I touch my belly and feel the baby

moving. Both of us are afraid it might be born on the train.

The first thing we do in Kiel is to buy a large pram. We don't have an apartment yet, but we're being put up in a little cottage that belongs to an affluent couple who are theatre supporters. The cottage turns out to be a small room with bunk beds, a tiny bath and a hotplate. That's where I spend the last few days before the birth of our child.

I'm lying in the garden. Everything around me is blooming and fragrant; I'm wishing it would always be like this. My appetite has suddenly become enormous. I eat almost constantly and make myself mountains of noodles in the villa's kitchen. For the first time in my life I'm free of gloomy thoughts and dreams. It's like being in a primitive, animal state: I get up in the morning feeling good, not worried about anything – that's the way I always wanted to be. And in the springtime garden in Kiel I succeed, for a short time.

As the delivery date approaches, I start to panic again. I can't believe that I'll have a healthy baby. Not me. I'm not one of those strong, healthy, radiant young mothers with their strong, healthy, pink babies. I really don't want a baby; I just want myself.

April 20 passes. Jan breathes a sigh of relief. But I get more and more nervous. The twenty-first comes and goes, the twenty-second, the twenty-third . . .

On 24 April there is a party in the villa. I'm sitting on the sofa with my big fat belly, surrounded by chattering women literally trying to outdo each other in telling me all the terrible things that can happen in childbirth. They talk about oxygen deprivation and heart sounds and forceps deliveries. I become very quiet. The hostess sees my distress and puts a bottle of Cognac in front of me.

'Have some,' she urges me. 'At this point it can't do any harm.'

I take a drink. The bottle is getting emptier. At one o'clock when we finally go to bed, I take the bottle and drink the rest. Shortly thereafter I feel a painful contraction in my abdomen.

That's not possible, I think. *It's probably just the Cognac or the party.* I turn on my side and try to go back to sleep. But the pain comes back. I don't dare wake Jan who's asleep in the upper bunk. He has to be at the theatre early in the morning. I get up quietly, pack my little suitcase, and plait my hair. The women at the party had said that's what you do. Then I sit on the edge of the bed like a schoolgirl, and wait.

Three o'clock, then four; slowly it turns light outside. It's quiet in the room but my heart beats very loudly. I go to the door and stand there with my little suitcase. Jan turns and mumbles something in his sleep.

'Jan,' I whisper timidly, 'Jan, I think we have to go to the hospital.'

Jan isn't the kind of man you wake up at four o'clock in the morning, no matter what.

'Try to go back to sleep,' he growls.

I lie down again, but it's no use. The pains come back at regular intervals.

'Jan!'

The clinic is nice and on this day I'm the only woman giving birth. They are all looking after me except the old midwife, who keeps dozing off in her chair.

They bring me something to eat, but I can't swallow it. Jan finishes off my food, even though he's not hungry either. The midwife feels my abdomen. 'It's a boy,' she says, and falls asleep again. Jan has also dozed off.

The hours pass. Then, suddenly, after an eternity of pain, I feel that something is happening in my belly. We're in danger, the child and I. Our lives are in danger.

'Jan! Get someone! Hurry!'

At the very last moment they save my baby, they save me.

When I come out of the anaesthesia, Jan is holding the baby in his arms.

It's a boy, and he's blond. A tiny smile flits over his face. Jan and I both cry. He's beautiful, and our very own. It's a miracle. 'Look, our son is blond!' I say. And this time Jan understands.

He rushes out of the hospital room and comes back with a pail full of red roses. 'I bought everything in the shop!' He beams. We count them; there are seventy-three. I am deeply moved, yet quick as a flash I figure out how much they must have cost.

That evening Jan calls my mother. 'Just imagine, Mama, he's blond. *Mazel tov.*'

Suddenly everything is all right. There are no more wounds. I am strong; I've done it; I am happy, invulnerable, armed against all danger, all the unhappiness of the world. No human being can harm me.

I'm floating on air.

The doctor is a big man, blond and broad shouldered, handsome. 'Aaah . . . our lovely Pole,' he says, smiling as he looks at my nametag.

Then he lifts Jakob up and looks him over. 'A gorgeous boy.'

I nod, pleased.

'What city in Poland are you from?'

'Kraków.'

'Kraków?' he says. 'I know it well. I was in Kraków as a soldier. During the war. You see . . .'

He still has my child in his arms.

I see . . . I close my eyes.

. . . The men in boots have turned their guns on us and are watching us. One of them is smoking a cigarette. He is as tall as a tree, and

under his hat you can see that his hair is shiny blond, his eyes as blue as the sky. He isn't smiling.

'WEITER! LOS!' I'm being pushed forward by the crowd, and I can't see the man in the boots any more. 'KENNKARTE! IDENTITY CARD!' They are checking documents. Right in front of us a young woman with a baby in her arms is dragged out of line by two of the men in boots. She cries and screams, but that just makes it worse. The blond man snatches the child away from her and throws it on the ground. Its head hits the hard cobblestones with a dull thud.

'Doctor,' I whisper weakly, 'if you had met me back then I wouldn't be here now. Please give me my child.'

'But what's the matter?' He looks at me uncomprehending, surprised, hurt. He still has Jakob in his arms.

The thought flashes through my mind that I'm not allowed to have this child, not allowed to do anything. I'm not allowed to be here, in this pleasant room with the roses, with my blond child. It's all a mistake. None of it is true.

The room starts to revolve – the doctor, the roses, the bed.

'Give me my child . . .'

'Give me my child . . .'

The nurse stands at my bedside. She is trying to take Jakob away from me.

'No, Nurse, please. Let him stay with me. Please, let him stay here.'

'But our little darling has to go to sleep now. And you do too.'

'No. Please. I can't.'

'Be sensible, Mrs Ligocka. *Give* me the child.' She looks at me, worried. Straightens her spectacles. 'Shall I get the doctor?'

'No, no! Don't.'

I'm sensible. I'm always sensible. I give her my child. The nurse lifts up the little blue bundle that was lying next to me and leaves the room with him.

I begin to cry.

I cry and cry and cry and cry.

I cry as though I have to spit out bloody scraps of memory. Never in all my life have I wept like this. I can't seem to stop.

I am gasping for air. Everything turns black.

Now they're standing around my bed – a young woman doctor and two nurses. Slowly I regain consciousness. 'You had a minor circulatory collapse,' one of them says. 'It happens.'

The doctor feels my pulse. 'Get a hypodermic, Nurse, and the circulatory medication . . . and a hot-water bottle. You can see she is very cold.'

They give me injections, drops, and the hot-water bottle. But it doesn't get better.

The older nurse looks at me with knowing eyes. 'Quickly, bring the baby to her,' she says to the younger woman.

They put the blue bundle back in my arms.

The older nurse looks at me, smiles. '*Niech yje Polska* – long live Poland!' she says. She is from Silesia, and this is the only Polish sentence she knows.

I stroke my son's little head. The last slanting rays of the April sun dance around the room and fall on his soft blond hair.

Slowly my heart begins to beat more calmly. I feel warmer. My weariness blends with the fragrance of the roses as I close my eyes and try to find that feeling lost within me – that feeling that is something like peace.

Jan is sitting next to my bed; he is pale, tense, nervous. 'What happened to you?'

I tell him about the doctor, but not about my memories. I have no words for that. Jan understands at once. He can imagine how I felt.

But he doesn't have time to stay. He is staging *The Tales*

of Hoffman with a cast of sixty. He puts his hand on my arm. 'Be happy with our little boy. Be happy with Jakob,' he says.

I nod and smile. He's right. Of course he's right. Yet the joy, the infinite peace, the beautiful crystal-ball feeling – they don't come back. I hold Jakob in my arms. I am happy with him – but the feeling of being invulnerable and protected is lost.

12

The cottage is much too small for two adults and a child.

Almost every day our hostess asks whether we've found an apartment yet. So, carrying the baby in a basket, we go looking for a place to live. The first apartment we see Jan says, 'Let's take it.'

It's small and dark, an underground hovel. I want something bright and beautiful for our child. As we're passing a sunny street that leads directly to the sea, I stop. 'This is where I'd like to live.'

'You're out of your mind!' Jan exclaims. 'There are only elegant villas here.'

But at the end of the street there's a house with a garden that extends almost to the edge of the water. It's covered in scaffolding and looks as though construction is still in progress.

'Please, Jan, let's just go and ask.'

Jan gives in, even though he thinks this is absurd. It turns out the house belongs to a family by the name of Jakob.

A good omen. They are finishing the attic for their son who intends to move in a year or two from now. Until then the place will be empty.

They rent it to us – three rooms, a kitchen, a bath and a view of the sea. The walls haven't been plastered or painted. So once again I roll up my sleeves, hang up lengths of material, set out bright-coloured wooden birds, dried flowers, toys and teddy bears – in short, I transform it into a cosy nest. We live there for six months – it's like a fairy-tale: husband and child and a lovely little house by the sea.

Autumn arrives and we have to move on, to Austria – Graz and Vienna; then back to Germany – Cologne and Frankfurt. For one winter we live in a vacation apartment in Spain. There, Jakob learns to walk and to say his first word, *adios*. After that to Sicily where the locals call Jakob *angelo* because of his blond curls. Then back to Vienna where we celebrate his first birthday with my mother.

Jakob has not been baptized. Jan never insisted on it; he has internalized both the Jewish and the Christian faiths like no one else I know. Sometimes he claims he is more Jewish than I am. We never talk about religion with my mother.

So we celebrate *all* the holidays with Jakob, Jewish as well as Christian ones.

We've been on the road for four years now, living in hotels, always just passing through, only guests. I'm working again and always take the child along with me.

We have accepted a wonderful offer for Jan to stage a Shostakovich opera in Copenhagen. The opera is *Katerina Izmailova*. I'm thrilled, because the costumes are a real artistic challenge. But sometimes working *and* taking care of Jakob is more than I can handle. Between rehearsals, while Jan is having coffee with the performers, I have to buy food for our child. Often I'm quite desperate and wish there were two of me.

The opera is a huge success. I think the costumes in Copenhagen are the most beautiful I have ever designed. They turned out so well even I was left speechless. Each dress was hand-embroidered; I transposed Russian art on to the stage. An entire wedding party, sixty performers, appear dressed in red. The murderous bride wears a red veil that flows about her like a cloud of blood. At the conclusion of the première everyone in the production bowed to the Queen's box. I was so thrilled, I didn't notice that all the rest of the cast had walked off and I was left standing on stage all by myself.

We were introduced to the Russian composer. Shostakovich

had been harassed by the Soviet regime all his life because some of his work didn't suit them; for a long time he was ignored before at last he became world-famous. He talks to us for hours about his youth during the time of the Russian Revolution.

Marlene Dietrich is appearing in Copenhagen's Tivoli Park. Both of us have admired her since we first met her in Warsaw. But this performance leaves us feeling depressed. She's as lovely as ever, but has lost her former radiance and seems a little shaky.

When Jan and I go backstage to say hello, we're surprised that no one stops us. Not a soul around. We knock on her dressing-room door.

'Come in,' she mumbles, haltingly.

Jan carefully opens the door. She is sitting at her makeup table, her back to us. Her wig is askew and her makeup is smeared. She doesn't turn round.

'I'm so tired,' she says.

We keep moving from one city to the next. Each time, even if it's only for three months, I try to furnish our temporary home as though we'll be there for ever. The constant travel is expensive because we have to drag all our belongings along, just like a circus.

Jakob is a dear, sunny boy and my primary joy.

I want my son to have a beautiful childhood. The best. I don't want to be reminded of my own childhood any more, but simply to do everything differently and better. For his first Christmas Jakob is surrounded by a mountain of toys. I can't think of anything nicer than buying toys. And although money is tight, I'd rather spend it on something foolish, something beautiful. Jan and I would never think of saving money to buy an apartment or a house. Where would such a house be – in Poland or in Germany? We don't know, and we don't worry about the future. We're just three people, passing through.

I often look at Jakob and think what a good thing it is that he doesn't know he's Jewish. He is blond, and we live in today's Germany.

Jan is a gentle, jolly father. He likes playing with his son and when he has time he changes nappies too. Except, unfortunately, he has little time. He always carries a photo of Jakob in his briefcase and shows it proudly to everyone. But when things get difficult he leaves Jakob's upbringing to me.

I can understand that. He has enough to do. We are fighting for survival in the theatre, outsiders trying to make our way in the 'wild' West.

Being a poor Polish immigrant in the affluent Germany of the sixties isn't easy. Sometimes people treat us as though we are Martians.

'Is Polish written in Cyrillic?' they ask. 'Are there polar bears in Poland?' Or they'll say, 'For foreigners you speak German quite well.'

In their eyes Poles are like poor savages. No one seems to understand that our poverty is the result of a dictatorship.

Jan isn't bothered as much by these humiliations; he ignores them. But I'm too often sick, can't sleep, get depressed and have anxiety attacks.

I would like to keep Jakob in bed with me, always. Several times during the night I get up to see whether he's still in his crib. Once when he swallowed some chewing-gum, I panicked and immediately called the poison control centre.

'Don't worry so much all the time,' Jan says.

It is a cold, foggy autumn, and we are back in Kiel, again staying in a house by the sea. When I don't have to go to the theatre, I'm alone with Jakob. I stroll along the beach with him for hours, listening to the hollow bellow of a foghorn, with a peculiar feeling of being cut off from all roots, of being nowhere, in nothingness. It's that life-is-a-film sensation: a woman wandering around with her child in Never Never Land.

The only way I can escape this empty feeling is by focusing

my attention on preparing Jakob's bottles, playing with him, or cooking something for him. When you have a child, you learn to cook with your heart. Luckily Jakob eats everything with boundless enthusiasm. How painful my refusal to eat on top of her constant worries about my health must have been for my mother.

But I never tell her that. I keep thinking, *Some day we'll talk about everything.* I believe that we have all the time in the world.

For Jakob's sake, I try to be cheerful, to push aside my fears.

As long as my mother is around, this is possible – to a degree. I can let her deal with all the difficulties and simply be a little girl who has a child. Usually I feel as though I have sore feet and must pull myself together in spite of the pain. Yet when I'm with my mother I can let go. I can lie down on the sofa while she bakes me a cake. I can leave my problems with her, even without actually talking to her about them – for instance, my difficulties with Jan. She says nothing. We would rather swap recipes than talk about feelings.

Only once is there a crack in the wall of silence. The man she loved has died. When she next comes to see us, she looks years older. She tells me how sad she was when she couldn't go to the funeral because his wife and children were there. After all these years it's the first time we speak intimately to each other. After that she resumes her silence.

Between us there is no way to communicate, there are no words. Only loving, tormented, disappointed silence.

She is, however, a wonderful grandmother. She and Jakob play the wildest games, crawling around under the tables together. On the spur of the moment she pours five pounds of sugar on to the floor of the balcony so that Jakob can play in the 'sand'. When he accidentally leaves his favourite blanket behind, she takes a taxi to the station, wearing a coat over her nightgown and delivers it to him. Jakob adores her. When she's with him, she can break into the sort of lighthearted laughter she never could share with me.

Sometimes he stays with her when I have to go to work.

I feel constantly torn between my career, the need to earn money, and the temptation simply to watch my child for hours on end. The pain of parting each time I have to leave Jakob behind is terrible. Again and again I go to a public telephone to call and ask how he's doing.

In spite of the difficulties, these years of wandering are professionally important to us. We form close bonds and establish ourselves on the theatre scene. But I am unable to build on my own professional successes, not even the one in Copenhagen, just as was the case with my writing in Poland. After a strenuous project I am always so worn out that I have to pull back, to get back the strength I have used in concealing my fears and anxieties. Then by the time I'm my old self again it's too late to pick up where I left off. They say that I may be among the most talented costume designers in the German theatre, that my work shows a special East European imagination and enormous intensity. But I simply can't manage a rapid career rise. I don't have what Roman has. He fought, he made a noise, he screamed. I turned everything inward, always felt I had to make myself small, silent and invisible. How can someone like me learn to be visible?

In Munich, Jan and I find work at the Institut für Theaterwissenschaft (Institute for Theatre Studies). Jan gives seminars on project realization, teaching students how to develop a play from inception to actual performance, and I show them how to make costumes and stage sets. The work is fun, and we like Munich. The city is home to lots of interesting people, and the weather is not as cold as it is in Kiel. Nor is it far from Vienna.

Jakob is now five, and I am seriously concerned about our future. He will have to start school soon. He needs to make friends, have a stable home, and should be allowed to grow up as a perfectly normal child. Up to now he's always played with

Reunited with Roman Polanski at the premiere of his production of Rigoletto *at the Munich Opera House (about 1976/7).*

actors, occupied himself with whatever there was backstage, constantly living in different apartments and different cities, eating on trains, and in general leading the life of a gypsy. It can't go on like that.

I ask Jan whether he wouldn't like to apply for a teaching position about to become available at this Munich acting school. I've seen how much pleasure he derives from working with young people. We'd have a regular income, a nice apartment, a normal life.

After moving more than twenty times I've become weary. I want to stay put.

It took six months to persuade Jan to apply at the school. He wanted the job so much that he didn't want to risk rejection. As a child he never got what he most wished for – so he'd rather give up without trying. Moreover, he had doubts about ever being able to settle down.

'I need my freedom,' he says. 'I want to direct plays.'

'And Jakob?' I ask. 'The child needs some regularity in his life. And we never have enough money.'

Jan nods. It's true. Our finances are always at the edge of catastrophe. We never know how long our funds will last.

'All right,' he sighs, 'I'll give it a try. But don't get your hopes up.'

Jakob and I are visiting my mother in Vienna when Jan phones. 'They hired me on the spot!' He sounds overjoyed. 'Now you can finally relax. And I've even found a marvellous little house surrounded by greenery, just right for us.'

'Are you sure?' I ask.

'Absolutely! It has a garden, a beautiful terrace, and lots of room. The village is nice, too, small, friendly, with a school and places to shop, and it's not far from Munich. It isn't expensive either.'

That's the deciding factor, of course.

The little house turns out to be half of a two-family house with square, dark stained-glass windows, plastic Venetian blinds, a ruler-straight hedge, and a tiny lawn. It stands on a cement-paved street along with eight other houses. My stomach contracts.

'Isn't it ideal?' Jan asks, opening the front door, which looks exactly like all the other front doors. Jan has already put up a name-card next to the doorbell.

'Just look, there are three bedrooms upstairs. We can each have a room of our own, and you'll finally have a place in which to paint. The living room even has wall-to-wall carpeting, and there's a workshop in the basement.'

I stare out of the window. Each of the windows looks out at the neighbours' houses.

'Come, I'll show you the village.'

The village has no market square, only a supermarket, a kindergarten, a school, a bus stop. Everything is square.

'Is it really not far from Munich?'

'Oh, only thirty or forty minutes. There's a bus.'

'Jan, don't you think we ought to look for an apartment in an older building in town? Then you wouldn't have so far to go every day.'

'Oh, that doesn't matter. I can read on the bus. No, no, you'll see, we'll be very happy here.'

But I sense we'll never be happy in this place. It feels like the end of the world.

13

'*Arbeit macht frei.*'

I flinch. But it's only our neighbour, saying hello over the top of our hedge. She nods at me cheerfully. I'm on the terrace about to plant a few pansies in a tub I just bought at the supermarket. Everyone around here has pansies.

'Good morning,' I say. She can't possible know what those words mean to me. She is stocky, robust and Bavarian. I'm sure she means well.

'Wouldn't you like to come over for a cup of coffee?' she asks.

We sit in her light brown kitchen with the flowered tiles. She offers me rolls. 'Just got them, they're still fresh.'

'No thanks,' I say.

'But you don't need to be on a diet!' She laughs and helps herself. 'A thin young thing like you. Are all the women in Poland this thin? You know, at first we all thought you were that nice Mr Biczycki's Spanish nanny. But then I found out that you're his wife!' She laughs heartily at her own wit.

I've never met anyone like her before.

'I think you'll have to excuse me now,' I mumble. 'I have to cook lunch, do a little more cleaning. But . . . please don't ever say those words again.'

'Which words?' she asks.

'"*Arbeit macht frei.*" You see, that's what it said over the gate at Auschwitz.'

'Auschwitz?' She's never heard of it.

*　　*　　*

Whenever possible I take Jakob to Munich. The bus trip is endless. We hang out in the city, go to a café, maybe a museum. But Jakob doesn't like art exhibitions, so we walk through the park for hours – anything, just to get away from the suburb.

Our house is still quite bare and not at all cosy. But I simply can't get myself to furnish it – I, who always loved to furnish every apartment we ever had. Nothing appropriate comes to mind, even though I keep trying. Everything there is so stiff, so normal, so banal. I feel like a mouse on a treadmill: doing the laundry, cooking, cleaning, mowing the lawn. There's always more to do, and whatever I do, I do it all wrong.

'You're exaggerating,' Jan says.

He is very happy with his new job and has finally discovered that what he likes to do most is to teach young people, to have an audience. All his life he has suffered from not getting enough attention. Perhaps that's why he went into the theatre in the first place. And I'm too busy to give him all he needs. But at school he is the centre of attention. His pupils love him. They come to our house all the time, and are encouraged to call him day or night. He's always there for them.

I can't stand having many people around me. It's as if I weren't there – Jan seems to have empathy for all the others, never for me.

At weekends he works in the garden or sits on the terrace with his pupils.

He's getting ever more settled, more sensible, more and more normal. Where is that enchanting lost boy I loved so much in him?

'Isn't it glorious?' Jan says, with a yawn. 'Our own home and garden. Come, Roma, let's mow the lawn.'

I don't want to mow the lawn. I just want to sit quietly in the garden enjoying the sunshine, and not talking to anyone. But I can't enjoy the sunshine when our next-door

*With her son Jakob
(about 1973).*

neighbour is bustling about, clearing her throat and rattling her coffee cups.

Jakob now goes to school.

I bought him a sailor suit – the same kind that Ryszard and I wore back then. It's one of the few childhood memories I like to recall. Jakob thinks it's silly.

At first he often came home from school crying. 'We have to pack up and leave,' he sobs. 'They all say we're foreigners and we're going to be arrested.' Each word is like the stab of a knife. How can I console him?

I assure him that this is all nonsense and that he is the best, the most beautiful and most intelligent person in the whole world. I want him to hear all the things that no one ever said to me as a child, and I'm convinced that if I say them often enough all his fears will dissolve. Unfortunately, Jakob senses the discrepancy between my words and what he hears others say. And he is beginning to believe the others.

In the meantime he's made friends, but things still aren't easy for him. As artists and foreigners in the suburbs, we simply don't belong. There are all those funny people who come to visit us. The neighbours find this peculiar. Children who come to our house are allowed to do all the things that are forbidden in their own homes – this, too, the neighbours hold against me. There's always a big plate of sweets on the table, and the children can jump and romp around on the furniture. I'm sure Jakob isn't unhappy, but he is painfully aware that he's different, just as I was 'different' at the Catholic elementary school. Jakob is good at sports. He attends Catholic instruction and has made friends with the pretty religion teacher who wears tight jeans and plays the guitar. No one at the school has an inkling that he's Jewish.

Sometimes, though, my over-protectiveness creates problems for him. I'm the only mother who still comes to pick her child up from school.

'Please, Mama, let me walk home by myself, like the others,' Jakob pleads with me.

Reluctantly, I give in.

Subconsciously, Jakob takes on my unspoken fears. He always senses what I feel, even when I assure him that everything is all right. Although Jan and I pretend we have no worries about money, Jakob quickly realises it's a lie. The older he gets, the more he realizes that the life of artists is full of constant, painful insecurity.

'I don't want to be an artist, Mama,' he says, looking very serious.

Jakob doesn't want to let himself be governed by fear, the way I am. For that reason, he is drawn to the most dangerous sports. But he worries about me at least as much as I do about him, just as I used to worry about my mother. Of course, I can tell that my excessive care annoys him.

Years later, I realized that the psychological wounds suffered by Holocaust victims also caused wounds in their children. But in those days I did not want to admit to it, so I didn't tell Jakob much about it. All my strength went into suppressing it. With will-power, and with love, I tried to shut out my memories. It didn't work.

The blue-tiled subway tunnel is deserted. The man has red hair and is wearing blue overalls. His arms reaching for Jakob are hairy . . . He pursues me through the subway station, through endless, brightly lit passages. I hold my child close, walk, then begin to run. I hear his panting directly behind me, feel his damp, hot breath on the back of my neck. I run for my life, for Jakob's life. Down on to the rails, into the tunnel. A train is coming. Its wheels turn slowly. I have to save my child, have to save my child, have to save my child . . . He grabs me—

I wake up drenched in sweat. Impossible to go back to sleep, so I go down to the kitchen, drink some tea, and stare out of the window at the neighbour's garden.

At seven o'clock on the dot the vacuum cleaner next door starts to drone. I wake up Jakob and make breakfast for him. A little later Jan comes thumping down the stairs. 'Oh, by the way,' he says, between gulps of coffee, 'you know that the key to the workroom downstairs broke off in the lock, don't you? I asked the locksmith to come over. He said he'd be here this afternoon.'

Once again I'm surprised by this new, practical side Jan has developed since he becoming a home 'owner'. I promise to take care of the locksmith.

At noon Jakob takes a little nap, and by then I've forgotten all about the lock. The bell rings. Sure that it's the woman next door, I sigh and open the door.

A red-haired man stands before me; even his arms are covered with red hair. He's wearing blue overalls. My heart begins to race. I panic and try to slam the door shut, but he holds it open. 'I'm the locksmith,' he says, with a heavy Bavarian accent. 'You have a key that snapped in the lock?'

I nod. I let him in – into my house, where my child is sleeping upstairs.

'In the basement . . .' I manage to say. Then I flee up the stairs into Jakob's room and lock the door behind me.

Jakob is fast asleep. Nothing happens. Nothing at all. I listen. Clattering sounds from down below, drilling, hammering, then, 'Mrs Biczycki? Mrs Biczycki?'

I don't answer, push myself against the door and hope fervently he won't come upstairs.

After a while I hear departing footsteps, and the front door is shut.

I breathe a sigh of relief and tiptoe down the stairs. The locksmith's bill is lying on the bottom step.

*   *   *

By now I'm merely playing roles: the charming wife, the good mother, a suburban housewife. At the parties to which we are more and more frequently invited I play the successful artist, wearing an original dress; no one can tell that it comes from the flea-market. If only for a few moments I'm happy to be among these beautiful, famous people who don't seem to have any worries, who are so different from my neighbours. I briefly allow myself to be infected by their gaiety. Still, these evenings are hard because it takes such an effort to maintain the mask.

The pictures I paint during this period are pale and lack vigour. I always feel guilty when I paint. Compared to all my duties and obligations it seems a sheer waste of time, time misspent.

I make my first attempts to work in television and film. From time to time Jan and I are hired to do a play somewhere. Then we pack our suitcases and leave. But here, too, I play a role: the energetic, self-confident costume designer, whose head is full of ideas and who knows what she wants to accomplish. Having to play-act constantly is like long-distance cross-country running when you're unfit.

Whenever we're on the road, my mother takes care of Jakob and the house. She likes being in the suburb. She cooks and bakes, plays with Jakob and helps him with his homework. I wonder if she has noticed that I'm slowly suffocating.

Perhaps, as before, she doesn't want to see it. Living a normal life is simply so tempting for us. After all, everything is as it should be: Jakob is well, Jan is content, we have many friends, a nice house.

Jan likes to give parties at weekends. In the summer the guests sit in our garden; there is conversation, laughter and lots of vodka. We are becoming better known in Munich, people introduce us to their friends in artistic circles.

But it's all only a game. And this feeling intensifies my depressions, my sleeplessness, and my pangs of conscience. *I just have to be stronger; then everything will be all right.* The harder I try, however, the weaker I feel.

'Why don't you go to see a doctor?' Jan suggests, and my mother agrees.

The doctor is a nice man. Jan met him in the theatre and has become very fond of him.

'Well, Mrs Biczycki, tell me what's wrong.'

I swallow, search for the right words. 'Nothing is working out,' I finally say. 'I can't eat, can't sleep. Sometimes I have the feeling I'm not here at all. I just can't cope with my life.'

The doctor gives me a brief physical examination; he doesn't have much time and I, aged thirty-four, don't seem to be very sick. He looks at me, somewhat perplexed.

'What's the matter with me?' I ask.

'Actually, nothing,' he replies. 'You have a nervous stomach, but many people have that. All in all, I would describe your condition as an autonomic nervous-system disorder. There's a good medication available for that, quite harmless, my wife uses it too. You simply take one tablet in the evening, then you'll sleep better.'

He gives me a prescription, clearly glad to be rid of me, and I head straight for the pharmacy. The medication is called Mandrax. I take it often and it always puts me in a good mood. My worries evaporate. Everything becomes soft. No more sharp corners.

Jan notices I'm taking pills but thinks nothing of it, just another of my whims.

'Oh, you took another of your pills. Great, you'll be in a better mood,' he says, as I wobble down the stairs.

A letter arrives: 'Your hedge is not properly trimmed . . . Please remove the pile of snow in front of your garage within 24 hours . . .'

Our dog Cupido, freshly bathed and dried, is lying on the

sofa when the man from the Society for the Protection of Animals arrives. 'People have been complaining that this dog is being neglected,' he says, shaking his head. 'Could it be that your neighbours have a grudge against you?'

They certainly do. We're only renting, we're foreigners, and on top of that we're artists.

So I try to do everything even better, even more by the book.

Without success.

More letters about the snow pile arrive. I show them to my nice Bavarian neighbour. She doesn't understand why they upset me. 'Just get rid of the stuff,' she says. She grabs a shovel and helps me remove the snow.

Jan also doesn't understand why I take the neighbours' harassment so much to heart. They accept him, I tell myself, because he's blond.

'You worry too much,' he says, and sighs. 'Don't take everything so hard.'

I go to the bathroom and swallow a pill.

After a while I find out that I'm not the only woman in the suburb who is lonely. Sure, the women here have everything they could wish for: their own houses, children at school, cars in the garage, husbands with jobs, matching sets of furniture, ironing machines in the basement, and freezers stuffed with food. But the woman next door, for instance, consumes mountains of cake and chocolate, and is getting fatter and fatter all the time. She and her husband get drunk every night in front of the TV.

An American series on the Holocaust is being shown on one of the TV channels. I find out about it by chance from a woman across the street who has always been very stand-offish. Somehow she must have heard that I am Jewish. That same evening she knocks on our door.

'Were you there? Were you part of it?' she asks in disbelief. 'Was it really like that?' The horror is still on her face.

Apparently she didn't know anything about the concentration camps before this.

I nod without saying a word. She and I never talk about it again, but since then her attitude towards me has been quite different, as if she now sees me as someone in constant need of help, like a handicapped person. But each of us remains isolated, alone.

At the supermarket, I see one of my neighbours slip a bottle of perfume into her coat pocket. Later this woman confides that shoplifting is her hobby. She's become accomplished at it. 'I even swiped one of the umbrellas from the café!' she says, with pride.

'Why do you do it?' I ask. She certainly doesn't need to steal: her husband earns enough.

'I don't know – there's so little going on around here,' she replies. Some of the other women do it too. They have a regular competition to see who can steal the most original object. One of the neighbours doesn't steal things. She goes to the city every afternoon, solicits men on the street, then goes to a hotel with them. She claims it's a lot better than stealing. At night when her husband comes home, she's at the stove preparing supper.

Shoplifting can be contagious. One day I arrive home with a grey styrofoam hat dummy that I took from one of the stores. I look at the stupid thing – I can't even use it. And I again feel that leaden weariness.

But whenever Jan and I are travelling life is brighter. No sooner have I left the suburb, than I can breathe again. We go to theatre openings, concerts, parties.

Often we receive invitations from wealthy people with an interest in the arts. In their beautiful homes, I can briefly and without envy forget my own life and live theirs.

On one of our trips we visit my cousin Roman in his palazzo in Rome. After his wife was murdered it became more difficult to stay in touch with him. He has visited us only once. But even now we don't have much to say to each other. He is surrounded by noisy people – people who are much too exhausting for me.

Now and then Jakob and I go to Monte Carlo. My friend Mira has a friend, an American Jew, who owns a fantastic villa there. One day she phones me. 'Get over here right away. Princess Caroline is getting married and we're invited. The wedding's going to take place practically in front of our door.'

Caroline has lilies-of-the-valley in her hair. The bridegroom is wearing too much jewellery. She smiles a bit forlornly. Things will not go well for these two. Everyone says so.

Monte Carlo is hot. The sea glitters invitingly, the aroma of mimosa hangs in the air.

We lie on wide loungers at one of the most elegant beaches, sunning ourselves. We've also rented a large, blue-and-white striped tent and sip cool drinks in its shade. Nearby, Princess Stephanie is flirting with three young men.

People go into the water in full gear: jewellery, makeup, artfully pinned-up hair.

At midday they have lunch at the Hôtel de Paris. The faces of the older women who sit there with their young lovers are so tautly sewn they can hardly eat. They wear expensive, brightly coloured dresses, and diamonds that sparkle in the sun. They remind me of the whores in Beersheba.

The servants in the villa anticipate our every wish. I move about as though this were the doll's house I wished for when I was a little girl, yet always aware that all these beautiful things belong to someone else. Often I try to imagine what it would be like to live a life like this – a life without cares, without fears.

Luxury means driving around in big cars, not having to take overcrowded buses, living in places where you don't feel your neighbours crowding in on you, and shopping in stores where you're treated pleasantly. Luxury means protection from being hurt. It makes escape possible and is a shield against fear.

Sammy, my friend's wealthy husband, catches my eye.

'Do you like diamonds?' he asks, putting his hand on my knee. 'You could have some too . . .'

His hand slides upward.

I move my chair a little. 'Not all people are meant to have diamonds,' I say, thinking, you wouldn't get any real pleasure from me, poor dear Sammy. I may have a pretty little skin, but inside it I'm a bundle of terror.

Sammy always orders the most expensive items on the menu: caviar, *pâté de foie gras*, loin of lamb. Like a good girl I eat everything on my plate, even though I know I'll be sick later.

After lunch my girlfriend and I go on a shopping spree: Armani, Gucci, Pollini . . . We buy shoes, dresses, handbags, skin-tight boots that reach almost to the hips, short brightly dyed leather jackets. What in the world am I going to do with all this stuff in Ottobrunn?

Sammy patiently takes out his credit card.

On the terrace at night we watch the big white yachts sailing proudly by. The housemaid serves us sole meunière fragrant with herbs; and wine that tastes of velvet and silk.

It gets dark; down in the harbour the lights go on. They form a huge bright diamond necklace.

I think of our unpaid electricity bill back home.

Each time we return home from such a trip, it's like being plunged into an abyss. I remember that I ought to clean the windows; I go down to the basement to do laundry and wash my clothes until the last bit of glitter has been rinsed out. Sometimes Jan will try to help me with the housework but in the suburb that's not acceptable and, anyway, he's always in a hurry. At the first opportunity he slips away, back to his job in the city, and I'm alone again.

Then I sit there for hours, staring straight ahead, unable

to move. Not until Jakob comes home from school am I able
to pull myself together and make him something to eat. But
once he's gone out to play, I sink back into a corner and turn
to stone.

'What did you do all day?' Jan reproaches me, when he
comes home at night. 'There's nothing to eat, and the house
hasn't been cleaned.'

That's when I lock myself in my room, take a pill, dissolve.

Recently I've been taking the pills at much shorter intervals. It's only medication. You take it when you need it. That's
all.

One day there's a man at our door, a well-known writer
from Kraków. He smiles, shakes my hand. 'Roma?'

Jan has directed many of his plays. But Jan isn't here; he's
out of town. Before he left he asked me to take care of Sławo
if he turned up.

I remember Sławo well. We would often sit in cafés
together when I was barely out of school and he was already
a recognized poet. He flirted with me then, and with others
too. 'May I smile at you?' he had asked. And had done so
often.

Since then he's made a name for himself in the world. I'm
sure he's become rich and arrogant. Now, as he stands on
our doorstep, I don't know what to do with him.

Sławo comes in. He lights his pipe, uncorks a bottle of
wine, and drops on to the sofa. We start to talk and don't
stop. Evening comes, night. We talk and talk – about Kraków,
Poland, the theatre, and about us.

By the time morning dawns and our neighbour switches
on her vacuum cleaner, we've fallen in love.

In the months that follow, there's a single-minded campaign
of conquest, letters, flowers, phone calls. Jan is still away
and doesn't know about any of this.

Sławo is Jan's exact opposite: deliberate, calm and self-
assured. Each move he makes, each thought, is planned and

executed perfectly. Sławo hates disorder and chaos. He always knows exactly what he wants.

And he wants me.

My heart has been waiting for this. Now it flies out to him. It's not just the aura of success that surrounds him. His self-assurance also gives me a feeling of security. Above all, though, he's a piece of home. All the things I've missed in the years I've lived in Germany come back into my life.

We have long conversations. He tells me about his childhood, which was spent in considerable poverty. He always had but one goal: to be rich and famous. And he's achieved it. His humour is biting, scurrilous and black – he even manages to make me laugh. And he is single, his wife having died a few years ago.

Sławo makes me feel he needs me and, above all, that I'm a lovable human being, not difficult, not sick.

I don't need the pills any more.

By the time Jan comes back it's much too late.

Jan sits down on our bed, his head buried in his hands. As always, his blond hair is dishevelled. He searches for cigarettes in his jacket pocket and, finding none, his hand lies helplessly on the edge of the bed. He stares at me, takes off his glasses. He looks tired, bleary-eyed, grey. His eyes are both incredulous and accusing. 'Why?' he asks, for the nth time.

'Because we can't go on this way. You don't need me. You've always said you don't need anybody,' I reply, with pretended self-assurance. The truth, which I haven't been able to articulate all these years, is: things are over between Jan and me, have been for a long time. There's an indefinable something, a danger that threatens me in this place, in this suburb, in this marriage – and I know of only one way to respond to it: to take my child and escape. Just as my mother did.

I had thought Jan would be relieved. He had had so much grief because of me. But the opposite is true. Jan never understood how lonely I was. And now he doesn't understand how I can leave him. He thinks the fault lies entirely with Sławo, blames him for what has happened. That's the easiest explanation there is.

'And Jakob? The house?' he asks. The creases in his forehead deepen.

'It's best that Jakob comes with me,' I answer quickly. I don't want to feel the hurt this causes him, so I keep talking. 'You'll visit each other. After all, we won't be living at the end of the world. As for the house, you know I've never liked it.'

'But we had a nice life here,' he says helplessly.

'I'm sorry. I didn't want any of this to happen. Maybe everything will turn out all right. Maybe I'll come back,' I say, almost believing my own words.

'Well, it's your life,' Jan says, without looking at me. 'I won't stand in the way of your happiness.' He sounds bitter. Again his hand searches for cigarettes. He finds them in the other jacket pocket and lights one.

My life, I think. *Is it about to really begin?*

14

More than anything else, I want to be alone.

I have moved to Stuttgart. But I have to go back to the suburb once more because I left something at our house. Something very important. I'm afraid to go back; there is danger there. But then I'm standing outside the front door, looking for my key. It's gone. I don't know how to get in . . . Yet suddenly I'm inside. No one there. Everything is as it was. The same old furniture. I try to open a cupboard. The wood creaks, the door is stuck; it takes all the strength I have to open it. The cupboard is empty, except for a little girl cowering in a corner. She grins at me. I recognize the little girl. She's me.

Slowly I wake from the dream, look around. Where am I? In the suburb or in Stuttgart?

I realize with relief that I'm in Stuttgart, in my nice new apartment. I decided to move to Stuttgart because it's near Munich. And not too far from Paris, where Sławo lives. I wanted to make it convenient for everyone. But in those first few weeks I wanted only to be alone. Alone with my child. Maybe that's what I've always wanted. The only life I'm familiar with: a mother alone with her child.

For the first time, I have an apartment of my own. Here I am, at the age of forty, feeling like a student with her own place for the first time. The apartment is on the top floor. It has many windows and is full of light. The rooms lead into one another, and the floors are made of beautiful old parquet that I lovingly wax and polish. The place now smells of floor polish – just as the Kierniks' used to.

At forty (1979).

The house sits on a hillside, the city spread out below. A cherry tree grows on one side of my terrace, spreading its branches over the balustrade. In spring the tree is a sea of blossoms, and in the summer you can stand on the terrace and pop the cherries into your mouth. It is summer now. I step outside, pick a few cherries, and reflect on my new life.

I have a good job as a costume designer with a broadcast company, and often work on two or three films simultaneously. So far I've managed to cope with both my parenthood and career. It's a new role for me: an independent, self-assured businesswoman who earns her own money, does her work competently and at the same time is raising a child. All the things one does these days.

Of course, the separation from his father was hard on Jakob, but he doesn't talk about it. He's become my friend, my pal. He tacitly accepts Sławo because he senses how important this man is to me; perhaps he also admires him. Sławo is nice to my son, but sees him as little as possible. At weekends Jakob often takes the train to Munich to be with Jan. He makes the trip by himself. It's important for

301

him to stay in touch with his father. Moreover, I don't want
to take Jan's son away from him; things are hard enough for
Jan. He's desperate, but he isn't giving up. He's convinced
that I'll come back to him one day. He thinks with time my
infatuation with Sławo will fade.

So far I don't know anyone in Stuttgart, except the few
people with whom I work. I take frequent walks by myself.
The city is beautiful, but the feeling of being a stranger has
never left me. There's no such thing as starting a new life.
But I won't realize that until later.

Sławo is usually in Paris, and sometimes I go there at weekends to be with him in his romantic studio overlooking the
Paris rooftops. He shows me the city and takes me to elegant
restaurants. I have always liked Paris.

I'm beginning to realize that it's not exactly easy to be
Sławo's lover. A famous writer is preoccupied with important thoughts and mustn't be disturbed. Sławo sometimes gets
up during the night and sits there, pipe in mouth, writing. I
stay in bed, afraid to move, because my moving will disturb
him. This is sheer torture for me.

I'm not allowed to do or wear anything that doesn't please
him. Sławo likes me to be inconspicuous and ladylike. And
if I laugh, it must be only when he laughs.

But our wonderful conversations make up for all this. We
talk a great deal with each other and he satisfies my longing
for Poland, for Kraków.

We don't talk much about me. His inner life is interesting
enough for both of us. And I flatter myself into believing
that I'm the only person with whom he can talk because I
understand him better than anyone else.

He also values my opinions. I'm the first to read his manu-
scripts; everything he writes is fascinating.

But because I'm afraid I might disturb him, I'm often so
tense that every part of my body hurts. I feel guilty when the
soundtrack at the movies is too loud, when Jakob has the

radio on in his room, when a truck roars by outside – all the things Sławo doesn't like. He always speaks very softly, but that is precisely what is so effective.

'I don't want to be disturbed,' he whispers, and my insides congeal. I feel guilty all the time. On the other hand, he phones ten times a day, comes immediately if I don't feel well. Mine is a quiet, gentle terror.

My mother has never been able to understand why I left Jan, and I couldn't explain it to her properly. 'But you have everything you've always wanted,' she said, shocked when I called to tell her I was leaving Jan and the suburbs. 'What else could you possibly want?'

I had no answer.

My mother is the last person to criticise anyone, and yet she has withdrawn; calls me seldom, writes rarely, and stubbornly refuses to visit me in Stuttgart. She doesn't understand me. After all, I had what she never had: a husband, a house and peace. She simply can't understand that I was dying.

And I *would* have died there in that suburb. Towards the end I felt I was no longer in this world. It's not that Jan had it in for me. He had his fears, and I had mine.

I had denied myself, I had become mute. But at the back of my mind was a ticking clock, reminding me that my life had been saved and that I had to make something of myself.

Autumn is here, and Jakob is attending a new school. We've established something like a normal life for ourselves in Stuttgart. I'm too busy to sit around thinking. For Christmas we go to visit Jan, and there I suddenly become aware of the total change in my life.

Sławo and I are making a film for which he's written the screenplay. Working with him is a pleasure. I also enjoy being the woman at his side.

When he is among people he is the personification of

intelligent silence, just sitting there, his pipe in his mouth, saying nothing.

Then Sławo and I start work on a second film, a feature film. The high point in my career. I have the chance to indulge myself in beautiful costumes because the story takes place shortly after the turn of the last century, a period that fascinates me aesthetically. The women in the film are clever, deceitful schemers, especially those who are beautiful.

Because I know Sławo and can guess what he's thinking while he's directing the film, I find working with him very satisfying. The actors, on the other hand, are having a terrible time. Silence reigns on the set. No one is allowed to criticize him. Work proceeds with everyone on edge. We film first in Austria, then in the picturesque fishing villages of Yugoslavia, and I revel in the colours and in the sea.

I manage to avoid being conspicuous, but in spite of that I am having an increasingly hard time coping with Sławo's perfectionism. Everything always has to go according to his plan. And if something doesn't, it's inevitably my fault. Before going outside, he ponders whether he should take an umbrella along, or which scarf to wear so that he won't catch cold. And when he and the crew take a break I am practically forbidden to move. By making me small and invisible he intensifies my childlike behaviour, my old fear of doing something wrong.

And yet, when a three-room apartment next to his unexpectedly becomes available, we immediately decide to take it. We buy furniture and I start looking for a Parisian school for Jakob. I want to be with Sławo, I want to live with him.

Spring has arrived in Stuttgart, and my cherry tree is blooming. Tomorrow is Jakob's twelfth birthday and Sławo is coming. My mother is also expected, her first visit to Stuttgart since I came here eight months ago. She has never met Sławo. Now the time has come.

Maybe at last we'll talk. Maybe I'll be able to explain everything to her. We'll have tea on the terrace. I'll show her the city, the shops.

The phone rings. It's Jan calling from Munich.

'Roma . . .'

His voice is so husky.

'I have something to tell you. Please sit down. It's about your mother . . .'

'What's the matter with her?' But I already know the answer.

'She's dead.'

The walls of my apartment cave in without making a sound and bury me. It's dark all around me, and silent. Still holding the receiver, I sink to the floor. Jan's voice is far away. 'Roma, are you still there?'

Yes, I'm still here. Why am I still there?

I wanted to die with you . . .

Later I see a letter someone has pushed under my door.

It's from Sławo.

'Dear Roma . . .' The letter in Sławo's large, neat hand-writing is long. As I read it, the words blur before my eyes. He needed lots of pages to convey artfully what he could have said in one short sentence: *We have to split up.*

My head is droning, my heart pounding. I can't grasp what I have just read. I read it once more, then again, and again: *I have to be alone.*

Alone? How can he exist without me? Who will sit on a pillow at his feet at night and tell stories about the magical old city that was once our hometown?

How can I live without him? Without the wonderful smell of his pipe? Without his striped shirts hanging like ruled school notebooks in my wardrobe?

I have to call him, to explain things. Explain everything. He must know that we can't live without each other.

I lie on the beautiful, gleaming parquet floor. There is absolute silence in my head. I no longer have a heart.

All that's left of me is this ache. I hold on to myself with both hands.

Get up. I have to get up. Make lunch. Jakob will be home from school soon. What am I going to I tell him? The pills. I'll take one. No, better take two. And later two more. And some in the evening. I have a full bottle left. After that sleep. Sleep.

Slowly I get up, stagger to the bathroom, take two pills. Who is that woman in the mirror? She looks like a stranger.

I go out onto the terrace, stand under the white cherry blossoms, and I know only one thing for certain – I will not fight to hold on to Sławo.

My mother is dead, and so is he. I'm a daughter in mourning, a lover in mourning who also feels a curious relief. That the love affair is over, that she will no longer continually have to apologize for what she says and does.

Why did Sławo leave me? The question goes round and round in my head for months afterwards. Of course I know the answer. He's simply afraid to have to take care of a woman and her twelve-year-old child. He doesn't want to form any ties, to take on any responsibilities. He wants to be alone.

And yet it's all my fault. My mother's death is my fault too. I was cold towards her over the last few months.

The pills are beginning to work. Jakob comes home. Lunch is ready, the table laid. I sit there, dangling my legs, smiling.

I keep taking more and more pills. When my doctor refuses to prescribe more, I find another doctor. The pills help me get through the day.

For Jakob's sake I pull myself together in the morning, radiate a mood of cheerfulness and confidence that is quite genuine – except it's possible only if I take the pills. I do my work. I function.

My mother is buried in a Vienna cemetery, not far from the grave of her beloved. It was a beautiful funeral.

Beforehand I had swallowed a couple of pills – it was the only way to get through it. Jan was there, and many of her friends had come. She always had many friends.

Standing at the graveside, I remembered absurd incidents I had long forgotten. The time on a tram when she used her umbrella to beat a man who was calling her names because she was a foreigner; then, as he was getting off, she hit him over the head two or three more times. And the time when she and Jakob had bought some magic tricks – how they had laughed when I fell for them! She had laughed so hard she had to hold on to her belly.

My usually quiet mother.

She died like that, quietly in her sleep. Like a flower.

If only I could have asked her to forgive me.

Then we throw earth and roses on her coffin and it's over.

Jan is worried about me. Probably because I'm walking somewhat unsteadily.

I look at him. He is pale and smokes too much. He is also mourning my mother.

'Shall I take you home?' he asks.

That almost makes me laugh. After all, I don't have a home.

'Yes.'

It's good having a friend. Now that my affair with Sławo is over, Jan and I have become friends. We're going on holiday together, and we'll celebrate Christmas with Jakob.

Jan takes my arm.

'Thank you,' I say, holding on to him.

It was like switching off the light in one room and turning it on in another. Immediately after I got home from the funeral, I went to the synagogue and cried the way she used to cry in the synagogue. I even took along her handkerchief.

I felt her presence everywhere, realizing then, and now, that in many ways I *am* my mother.

*   *   *

Everything about me has changed. I have become much gentler and nicer to people, the way my mother was. And only since her death have I had any real friends. I can do things for them, I welcome them to my home day or night, I can look after them and cook for them, the way my mother always did.

I now light two candles on Friday evenings and I say the blessings for Jakob and me. *Shabat shalom*. Just the way she did.

But still there is no peace within me.

I am addicted. I can't live without the pills.

Ever since the day my mother died and Sławo left me, I have scarcely been able to sleep, even when I take the pills. Mornings I get up as usual, send Jakob to school, exude harmony. But almost before he closes the door, I rush to get my pills. Only then do I feel strong enough to do the house-work, or go on a few errands.

I no longer work at the TV station. Luckily my mother had saved a little money, and I can survive on that for the next few months. Any real job is out of the question. I live from one pill to the next. Soon I take two at a time, even in the middle of the night, and I quickly swallow more before Jakob comes home from school. Then he leaves again. He has friends and is busy with his own life. In the evenings, after I have taken two more pills, I test Jakob on his vocab-ulary, talk a little with him, or we watch television together. Jakob doesn't notice any of the signs of my addiction.

When I go to bed, I doze off briefly. Then I lie awake until the dawn, when I sleep for a few more minutes. After that, the whole business starts all over again.

'Stop it!' my grandmother says sternly.

'Yes, Grandmother. I will. Tomorrow.'

I dream I'm looking into the mirror. My face is made of sand. I touch the sand and it dissolves between my fingers.

Waking up is always brutal. The light streaming through the windows. I can't stand it; it hurts. And the noises, I can't stand them either. They bore into my head. My thoughts are also too loud, a babble of voices. Everything is too loud. Everything hurts. Only the pills lessen the pain. When I swallow them the light becomes gentler, the voices softer, the world bearable.

For a long time now the pills have not left me dancing on air. And my grandmother doesn't speak to me any more. I just talk to myself. Take a pill, I say to myself, so that you can survive the next three, four hours.

Soon it's only two hours.

My fear is like a hungry animal. I have to keep feeding it. After that it sleeps for a while. I have known for a long time that I can't exist without the pills, and yet I have to forget that I know. When the little bottle is almost empty I panic. That's why I always keep some in reserve.

It's a desperate quest, but with practice I've become a real expert. There isn't a trick I don't know.

I show up in a doctor's office, neat and well dressed. 'Doctor, I'm not sleeping well. I'm tense because of my job, and this medicine helps. I take it now and then, not often, to relax . . . You know, my nerves . . .'

I think up a thousand excuses and they all work. The doctors all believe me. The only one who suspects anything is our old family doctor, who has known me for a long time. He looks searchingly into my eyes and asks, 'You won't abuse them, will you? I'll be glad to renew your prescription, but you know it isn't good for you to—'

'Of course,' I assure him. 'I promise I won't take them often.' The next time I turn up at his office, I take a nearly full bottle out of my handbag as proof of my innocence. I've kept the bottle especially for this purpose. 'You see,' I say, 'these are the ones you prescribed for me last time. I've taken only a few so far.' He chooses to believe me. Actually, I've consumed at least twenty full bottles of pills in the meantime.

Naturally, to avoid suspicion, I'm forced continually to change doctors. When I've gone through all of them, I turn up at the office of the first one again. But by now they're all suspicious.

I buy the pills in different pharmacies, but there aren't many pharmacies in Stuttgart. I act out entire movie scenes in these drugstores.

'You know,' I say to the pharmacist, all upset, 'I've been staying temporarily with my sister. Unfortunately she isn't at home just now and I've left my prescription at her place. My train is leaving in an hour, and I have to be on it. Couldn't you make an exception?'

I know all the pharmacists within a radius of thirty miles – know exactly at what time of day and where I have a chance of getting what I want. Saturday is best because that's when they're all very busy.

But things are getting tight. I need lots of pills. Always more and more.

Sometimes when I look in the mirror I'm surprised to see how thin I've become. I'm also getting progressively weaker. Even with pills sleep is now out of the question.

I hardly ever go outside any more; the crowded streets frighten me. I dash out to do some shopping then immediately get back into bed. From bed to couch, from couch to kitchen. When I occasionally go to the cinema with Jakob, I'm overcome by claustrophobia. In the darkness I slip a pill into my mouth. By now I can swallow them without water.

I have no friends left, don't need any. The pills are my only friends. I am separated from other people by a glass wall. When I talk to someone, I have to talk through it.

After three or four months of this addiction my memory

is lost in fog. I remember nothing, except that Jakob is doing well. He has everything he needs. As for me, I have dissolved.

That summer, almost against my will, some old friends take me with them on holiday. They say I have to get away because I always look ill. Jakob stays with his father while we go to Madeira.

The rocky island is hot, cacti flourishing everywhere. There are no beaches. Alcohol is ridiculously cheap and most tourists take full advantage of that. Madeira used to belong to the British. They laid out a country club and built beautiful houses, tending everything meticulously. But then came nationalization and, after that, deterioration. There are slums everywhere; garbage piles up in the streets. Hordes of dirty children pursue you wherever you go. Even Churchill's former villa is totally dilapidated; the windows and doors hang open, his books lie around in tatters, and the garden looks like a park after a wild celebration.

And yet Madeira is paradise for me.

You can get anything you want in the Portuguese pharmacies, without a prescription and without anyone caring. The first time I go into one I see they have my pills; I know them all by name now. When I shyly point to them, they give me as many as I want. I drag the stuff back to my hotel by the bagful. Soon I have enough for six months and I feel as though I'm in the land of milk and honey.

For two weeks I stroll around the hotel swimming-pool because there's nothing else to do on the island.

I go obediently to the dining room with my friends, poke at my food a bit and pretend I'm eating. No one seems to notice. One of my friends is a doctor. But she doesn't say a word about it. Only once, after the waiter has again removed my full plate, does she look at me thoughtfully. 'You ought to see a doctor when you get back from holiday,' she says casually. 'Anorexia nervosa is usually a condition *young* girls have.'

On a humid morning in the middle of August, the fog around me lifts for a moment and the veil of apathy is torn away. We're at the breakfast table when the husband of one of my friends comes over to our table and waves an English newspaper at us. 'Guess what,' he says. 'There's a general strike in Poland. Members of Solidarity, the workers' union, are at the barricades, protesting against the government.'

I grip my chair. He reads to us from the newspaper, but there's not much information about what's going on in Poland. The local television station doesn't mention it at all.

I jump up with excitement. 'I want to go home!' I exclaim.

We have to wait. Our flight doesn't leave for a few more days.

'Ms Ligocka! Imagine meeting you here!' A familiar voice. It's my boss at the television station. I've been back in Stuttgart for a couple of weeks and accidentally run into him on the street. I'm embarrassed to see him, mumble an excuse, tell him that my mother died, and that I am not feeling well because of that.

'We have lots of work for you. We miss you,' he adds, looking concerned. 'Please let us hear from you soon. Call me. Promise?'

I promise.

My supply of Portuguese pills is dwindling, and I sense the panic returning. In a few days it'll be Easter.

Jakob and I have been invited to a Greek Easter party by Despina, a former pupil of Jan. For the first time in a long time I feel like being among people again, and Jakob is looking forward to it too. These days, I'm almost completely alone with my pills and my child, and I can hardly bear it.

It turns out to be a lovely party. All of Despina's Greek relatives have come – grandfathers, children, uncles and aunts. We are seated at long tables, eating, singing and drinking wine. But

I hear their voices as though they were coming through a curtain of mist, and I'm unable even to drink one glass of wine. If I do, all those pills I've taken could kill me.

Suddenly it becomes clear to me that I am a slave. I think of my life, my own, precious, God-given, unique life in which I have for so long stopped taking part.

So no more pills. No more dependency. I've stopped. And it's hell.

Again I fight for every hour, not from pill to pill, but away from them, hour by hour, step by step.

In the television studio (about 1981/2).

The first night I feel as cold as if I had been chased out into a clear freezing winter night, then into the blinding brightness of a street-lamp. My teeth chatter. My skin hurts. I writhe in pain. One firecracker after another explodes before my eyes. Slowly the fog disperses. The more the effect of the pills lets up, the more painful the clarity. Thoughts chase each other, clear sharp thoughts – so many that it seems as if my head will burst and I'll go mad. Words, a flood of words – Latin, German, Polish, old children's songs – all swirl in an icy spiral.

I sit and write poems; lie on the floor with cramps; feel sick to death; almost collapse from exhaustion, and I know I won't be able to sleep because I refuse to take any more pills. Whatever I eat, I immediately have to throw up – if I don't eat, I vomit bile.

I talk to myself, take care of myself as I would a sick child. Look at the clock. Keep looking at the clock. It's morning.

It's noon. You haven't taken any pills . . . for two hours. Three hours. Eight.

You're cold? Cover yourself. Your throat is dry? Drink something. Be good to yourself. Be patient. Be patient with yourself. Look at the hands of the clock. Time is passing.

Want to eat something? You can't? Then don't. Keep going. The little bottle of pills? Still within your reach. You can take them anytime. It doesn't matter at all if you do or don't.

But I don't. The nights during which I lie awake seem endless. My stomach aches, my muscles burn. A high shrill sound, like that of a chain-saw, drones in my head. Is the little bottle still here?

I don't take the pills. I drink tea and, clutching a hot-water bottle, I crawl under the heavy white wool blanket. A present from Sławo.

And I have to be quiet so that my child won't notice anything.

Once Jakob comes sleepy-eyed into my room as I'm lying on the floor, writhing with pain.

'What are you doing, Mama?'

'Oh, just some exercises,' I groan, and try to kick my legs.

I don't know how long the withdrawal lasts; I've completely lost any feeling for time, just like that time in the cellar in the ghetto.

But the clock keeps ticking, and then it's over. One day I know that I won't take any more pills, ever again, even if I can't sleep for an eternity. I look in the mirror and for the first time I recognize myself again.

I weigh ninety-nine pounds.

Today I realize I could have died going cold turkey like that. You should detoxify the body gradually, in hospital, over a period of weeks. I was lucky. As so often in my life.

15

War again. On 13 December, politics suddenly enters my life. I don't usually listen to the radio, but just by chance early one morning I tune to Radio Warsaw and hear the announcer say: 'At five o'clock this morning, martial law was declared in Poland . . . The army is taking over.'

Those gangsters.

A speech by General Jaruzelski follows the announcement. When I switch on the TV, I see tanks rolling through Warsaw. It is snowing – a cold winter in Poland, and people are lining up in the streets for bread.

That's how it was back then, I think. It is hard to believe – while I am sitting in my warm apartment in Germany, my own country is in a crisis. There are endless rumours: this one or that one has been arrested; others have escaped. Later I find out that many of our friends – friends who, not too long before, had come to visit us – have been arrested and jailed.

We are sitting in front of the TV with tears in our eyes – Jakob, my Polish friends and I – feeling the way the Czechs must have felt back in 1968 when Russian tanks entered Prague.

I immerse myself in politics; I pore over books, make telephone calls, have long discussions. I learn about the Universal Declaration of Human Rights, which guarantees, in black and white, freedom from bodily harm, freedom of speech, freedom of movement and residence, and freedom from persecution because of race or religion. All this is new to me, and I am thrilled and inspired to learn of its existence.

This document also protects *me* and *my* rights – rights I didn't know I had.

At the same time I see that there are people who need my help, and for whom I can do something.

I am no longer lonely. With a few friends I start a small human-rights society in Stuttgart. I am especially committed to helping women in the Communist Eastern part of Germany (the GDR), women who, after attempting to escape to the West, have had their children taken away from them. They are never told where their children are, or given the names of the foster families with whom they have been placed. Many of these mothers will never see their children again. I spend nights writing letters to Erich Honecker, the leader of East Germany, to the UN, to the newspapers. How easy it is to go without sleep when you are writing letters that might help someone.

I establish contact with many people all over the world, wonderful and courageous people.

During this time I also discover the works of Vladimir Bukowski, and he becomes one of my heroes. As I learn about his life, as well as the tragic stories of so many others, it becomes clear to me that some individuals will, deliberately and of their own free will, endure pain and fear, go to prison, sacrifice their own freedom for others.

And the more I learn about the Communist regime, the more I understand what has happened under the Third Reich. I see the parallels, the connections between the two dictatorships, the common language of tyranny, and the similar methodologies of manipulation. But all this understanding is on a purely intellectual level. I still don't want to deal with my past.

'Don't think about it,' they said to me long ago, and I absorbed the lesson.

Nevertheless, I am maturing rapidly. What others learned in their twenties, I am learning in my mid-forties – to express myself openly, to get involved in the world, to take on responsibility.

In October of this year is the Book Fair in Frankfurt, when publishers from around the world gather to buy and sell their works. Dissidents have recently come to Germany. There is great political tension in the air, and the Book Fair is the place to meet. Of course I go.

I am standing at the booth of the Polish underground journal *Kultura*, which is published in Paris and offers uncensored reports on the political situation in Poland. The men standing around me – intellectuals and dissidents – are all smoking and talking in low voices. They wear green parkas, beards, turtleneck sweaters. I think of them as heroes. Many have come directly from prison; others have been expelled from Poland and cannot go back.

I leaf through books that are banned in Poland and examine photocopied texts and fliers. The adjacent stand has Russian literature; Vladimir Bukowski's latest book is on display. I am eager to meet him, but the poet is nowhere to be seen. A young man in a white shirt with short blond hair, high cheekbones and bright blue-green eyes is sitting behind the table that displays Bukowski's book. His nametag reads 'Andrzej'.

'Is Vladimir Bukowski here?' I ask him.

He shakes his head. 'I'm afraid you'll have to make do with me. I'm his Polish translator.'

'Well, then, you have no choice – you just have to have a cup of coffee with me,' I say.

'Why should I? I don't have time for that.'

I feel myself blushing. 'Because – because – because I'm Roman Polanski's cousin,' I stutter in embarrassment. What a stupid thing to say.

The young man laughs. 'If that's so,' he says, 'then we shall indeed have to have coffee.'

The cup of coffee turns into a day and a half.

Andrzej and I have fallen in love.

He is eighteen years younger than I, the first man in my life who doesn't need me. I enjoy not being needed. He simply takes me as I am, and I don't have to do anything. Suddenly everything is uncomplicated. We go for a walk, we talk, or we don't talk.

'I have to leave now,' he says. 'I'll see you.' And he is gone.

He has to attend a meeting of the anti-Communist Internationale, and after that he is going to Paris. Andrzej is a war correspondent, translator and dissident, all in one. He smuggles forbidden literature to the East and establishes contact between various dissidents. He is constantly travelling, a man for whom a steady relationship is out of the question. But that's what I like about him.

As soon as I get back to Stuttgart, I sit down to write him a long letter. When the phone rings, I pick up the receiver, annoyed at being disturbed.

'I'm an idiot, I should simply have taken you with me. But I could stop off in Stuttgart on the way to Paris. To be honest, I'm already on my way; I'll be there in an hour and a half.'

An hour and a half to wash my hair, straighten up the apartment and cook. Then he is at the door.

I never know when Andrzej will come or when he will call, but for the first time in my life I don't sit around waiting and I don't ask questions. To my amazement, I am not even worried about his safety, although he is constantly taking risks. There are no more inner conflicts and no agonizing discussions about our relationship. That isn't even an option with Andrzej; he would consider it a pure waste of time. Other things are simply more important.

I paint a lot, these days. Of course, I also have to earn a living. I work at the theatre, the film studio and the television station. But this sort of work doesn't quite suit me any more. The irrelevance and the hypocrisy of show-business are a contradiction of what is happening in the world: in Poland, in the GDR, in the Soviet Union. While I am designing beautiful costumes at the municipal theatre, I try to get my colleagues interested and politically involved, but no one shares my concerns.

Kraków, Summer 1994: Roma attends the opening of her first major exhibition with her son Jakob.

A new type of show-business culture is developing and the entertainment industry is growing by leaps and bounds; yet the content of the television programmes is empty and ugly. This is no longer my world.

The discrepancy I see between the engagement of a few dedicated individuals and the carefree infantile western lifestyle leads to my first real break with my profession. The work I am doing seems insignificant.

I feel ashamed sometimes about spending less time with Jakob because of my work, but he doesn't need me so much any more. He is almost grown-up, and will soon be leaving school.

Andrzej often takes me along to his secret meetings. He also uses me as a sort of mail drop. He leaves books with me to be picked up by someone who will then see to it that they are printed somewhere in the East, or tells me where to send money we have collected. Once we go to a meeting of dissidents on Lake Lugano in Switzerland. We sit by the shore of the lake till late into the night, telling stories and talking. A rebellious bard plays the guitar and sings songs about walls that will fall, fall, fall. There is a lot of drinking.

Jakob also gets involved. He paints banners, and with some friends starts his own group. He collects signatures, writes articles for the student paper, and often argues with his teachers about politics.

Then what no one thinks possible, happens. The wall comes down. The Iron Curtain opens.

I see Andrzej for the last time. He comes to visit me. I am scheduled to go into hospital for abdominal surgery. When I tell him how frightened I feel, he is deeply affected for the first time since I met him: his self-assurance and his easy-going attitude are gone. Yet we both know that our relationship is over.

While I am still in hospital, Andrzej goes to Warsaw to start a new life there. We talk on the phone now and then. Once he calls from Afghanistan, another time from the White House in Moscow, just as the tanks are rolling into the city during the *putsch* against Gorbachev. Our love has turned into friendship.

I didn't know that one kind of relationship could change into another so painlessly, so gently. Of all the men in my life, Andrzej is the only one I remember without pain.

It is time to go back to Kraków. In December 1990 Jakob bundles me into his little car and we take off.

At the last minute, however, I am suddenly afraid. But Jakob insists. 'I want to see your city and visit my grandfather's grave.'

We drive across the border and straight through Poland. The Polish roads are as bad as ever. My heart beats faster, but no one stops us.

We arrive at the Kraków market square around midnight. A light layer of snow covers the church towers, the old houses and the cobblestone pavement. It is quiet. I am breathless with joy.

How wonderful it is to be able to show Jakob around, to tell him about the past, the way my mother used to tell me – the shop in which one bought hats in those days; the café where I always used to sit and where I was proposed to; the memorial for the Polish poet Mickiewicz where lovers used to meet; where my mother and I used to live; the cabaret.

On our first day in Kraków I look up my old friend Piotr. 'There you are again,' he says quietly, as though after all this time it is not unusual to see me on his doorstep.

There are so many absences. Marynia has been dead for many years.

And Manuela is dead too. For a while she continued to perform in Warsaw, people say, then she disappeared.

The grave of her great grandfather.

But my old girlfriends are still there. Barbara and I hug after almost thirty years. We have so much to talk about. When her beautiful sister died, Barbara raised her two young children. After all these years she tells me at last about her father. No one has been allowed to mention his existence because he was a member of Poland's exile government in London during the Stalin period. Barbara has become a painter and graphic designer and taught at the Art Academy for many years. She is very active in the Solidarity movement.

The Jewish cemetery is overgrown and wild, almost like a jungle. I think we will never find my father's grave. 'Grandfather will show us the way,' Jakob said. And so it is.

We also find my great-grandfather's grave. His grave is one of the few left intact when the Germans desecrated the cemetery and erected the Płaszów camp there. Now it's the only surviving gravestone in a brown, damp field.

16

Don't think about it, my mother said.

A cold grey dawn. We're standing at the edge of a gorge, looking across to the other side, just a few of us. My mother is there. Jan too. We're all dressed in warm clothes, overcoats, carrying suitcases and bundles. Jakob is there, but he is an adult.

On the other side an old Jew bends over a little boy lying on the ground. The Jew fills his hands with sand and pours it into the boy's mouth. The boy tries to defend himself. His little fingers grab at the old man's chapped hands, but that doesn't seem to deter the Jew, who keeps pouring the sand into the child's mouth, more and more without stopping. The boy's resistance gets steadily weaker – he merely lifts his arms, lets them drop again – lifts them, lets them drop – weaker and weaker . . .

The sand keeps trickling from the old man's bony hands. After a while the boy just lies there. Completely still.

We turn round and go off as if we had been onstage.

'He's dead, isn't he?' I ask my mother.

'We should have rescued him!' I shout soundlessly. 'Now he's dead!' I want to shout, but can't – I have no voice.

'So it goes,' my mother says. She hunches her shoulders and tries to hide her head. 'It's always like that,' she says, and suddenly she's far, far away. 'Don't think about it,' she says, from far away. 'It's always like that.'

The memory returns to me in my dreams, but I don't want to remember. My whole life I've fought it, locking it away securely in a dark chamber of my heart.

But then something happens, that changes everything. I get an invitation to the première of a film from the mayor of Kraków.

I have now known for months that the American director Steven Spielberg is shooting a film in Kraków about the war.

'Aren't you interested?' my friends ask me.

I tell them that I can't deal with war films. They always make me cry. And, besides, what will an American know about what happened back then? What can he possibly know?

The rumours become more concrete: Spielberg is making a film about the Kraków ghetto. The première is scheduled for March. All survivors and their families have been invited. Hence my invitation. I don't want anything to do with all that.

'When are you going to Kraków, Mama?' Jakob asks me.

'Jakob, please, you know I can't bear to see it. I'd have to get up and leave in the middle. You know me.'

But Jakob insists. 'It's not a question of whether you can or cannot. You *have* to go. You simply *have* to.'

And so, I do: row 12, seat 22. I will never forget the numbers, because I will never forget the film.

All around me are people in elegant dress, prominent people from the Church, the arts, and politics: bishops, generals, rabbis. Almost the entire Polish government is there. In the semi-darkness I can make out the face of President Lech Wałęsa two rows behind me. The atmosphere is somewhere between that of an Oscar ceremony and a State funeral.

Scattered among this illustrious audience are other faces: pale, insecure, a bit lost, most of them grey-haired. The people the film is about.

In the ghetto. Dark apartments. Crowded. Suitcases. Shouting. Tears. Boots.

Yes, that's how it was, I say to myself. This isn't fake. It's true.

The camp in Płaszów. The engineer who is building the barracks. In the film it is a woman inmate. Because one of the barracks collapses, she is accused of sabotage and executed. I think of my uncle, the engineer Krautwirth.

Separated by the camp's barbed-wire fence, a couple are secretly married. I recognize you, Aunt Sabine.

Then a tiny figure suddenly comes towards me, glancing furtively before disappearing into a dark hole.

A little girl in a red coat. Her black eyes looks straight into mine. She disappears between the floorboards. The same way I once did.

And I know both who the person is I have been looking for and from whom I have been so desperately trying to run all these years. Suddenly I realise who I really am.

I don't want to cry in front of all these strangers, these important people, so I hold my breath and watch, watch as the world is destroyed on screen.

A second film is playing in my head. Suddenly I see not only my grandmother, I see them all: my uncles, aunts, Irene, Krautwirth, Sabine, my father and my mother. Everyone.

After the screening, white as a sheet and unsteady on my feet, I go to the reception. A friend who helped organize it for Spielberg takes one look at me and stops short. 'So it was too much for you after all,' she says, taking me in her arms. I hold her tight. It helps to have her arms round me. I try to say something, but my mouth is dry and my throat is choked.

'That was me!' I am finally able to say. 'That was me!'

She stares at me, dumbfounded.

'What do you mean, "That was me"?'

'The little girl in the red coat. In the film. No, not in the film. In reality. Really!'

Someone hands me a glass of vodka, then another, and another.

Then Steven Spielberg enters the room. He is smiling.

My friend tries excitedly to introduce me to him. 'This is Roma. She—'

Spielberg shakes my hand mechanically, smiles again. He is in a hurry. He has to get to the airport.

'She is the little girl in the red coat!' Ania calls after him. But he can no longer hear her. He is already gone.

It is early Friday evening. Soon I'll be lighting the candles and reciting the blessing. *Shabbat shalom.* Sitting at my desk, I am looking out at the gradually darkening sky, a blank pad of paper sitting before me.

I am thinking of my grandmother. *Where are you, Grandmother? You haven't been coming to visit me lately.*

'Who says I'm not here?' an insulted voice asks. 'What are you doing?'

'I'm thinking,' I respond. 'I want to remember. I finally want to tell everything. Our story.'

'Didn't you want to forget it?'

'No,' I say, and take a deep breath. 'I want to remember. I would like it to be a book.'

'A book? For whom?'

I think about that for a moment. 'I don't know,' I say. 'For Jakob, for me. For the others. And above all for you.'

My grandmother says nothing.

'I want to tell the story,' I say, 'the story of the little girl who is crying deep down inside me and who is

In her studio (1999).

325

still afraid. And you, Grandmother, I'll have to write about you. I'll have to let you die all over again. Can you forgive me?'

She doesn't answer.

Then she says, 'Do you still remember what we said to you in the ghetto back then? "Don't look. Don't turn round. Don't think about it."'

I remember it well.

'But now it's time,' she whispers. 'Look. Turn around. Think about it. Tell the story.'